AF148117

New Approaches to Religion and Power

Series editor: Joerg Rieger

While the relationship of religion and power is a perennial topic, it only continues to grow in importance and scope in our increasingly globalized and diverse world. Religion, on a global scale, has openly joined power struggles, often in support of the powers that be. But at the same time, religion has made major contributions to resistance movements. In this context, current methods in the study of religion and theology have created a deeper awareness of the issue of power: critical theory, cultural studies, postcolonial theory, subaltern studies, feminist theory, critical race theory, and working class studies are contributing to a new quality of study in the field. This series is a place for both studies of particular problems in the relation of religion and power as well as for more general interpretations of this relation. It undergirds the growing recognition that religion can no longer be studied without the study of power.

Series editor:

Joerg Rieger is Wendland-Cook Professor of Constructive Theology in the Perkins School of Theology at Southern Methodist University.

Titles:

No Longer the Same: Religious Others and the Liberation of Christian Theology
David R. Brockman

The Subject, Capitalism, and Religion: Horizons of Hope in Complex Societies
Jung Mo Sung

Imaging Religion in Film: The Politics of Nostalgia
M. Gail Hamner

Spaces of Modern Theology: Geography and Power in Schleiermacher's World
Steven R. Jungkeit

Transcending Greedy Money: Interreligious Solidarity for Just Relations
Ulrich Duchrow and Franz J. Hinkelammert

Foucault, Douglass, Fanon, and Scotus in Dialogue: On Social Construction and Freedom
Cynthia R. Nielsen

Lenin, Religion, and Theology
Roland Boer

In Search of God's Power in Broken Bodies: A Theology of Maum
Hwa-Young Chong

The Reemergence of Liberation Theologies: Models for the Twenty-First Century
Edited by Thia Cooper

Religion, Theology, and Class
Joerg Rieger

Theological Perspectives for Life, Liberty, and the Pursuit of Happiness: Public Intellectuals for the Twenty-First Century
Edited by Ada Maria Isasi-Diaz, Mary McClintock Fulkerson, and Rosemary Carbine

Messianism Against Christology: Resistance Movements, Folk Arts, and Empire
James W. Perkinson

Also by James W. Perkinson

Shamanism, Racism, and Hip-Hop Culture: Essays on White Supremacy and Black Subversion. (2005).

White Theology: Outing Supremacy in Modernity. (2004).

Messianism Against Christology

Resistance Movements, Folk Arts, and Empire

James W. Perkinson

palgrave
macmillan

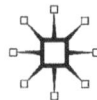

First published in 2013 by
PALGRAVE MACMILLAN®
in the United States—a division of St. Martin's Press LLC,
175 Fifth Avenue, New York, NY 10010.

Where this book is distributed in the UK, Europe and the rest of the world,
this is by Palgrave Macmillan, a division of Macmillan Publishers Limited,
registered in England, company number 785998, of Houndmills,
Basingstoke, Hampshire RG21 6XS.

Palgrave Macmillan is the global academic imprint of the above companies
and has companies and representatives throughout the world.

Palgrave® and Macmillan® are registered trademarks in the United States,
the United Kingdom, Europe and other countries.

ISBN 978-1-349-46168-4   ISBN 978-1-137-32519-8 (eBook)
DOI 10.1057/9781137325198

Library of Congress Cataloging-in-Publication Data is available from the
Library of Congress.

A catalogue record of the book is available from the British Library.

Design by Newgen Knowledge Works (P) Ltd., Chennai, India.

First edition: December 2013

10 9 8 7 6 5 4 3 2 1

Dedicated to the All the Creatures—Human and "Other"—Whose
Living Beauty Refuses to Capitulate to the POWERS.

Contents

Figures

Acknowledgments

This book has its immediate departure in my relationship with my wife of ten years, whose ever restive search, alongside my own, has been the great gift of my life. A Filipina of most marked soulfulness, Lily's quest for what is truly just and sustainable on this damaged and wailing planet has ever checked my own, when I have gone lazy or naïve. The cultural "matrimony" of irrepressible humor, florid love of color, palm-tree-pliant resilience, and exquisite sensibility she bears, gives every day meaning to the indigenous romance this work in part represents. In writing, I can never be entirely sure whose song I am singing. But let the reader (and the husband) not be misled. Beneath the delicate tuning of cultures yet carrying memory of their birthing from demanding soils, there is a ferocious resourcefulness. I grow ever more astonished at the deep ancestors of our race, the more I wrestle with our contemporary surfeit of war, poverty and ecological wreckage! To all who have given sustenance on the way to this place and moment: hail. And they are not only human.

I confess a shrunk soul, struggling to learn languages long lost. I have labored in the process of this writing to bring a house plant back from death through daily care and gentle talk—trusting against my hard modern heart, that someone was "home" in the leaves and stem and loam. I have begun growing heirloom corn. I cry to the sun. I put out food for spiders and squirrels. And all of it looms as so much futile effort, while limbs are torn by bombs I pay for thousands of miles from my home, and homeless ones a block away spend the meager dollar I sometimes give back, knowing their loss has probably fueled my own comfort through all the intricacies of racialist housing policy and banking practice. I know the names of a few of these "other ones." I fight politically against the plundering in ways I know how. But mostly I eat and write, and dream, oblivious.

Yes, I thank parents and friends, colleagues at Ecumenical Theological Seminary and Seminary Consortium for Urban Pastoral Education, all my coconspirators in resisting corporate takeover of Detroit and the country, fellow poets at city venues, artists whose riots of imagination keep my own amazed, authors and teachers who regularly send my spirit on trek or plunge me into rage at the pillage that rampages unchecked. But here especially, I want to serve notice of kin whose fins and antennae, roots and wings and fur, my culture and Christianity has never known how to acknowledge, much less feed in kind. To them, a soft thank you, and a resolve to live fiercely, create relentlessly, grieve unabashedly, and finally give unreservedly of my own substance and body, when the time comes, "to be eaten" even as I eat!

The original version of this book was revised.
An erratum to this book can be found at DOI 10.1057/9781137325198

INTRODUCTION

Junk Installation: Messianic Art and Social Movement

Art is medicine, and then you can take it beyond... (Tyre Guyton, comment while painting car hoods on Heidelberg Street).

He answered, "I tell you, if these were silent, the very stones would cry out (Lk 19:40).

On the Street in Detroit

When the situation is dire and response is critical, the messianic appears as "shock art." Since I am writing about a particular kind of sign in particular spaces and times, I begin where I live. This book finds its founding emblem in brightly colored folk-faces painted on rusting car hoods displayed on a ghetto street in inner city Detroit. The artist is Tyree Guyton. The street is Heidelberg—now become internationally (in)famous as site of these startlingly colorful apparitions. The faces he calls, "faces of God" (Figure I.1).

Leering wildly from dozens of upended panels of dented sheet metal scavenged from nearby junk yards, this art is not part of the "ruins porn" for which postindustrial Detroit has gained a certain recent notoriety (and shows up now on YouTube as the icon of chic desolation for those who do not have to inhabit the images). No, here an entire block has become outdoor stage for a running battle with authorities since the late 1980s. Guyton, growing up poor and fatherless in a family under duress on this German-named byway, deep in the old black neighborhood of the near east side called Paradise Valley, is a local phoenix. His project has twice been wrecked by official decree. Dodging bulldozers where others dodge bullets, he has grown a community. In his project's first incarnation beginning in 1986,

Figure I.1 Heidelberg Project car hoods.

the house next door to his own "spoke to him one day" and thereby over-night became the central frame for an insurgent reappearance of garbage—found objects, scavenged from weed-wracked lots, splashed with paint, nailed onto the wood structure like a postmodern cross, seething with meanings obvious and occult, writhing across the eye with a death that refused to die. Dolls and clocks, suitcases and rakes, stuffed animals and steering wheels, old telephones and new street signs—whatever had been discarded was fair game for the gravity-defying frame-up and bold emblazoning. Bicycles climbed tree limbs upside down; shoes dangled from the high branches—symbol of what Guyton's grandfather remembered as the soles (souls) of those lynched back in the family's deep-South past. "Dead" vacuum cleaners lined up in battle-formation like sentinels on drill parade in the side yard—evoking shades of Ezekiel's bone-valley and the command to prophesy...! And polka dots covered the street surface in a riot of inverted balloons! As one wag crooned, you turn the corner here, in this section of Detroit's bitter blight, and it's suddenly like "someone just turned the sun on!" (Figure I.2).

Figure I.2   Heidelberg Project OJ House front.

After the first bulldozing—multiple machines knocking over the house in a mere 15-minute barrage, accompanied by a helicopter and blaring police horns—Guyton and friends staged a funeral, buried the house-body with all its chromatic blazons shouting like so much multicolored blood, and hunkered down into the lesson. Within months, the grandfather died, whispering, "You can't stop!" And Guyton didn't. He had already been, a few years before, dismissed, from one of the city's premier art programs, as too renegade. This was now one more "pound down" of heavy manners on outlaw meanings that he would simply refuse to abide. Instead, at his instigation, the suppressed polka dots came roaring back from the underground like a raging cotillion of ancestors, suddenly showing up on every blighted structure all across the city-scape, compliments of guerrilla "taggers" working midnight shifts in anonymous comeuppance. A 1956 bus carcass, resurrected from its scrapheap, was ferried into the 'hood, swarmed by neighbor kids wielding brushes, and rendered like a bullet-spray of color, machine-gunning every least glance with a war of dots. Looking like a jelly bean jar on its side—in honor of his departed grandpa's favorite snack—the bus commemorated at once Tyree's birth-year and Rosa Parks' initiation of the Montgomery Boycott, as well as the refusal of either figure (and of all this resurgent tint!) to stay in place. Another city-assault in 1999 erased another one-third of the creativity, but neither court-summonses nor neighbors' derision could halt the upwelling of percussive brightness (Figure I.3).

Today, the installation evolves. A hummer doused in pastel pink and half-buried as a sign of its coming "peak oil" demise—led by an upright pink bicycle bearing an arrow stating, "this way to the future"—served to mark Detroit's hosting of the 2010 US Social Forum. This gathering of twenty-thousand activists from across the land for a week of skills-sharing and vision-trading reveled in sheer celebration of D-Town innovation. Guyton-like glam proliferating on the eye-slamming sides of buildings throughout Detroit (as indeed around the globe wherever his tactic has gained a following) mirrored the movement: a Do-It-Yourself insurgence animated by inner city residents populating the postindustrial abandonment with proliferating gardens (more than one

Figure I.3 Heidelberg Project street polka dots.

thousand as of the Forum's opening), and a proliferating population of entrepreneurial youth busily creating their own media-tropolis outside the corporate image or dollar. Meanwhile on Heidelberg itself, a white fellow artist had moved in across the street years earlier and begun putting up his own corral of resurgent detritus—charred timbers from a long-defunct auto plant presiding like a trinity of *nkisi*-statues awaiting the nails of healing, auto guts and plumbing parts winding around the grounds begging divining like the innards of an animal, bright cryptograms in languorous longhand on every wayward shard (such as liquor bottles hung around the edges of a big TV set bearing the inscription, "Found: Weapons of Mass Destruction").[1] And Tyree's own spectral puns continue to propagate—4 × 8 plywood paintings of a single high-heeled shoe, boldly marked with the word "God," marching across a vacant lot, proclaiming a coming "stomping" for a bureaucracy of corruption; an old stove crammed with used Nikes like a porcelain exclamation point warning of holocaust; mirrors or TV sets scribbled with vermillion riddles. All of it landing, like an uppercut to the eyeball, jamming death and life into the same sign, in militant silence asking out loud, "How do you read?" (Figures I.4 and I.5).

Figure I.4   Heidelberg Project buried hummer.

Figure I.5 Heidelberg Project street north view.

On the Page in Palestine

And such indeed is the theme of this writing. This is a book about "Christ"—or more classically stated, *christology*: the ground or logic or discourse on a certain "hallowing" or "haunting" of a human being judged iconic and momentous for the entire enterprise of "being human" in history. More precisely, I mean to lift up a *logos* about *christos* here as the "marking out," in various media, of a defiant modality of signifying in a situation of struggle and early demise. And the absence of the definite particle "the" before the chosen designation "christ" is meant to be troubling and suggestive. The "anointing" (in Greek, *christos*) in question is not simply "one" (as in "anointed one," "the Christ"), but a "commonality of enablement" or even "commons of the spirit," visited on an individual for a communal purpose, emerging historically in early Israel's experience as a means of specifying focus and magnifying significance. Leaders were marked out and designated such in a public ritual by the pouring of caul-fat from animal sacrifices on the heads of those specified for focal attention (transferring the vital animal "powers" to the one anointed). That is to say, ancient "christening"—plying

the human body with the juices and life-force of an "other" body—
was a mode of artistic signifying. Smearing skin with the glistening
substance of dead ancestors (oils of emulsified plant and animal bodies representing the primal remains of the earliest ancestry we have)
served as a dramaturgical sign of purpose. We might even say the act
imbued the one so marked as more than just one—as a multiple, bearing an entire ecology of powers.[2] And it was not even limited solely to
humans. Indeed, one of the term's primary meanings is "to paint," and
the earliest biblical instance of "anointing" is what Jacob does to the
Dreaming Stone of the Canaanite highlands whose terrifying[3] visions
of the night led him to consecrate the rock-set-up-as-a-pillar as "God's
House" ("Bethel") (Davidson 1970, 519; Gen 28:10–22; 35:14). And the
riff offered here on such anointing—as the creative figuring of a certain
ancestral surplus (the dead "who do not stay dead," as Toni Morrison
might venture)—is critical, as we see in the following text.

The exploration to follow will claim that the favored medium of such
a portentous "signing" is not merely the flesh of a certain human named
"Jesus," but a representational artifice about the meaning of his way of
living—prefaced by those he learned from, and continued by those who
learned from him. Its quintessential image is the creative judo done
by agonized humans on desperate circumstances, making pain yield
beauty in spite of itself. We are not used to thinking of the *Ur*-Texts
of *Yehoshua* as art—but these gospel craftings of the following of Jesus
are the only sources we have for what we mean by christic apparition.
Here, I am thinking especially of the recent work on Mark's gospel by
activist educator, Ched Myers, whose painstaking 500-page elaboration of a socioliterary method of exegeting the text makes abundantly
clear the way this first witness to a particular life lived against the grain
of empire is indeed a prodigiously artful achievement—as much the
mandala of a seriously revolutionary movement, continuing into the
present, as the mnemonic of a fetishized figure of the past (Myers 1988,
116, 448 ff.). The classical text of incarnation is in fact a sharp angle of
artistic conjuration intending proliferation—whether in written forms
quickly multiplying in the first century as the gospels and epistles of
early disciples like John and Paul (and indeed dozens more, canonically accepted and not), or at a much further remove and later date in
time like today, in slash-and-burn color such as Guyton and crew spew
on urban blight. Christology can be as well read from a dis rap spit by
eloquent anger inside the trap of urban adolescence as from a parable
fashioned in the Galilee outback by a renegade prophet on run from the
authorities; as hauntingly "sent up" by a jazz note stalking midnight

losses in a forgotten club south of Eight Mile as by a hymn to the *logos* of all-things-created prefaced to the Book of Signs known as *KATA IΩANNHN* (the actual Greek title to John's gospel). Such is the argument to come.

And I argue that these are all—yes, *all!*—merely local augurings of a diverse but global phenomenon. Once entertained, discerned, and practiced, the perceived presence (*parousia*) shows its face everywhere as a way of defying domination in service of a wildly beautiful creativity: antique amulets of the outback of Ethiopia under imperial Rome or the reliquary of a teenage martyr in Provence granting hope to peasants, *yagé*-induced incantations evoking shamanic visions of healing contesting missionary aggression in the Amazon or Celtic "illuminatory" craft on a vellum page, giving a druidic/talismanic halo to otherwise "orthodox" christological subjects in early medieval Ireland. In a word, incarnation will be entertained here as an artfulness that possesses, gaining historical purchase in social movements that refuse merely to be possessed (by domination). And *christology* will proceed then as a mode of reading the logics of those contested possessions, a giving of sense to the signs, emerging from the wrack and ruins of history, that animate such resistance movements with the unrepentant energies of those suffering and slain unjustly. Obviously, saying such departs somewhat dramatically from classical christology with all of its concern to secure a monopoly of meaning to a singular life lived and killed under Roman hegemony in first century Palestine. So let me set out a preliminary warrant to the argument.

Method in the Messianism

We live in a time when intellectual certainty about the difference between modernity and all else that has gone before has begun to second guess its claims to either uniqueness or superiority. In recent years, in the neck of the intellectual woods I hang out in, "political theology" has emerged as a hot topic on both sides of the divide between religious reflection and secular theorization. In one sense, what follows here occupies a small niche in that larger debate. While some thinkers would query the appropriateness of the term "theological"—angling in favor of a more generalized and less parochial term like "religion" (though itself under challenge as also code for colonial hubris and misprision)—the adoption of the central term of Christian reflection offers a certain historical specificity that is germane. The very fact that theorists around the globe are engaged in exchanges about such issues arises as an effect of the troubled and ongoing history of Western expansionist policy across the entire landscape of colonial struggle. That expansion took place under the direction of a quintessentially Christian conviction of mission responsibility and theological certainty. "Theology" accurately identifies the terrain of epistemic elaboration that first leveraged the modern colonial enterprise, both among its explicitly clerical apologists and on the ground among its varied commercial protagonists.

When a polity such as the United States began to articulate a space of disestablishment between church and state, the experiment laid down a line of differentiation that became definitive for most of the theoretical notions of modernity that followed. "The secular" and "the religious" were imagined as domains that in principle could be maintained as separate in the formality of their respective powers, if not always in the content of their practices or the influence of their discourses. That a more recent hermeneutics of suspicion has had to entertain doubt even about the very form of its own constitution (that it too, might be quasi-theological) only reinforces the point about the particularity of the theological that now demands closer accounting as a haunting even of the most rigorously entertained commitments to secularity. It is not religion in general that ghosts the grounding under theorizations of the modern political state, but more accurately "Christianity." And thus a concern for the productivity of a concept like political theology—even in pursuit, for example, of greater clarity on a purportedly hybrid political formation like a "democratic" Islamic state—remains a concern suffused with "Christian" imagination. It is after all the Greek *theos,* not the Arabic *allah,* that anchors the ethos of the term.

The effort here then zeroes in on the centripetal force suffusing that "theological ghosting" to render explicit and thematic the messianic presumption that colors the whole (indeed today, "ghosts" it in the tones of a nearly invisible miasma of messianic "whiteness"). The theological—in our concrete historical itinerary of continuing Western hegemony—inevitably carries a charge of the christological. If Mark Taylor is concerned in his recent work on this terrain (*The Theological and the Political*) to articulate the "politicality of theology" then I am pushing the discourse here toward an even more sharply focused "politicality of christology," for which I prefer the somewhat less obviously loaded (but no less particular and weighted) term "messianism"[4] (M. Taylor 2011, 3). But where Taylor's book offers a sophisticated quadrille of what might be called transimmanence theory, working through the complicated steps of the likes of Foucault and Bourdieu, Butler and Schatzki, Agamben and Nancy and Spivak in five "theophanous" chapters of quite compelling beauty, here I rather seek to mambo suggestively through the vernacular practices of subaltern peoples, beginning with the biblical traditions of such and hop-stepping adventitiously forward. Taylor's predilection for the "prodigious force of artful signs deployed in spectral practice" is prescient and delineates a similar emphasis in this work (especially as that artistry is given historical purchase in social movements of resistance "weighing in" against the weight of the social ontology subordinated peoples are forced to inhabit and habituate; M. Taylor 2011, xii). Indeed, in one sense, this work is a grateful riff on his, taking up a bit of the gauntlet and some of the articulation he himself offered to other scholars in closing his work (M. Taylor 2011, 224–225).

I argue that christology must also be shifted away from doctrine to sign. In its subaltern emergence as a "Little Tradition" idiom, it is better comprehended as an artful form of judo performed on violence—coiled inwards with intense subtleties and gestured outwards with often disguised but equally intense ferocities. Its signal feature will show up as the conveyance of a charge of unresolved history, cast in official theological terms as "resurrection," but open to other figurings in the cultural codes of other movements struggling under other forms of duress than those of occupied Palestine of the first century. Cast, for instance, in the black vernacular of the earliest modern "settlers" of this continent[5] who made common cause with native inhabitants in 1526 after going *cimarron* from Spanish enslavement, I would call this is a *messianism of haints*. But however it is cast, recognizing such today requires the discernment of a seething[6] surplus of unlived aspiration, prematurely buried in the grave, but now ghosting the living with an unfinished groan. This is a surplus upwardly fracking social order with an inverse injection of prodigious artifice, galvanizing movement against the impossibility of hope, granting inarticulate motion a calligraphy of explosive expression or sly coloration. It opens a slight trace of dawn at the very heart of an existential midnight, releasing beauty from the prison house of orthodox censure and spirit from capitalist dismissal, in groping toward momentary embodiments of "other worlds" and ways of being together on the planet.

To return for a moment to Guyton's "hood-winking" representations of Motor City struggle with which I began this reflection, it is worth noting that my reading of his art as christic is not imposition or cooptation from without. Guyton himself regularly invokes Christian imagery and sayings, and in his signature video of the project (significantly entitled "Come Unto Me"), quotes the passage in John 9:1–11 where Jesus puts "mud" (some of the soil found under his feet mixed with his own spit) on the eye of a blind person he is attempting to heal. Guyton does so while the video footage depicts him scavenging car parts from neighborhood junk yards which he will mix with his creative coloring and then "put" on the eyes of his supporters and critics alike, asking, in effect, "Do you now see?" But Guyton will likewise refuse to be contained by the discourse he invokes, continuously moving the Christian signs out of place—putting crosses on doll houses on the sidewalk or the word "God" on a picture tube cantilevered out of an abandoned house window or on any number of other objects he arranges throughout his installation.

And the "faces of God" he slashes onto car hoods are such not because they are recognizable faces of Jesus. Their christic power is rather, I would argue, borne by their awakening strikes of color. The percussive force of the brightly juxtaposed yellows and reds, blues and greens—in features whose textures are raw, *brut,* and capable of signifying complexly from a minimalist folk vocabulary of lines and shapes—is force indeed. It is the flash of their contrast, the bold simplicity of their stark primality, that accomplishes the effect I am calling "christic." They awaken inchoate energies into ribald leanings and inclinations that want to shout against every convention of containment and down-pressing. Eyes suddenly sparkle with epiphany, tongues with poetry! Or indeed, with complaint! In effect, Guyton's bold palette and harsh juxtapositions continuously open that inner city neighborhood to its underground energies not just of celebration, but of contradiction, dissent, and begging to differ—which is exactly what they did do, from day one. Much of the community protested his early designs as "refuse"—a literal insult to the eye. One neighborhood picketer even opined in response that "art belongs in a museum, caged up like an animal" under lock and key. Guyton responded in counterpoint by commending the resistance. At least the silence had been torn open, and the subtext given a public airing. This was "subaltern logos" unleashed—messy, groaning, combative, but alive. Other neighbors confessed rather a kind of "resurrection": young people destined to become drug dealers by ten years of age and die early, now catching sight—and having a literal hand in—a different vision of life, animated by paint brushes and color, using only what was already underfoot.

Guyton himself is ever prescient in his own confessions. He names his grandfather as inspiration—the literal in-filling of whose spirit enabled the project in the first place. Grandpa Mackey (as he is known) first championed Tyree's art-impulse in a poor family afraid of the lack of economic prospect of an art career. And while the enterprise in a real sense killed the old man with heartbreak after it was first bulldozed in 1991, it is his spirit and irrepressible-ness that lives on through the coloration. "Color" indeed, as the body of resurrection! Percussion as its mode of being! And Tyree as poet-of-the-hand, figuring the anti-death in ever-renewed frames of resistance (and perhaps there is even room here to see the channeling of outrage over his loss of three brothers to street violence over the years). Initially a lone-ranger existence of "speaking against" the wall of urban decay and municipal law and art school norms of "art." But soon gathered into a movement-following that today has waxed international in scope and finds its deepest anchor in an emergent DIY ("do it yourself") sensibility challenging the police-state coercions of big government and big finance across an entire planet (like the sign of an upstart David against a huge market-force Goliath). This is a "grow-your-own-beauty" aesthetic whose co-dependent arising (to borrow a Buddhist term) includes an anti-agribusiness "grow-your-own-food" economics and alternative-media "grow-your-own-story" politics—a ground-swelling movement of "multitudes"[7] whose true potency we are just beginning to sense in upwellings as diverse as the Arab Spring abroad and locovore orientations at home. And I want also to name it—in a provocation whose justification is the rest of the book—"christological."

Messianic Effects

Now consider what Guyton's wanton paint-bombing accomplished. The city weighed in heavily, came down hard—bulldozers, police, and helicopter surveillance. Tyree's artistic "incarnations" on that decimated block set off a chain of responses that ultimately revealed the city as "principality" in the language of spiritual discernment (being reclaimed in our day by the likes of William Stringfellow, Walter Wink, and Bill Wylie Kellermann as we see in chapter 5). Heidelberg became a site of sudden epiphany, art meets empire. The provocation had succeeded in making apparent a whole series of interlocking causalities that determine why some people have a monopoly on office buildings and suburban residences, "authorized" bullets and hired bulldozers, while others suffer in the anonymity of urban blight. Guyton himself—in the video production extolling his work—underscores the reality. While dashing a crumpled car-hood with the bold strokes of a God-face, he comments, "the art you see is the 'front' or facade; underneath is the spiritual reality of war." Growing up, a paint brush for him was the possibility of creating freedom. The first time Grandpa Mackey placed one in his hand at age nine, it "burned," he says—perhaps a tiny tactile version of Moses' visual experience of flaming foliage. It was also "medicine"—a mode of healing exorcism. But it was likewise something you could "take beyond," in Guyton's words, to begin to query the boundaries of your world, the containment that chokes off energy and warps identity. From his expulsion from art school, through the multiple bulldozings of his installation, to hauling the city into court and fighting over charges and fines, Guyton has regularly touched the "beast underneath" the sullen silence of urban blight. This is the subtext of oppression: the covert assemblage of seething forces ghosting the machinery of big government and big capital. It is a complex interlinkage of powers—a racialized housing market,[8] postwar white flight, corporate relocation and asset drain to separatist suburbs, colonialist policing, etc.—whose labyrinthine ruthlessness is nearly impossible to make clear.

But suddenly, in the cold November air of 1991, that juggernaut of forces was conjured into daylight through the encounter of bright street art with big machines and blue badges in a couple of hours of unmistakable "state repression." Yes, neighbors in the hood had complained and served as the street-level surrogates of those large-scale "powers," and yes, they even had "cause"—their uncomfortable experience, as the installation gained fame and drew visitors, of living in a fish-bowl of outsider gaze and disruption, wandering through their neighborhood on a daily basis (Beardsley 2007, 42, 46; Herron 2007, 3–4; Jackson 2007, 26, 31). But the choice between relentless immersion in the harsh silences of imposed impoverishment or continuous negotiation with naïve (suburban) voyeurism and media attention is hardly a worthy choice. Tyree forced the issue—and today that neighborhood has gained a "followership" of disciplined supporters, organizing for material support, staging community activities of all kinds (a small garden of vegetables, regular days of performance for young street artists, plans and funding for a center offering education and inspiration, etc.) and continuing to probe the broader urban (and indeed global) context concerning the policies and priorities that decimate inner city neighborhoods.[9]

Such is by no means utopia, nor is Guyton easily packaged (and thereby "disposed of," as Dorothy Day would challenge) as a "saint." But the now quarter-century saga of this project does stand as sign and can be easily read as gospel. But in so doing, it is equally critical to hold what we mean by New Testament "gospel" accountable to the wild beauty, renegade humor, and blight-busting brightness rising phoenix-like and uncontainable from the burned building hulks and the refuse-as-palette met with on Heidelberg (indeed, I use the video that tracks

Heidelberg's history, in courses I teach, as a riff on Mark's version of the Jesus-story, reading back and forth between the two in a cross-signifying manner that is mutually revealing of the stakes of trying to be human in an infrahuman situation). I am hard put any more to say which augurs more deeply or stirs more passionately my own desire to "mean something" and live fiercely on behalf of "spirit." And this for me is the crux: how one "reads" and how one is "read by" (and enlivened and moved and compelled to action by) the *animation* of things. I am interested here in what might be called a *messianism of animation*—what postcolonial theorist Gayatri Spivak has lately dreamed of as "animist theologies of liberation," beholden not to old doctrines and decrepit orthodoxies, but to living ecologies and justice (Spivak 1999, 382–383).

And the issue is not just "messianic flesh," like that of Jesus of Nazareth, but the articulation of subaltern spaces for revivification and movement. How provoke the third eye to grasp a hidden transcript—what might be called "renegade rearrangements of possibility," prying open "breathing room" for insurgent energy? Such is Guyton's project. Like a sudden clearing in a napalmed forest, Heidelberg Street has been recast as a huddle of leering witnesses holding a clandestine meeting in a war-zone, recreating the block as a conspiracy. Attempting to give word to the effect the houses and art assemblages have while one is walking this block, we might say this is a "cathedral" of chameleon dilapidation—ruins and flotsam shamanized into dancing colors spitting riddles. Rather than a Gregorian chant "echo chamber" of dead Christian saints staring down from the walls in an imperial basilica of ancient Rome, this is trash art under a junk aesthetic, "squatting" and signifying at the edge of two sidewalks. Its secrets enter not through the ears, but the eyes and skin. The experience of the energies arcing between these stark "ghetto" apparitions, tattooing the air with jagged mirth, is like being in a hall of mirrors—except they never reflect the same way twice, nor do they simply affirm the on-looker. Here is guffawing irony! Laughing puzzles, tweaking idols, and idolatries! This is the grave-revolt of disappeared homeless and displaced children, coming back in bodies of dead commodities and living paint! The staunch march of raucous polka dots on the street-surface is like the track of a strange ancestral visitation, whispering with rumor, jeering in gossip. The houses themselves peer down like menhirs, mute with memory and prophecy... or with recognizable soliloquy on recognizable officials or conceits (Detroit City Council doings are frequent targets of some of the visual puns and bright epithets)! In religious studies terminology, the result is a form of "urban shamanism," with Tyree as vibrant medium, awake to the codification of information and energy locked up in the discarded bodies and abandoned hulks of the inner city ecology. Under his hand and sense of dramaturgy, their witness is unlocked and made vivid for the daily struggle to survive.[10]

But Heidelberg represents also a montage community. The art here is no longer just Guyton's vision or juxtaposition, but an entire open commentary—visitors invited spontaneously to add their own dots to the houses or street, or stuffed animals and sharp ideas to one of the installations. It stands as a "living museum" of the people, who not only visit but also leave on deposit, their own "word" or image or (literally!) the shoes from their feet, destined for a paint brush and display. This work does not only serve but also incorporate; it is not simply "for" but "of" the community (B. Taylor 2011, 4). It is at once a shrine and a manifesto to a rising from the ashes of an entire city—alternative to down-top design and authorized policy and the despair of poverty alike. Its seething presences are indeed messianic—and signal the insurgence this book seeks to celebrate.

But isn't putting such a claim at the fore of a work on christology mere bombast and hot air—a send up of canonical norms and theological "certainties" so wild and oblique as to be laughably cavalier?

Messianism Against Christology

This work has grown out of a course I've taught for more than a decade now. Its precise purpose is to situate christology in relationship to its own cultural particularity and codification—from biblical versions of the same, forward through its varied historical wanderings and missionary promulgations—to try to facilitate a different Christian response to the rest of the world than has been the case for much of its history. It is patent that most of the one-fifth of the world's people who today claim to be Christian do so out of a conviction that Christianity is somehow truer than other religious convictions or practices. Whatever else it purports to be, Christianity is at least a mode of felt and lived religious superiority—all disclaimers of arrogance or protestations of modesty to the good (i.e., the typical evangelical "I'm-just-a-worm" deference to divine sovereignty). And that deep sense of primacy has colored Christian approaches to relations with others historically.

But what is "religious," what "cultural," and what "economic" and "political" are not so easily separable. Religious convictions of supremacy do not simply stay put in the pew. They animate—and are reinforced by—material relations of domination and subordination.

The Iraq and Afghanistan wars of late, for instance, were initiated in the name of US national security, but build implicitly and continuously on taken-for-granted notions of cultural and religious superiority in securing (tacit, if no longer enthusiastic) support from the US populace. They are simply the latest "race" wars over resources, legitimized by an inchoate religiocultural conviction of superiority and entitlement that is not easily separable from the rest of what goes by the name of "modern Western civilization" or simply "our American way of life."

The damnable real-life effects of this Western messianic complex—promising one or another version of universal salvation (whether spiritual or political or economic) and encoding an intractable presumption of supremacy—is all too evident in even a cursory survey of modern history. In its name, native peoples have been genocidally "reduced" and disappeared from their lands, Africans genocidally enslaved and racialized as a replacement labor force, and more recently, an entire globe annexed and plundered in the corporate project of economic takeover and cultural reengineering that has come to embody that earlier Christian conviction of superiority and entitlement. Of course, the five-hundred-year development of this sociopolitical juggernaut enshrined in a particular religiocultural hegemony is complex, multidimensional, and ever morphing. My gloss on modern Western development as an almost irresistible cultural force elaborating a continuity of political and religious violence is mere gloss. But it invokes, for this work, the ever-throbbing foreground (of arrogance) and unrequited background (of anguish) against which I want to think "christologically."

Given such, my own purpose here (among others) is one of seeking to open up space for genuine encounter and activist solidarity (in a search for greater global justice) between Christian forms of resistance and similar initiatives animated by "little tradition" cultures rooted in local ecologies.[11] But doing so, I would assert, requires incessant vigilance against an ancient but profound imperial impetus to *presume* Christianity as the greater truth, simply by definition (what Christianity supposedly *is*). My concern for such emerges especially out of personal and practical experience of dealing with the modern offspring of this Christian presumption of superiority—the kindred forces of white racial supremacy and middle class convictions of economic entitlement—as these recurrently surfaced in my relations with my lower income neighbors of color in inner city Detroit where I have lived for more than 25 years. There I have been vigorously called out (or subtly put in place) any time I have inadvertently channeled a bit of flatulent white arrogance. But I have also just as vigorously been invited to plunge into a surprising and rewarding practice of mutuality and shared struggle whenever I have managed to respond creatively and respectfully to the necessities of the moment. (And the allusion here to a kind of "baptismal initiation"—with its attendant necessity for something like "exorcism"—is critical and key.) This 25-year regimen of deeply encountered and often harshly negotiated "difference" has become the crucible from which most of my theorizing and conceptualizing now emerges. As I have written in depth about this experience of race and its discontents elsewhere, here I only hint in the briefest of rehearsals.

An early evangelical experience of "born again" fervor, followed by baptism into charismatic spirituality and commitment, led to motivation as a 23-year old to move into an impoverished Motor City neighborhood as part of a residential Christian community, "hell bent" on helping inner city folk deal with their decimated circumstance. Only gradually, over the course of a decade, did that patronizing arrogance fade before the intransigence of the forces pillaging the neighborhood. Slowly, the hardness of ghetto life pried scales off of eyes blinded by white presumption and prejudice. Black community members and neighborhood residents alike knew deeply the reality of the economic powers enacting racial perceptions and the political will that would keep such in place. And they took a much longer and more tragic (and comic) view of the possibilities of change, the necessities of survival, and the pleasures of small triumphs. Once I was finally awakened to the intensity of the battle daily waged in that neighborhood among those laboring under the stereotypes and inside the social structures in which dominant society had incarcerated them, my own impulse to "help" withered to more human scale, and the desire to learn took its place.

What began to appear with ever clearer aspect was the immense creativity and heart-rending ferocity with which so many of my inner city neighbors regularly engaged life. Some of that *élan* was coded as "Christian" and transacted as "church," but most of it was lived out simply as a style of communicating, a mode of improvising, and a "colorfulness of being" (literally and figuratively) that was simply remarkable. Genius in making desperation yield beauty in spite of itself was in evidence all around me in measures large and small, and I was astonished at both my neighbors' precocity and my own incapacity, in kind. I fell in love in response and was therein plunged into an initiatory reformation that has not ceased to alter my sense of self—and way of living—ever since. It is that willingness to be altered in response to an "other" way of being that looms now as the touchstone for my thinking about most things visionary and valuable (such as religion or in this case, christology).

Shaped by the predilections that have resulted from this particular history, the book that follows here is a collection of essays exploring questions of justice and sustainability, representation and identity, art and symbology, as these arise in various historical moments both inside and outside normative christological discourse about Jesus. The basic thesis is that messianic talk about Jesus began in what anthropology would identify as the "Little Tradition" idiom of first century Palestinian peasants, conserving memory of an older way of living more sustainably on the land, but gradually shifted over into official "Great Tradition" christological discourses, as the messianic Jewish peasant movement transformed itself, first into an urban Greco-Roman religion after the Jewish War (65–66 CE), and then into an imperial cult after Constantine (313 CE). In such a transformation from subordinate orality to dominant and dominating literacy, from vernacular story to classical doctrine, messianic resistance to injustice, as often as not, had to go underground and adopt ironic subversion as its modality, in counterpoint to its own cooptation by organized wealth and power as a discourse of apology for the reigning sociopolitical order. "Christology," in such a perspective, has to develop a sense for the hidden transcript of resistance, camouflaged inside or underneath, the public transcript of canonical agreement. Or said another way, the problematic is that of "minor messianisms" and vernacular "counter-christologies" opening living space underneath or alongside of a dominant and dominating Christologos. The book is an exploration of that subjugated knowledge and its varied arts of practice.

Overview of the Walk-Through

At the most basic level, the effort here can be comprehended as a vernacular critique of the christology that emerges historically from the fourth gospel. The Logos-Hymn appended to John's narrative line opened the door to an emphasis that proved very strategic for empire, as we see. It began a pilgrimage of focus from "folk arts" and "social movement" to "philosophical containment." On the other hand, however, John's way of narrating his story under a regime of messianic "traces" (his so-called Book of Signs, organizing the first 11 chapters) is suggestive for my own organization of material. Most of the effort expended here concentrates on retrieving from the tradition's formative texts and time, a reading of Christology "from below" and beholden to a messianism rooted in the land. Since so much of Christianity takes its direction from this formative period that generated both the canonical scriptures themselves and their orthodox interpretation, the heaviest weight of work will focus on these *Ur*-texts and developments. The concern is to open new vistas of perception, not offer a definitive interpretation. It could hardly be otherwise when the topic is folk arts and peasant movements, the subject typically "subaltern," and space quite limited.

What follows then is a sequence of chapters beginning with a general overview (styled as "Wildlands Memorialized") of the way I exegete "messianism" and "the messianic" as a counter-reading to orthodox Christology (chapter 1), and then proceeding through three areas of focus. The first part keys on the "messianic signs" that shape the tradition *biblically*, looking at the particular Hebrew figures Jesus drafts into artful invocation animating his own teaching (chapter 2), and then tracking the way his followers craft their memories into gospel narratives of movement events and emphases (chapter 3). Here the privileged art forms are "Ancestral Invocation" and "Parabolic Incantation," respectively. Part two traces the subtle but seismic shift in context and content, when a rural Galilean movement is pulled into an urban imperial orbit and reformulated under a literate concern for *theological* canonicity and orthodoxy. Pauline theorizing of imperial aggrandizement as an operation of "principalities and powers" and Johannine recourse to the logos-doctrine (Jh 1:1–18) begin to install "Metaphysical Speculation" as the new art of confessional commitment. But this is also a moment when the tradition necessarily galvanizes a counter-tradition in which rural folk-practice must "occult" its own local land-orientation and village-ethic that are increasingly at odds with the universalizing vision of imperial orthodoxy. Ethiopian peasant use of "Talismanic Depiction" supplies a kind of test case for a vast history and repertoire of indigenous arts of resistance, through which canonical subject matter is regularly conscripted into clandestine struggles for survival.

Part three will then sample a number of these "messianic" survival arts and the various movements and alternative lifeways that made use of them at given moments of *historical* subversion. The range is adventitious, running from Celtic illuminated manuscripts to Provençal gilded relics, from Haitian possession-cult dramaturgy to Ecuadoran rain-forest shamanism, from Filipino revolutionary liturgy to Mexican street-procession. The genres of artful resistance examined include "Manuscript Illumination," "Reliquary Embodiment," "Possession Dance," "Visionary Chant," "Folk Poetry," and "Street Theater," each briefly "read" as a vernacular mode of engaging the messianic.

And finally, in a concluding chapter, we swing back up to contemporary Detroit and its prospects of reinventing itself as a new kind of urban-rural hybrid, reinserting a ten-thousand-year trajectory of unsustainable "development" (the city) back into a measure of accountable exchange with the ecology, which is the very matrix and "mother" of its continuing possibility—and doing so under tutelage and in time with the "Insurgent Beat" of an irrepressible hip-hop aesthetic. As originally conceived, the book would have devoted more time and detail to each of these examples gleaned from the history of Christian expansion around the globe. But in the actual writing it became apparent that sketching out the early career of the Jesus movement—from its origins in Hebrew struggle, through its Galilean phase, and into its change of context and focus in adaptation to the Roman Empire—would require much of the space available. In consequence, this third part is being offered as a kind of appendix in ebook format, at once addendum to the "thicker" analysis of the formative period of the tradition and prolegomena to a wider study of people's movements and arts that it can only barely begin suggest.

CHAPTER 1

Wildlands Memorialization: Messianism Mapped

Jackson likes to tell the story of the old Sioux Indian who watches a pioneer plowing up the prairie sod, stoops to examine the furrow, straightens up, and says, "Wrong side up" (Eisenberg 1999, 328).

And the Lord said, "What have you done? The voice of your brother's blood is crying to me from the ground (Gen 4:10 after Cain has killed Abel).

Writing about Christianity at this particular juncture of history demands a certain focus. In a US landscape soaked in half a millennium of colonial bloodletting, whose conquering culture has yet merely to acknowledge, much less redress, that unrelenting violence, confession stands paramount. Recent work by native scholars, such as Shawnee/Lenape Steven Newcomb's *Pagans in the Promised Land: Decoding the Doctrine of Christian Discovery,* has begun detailing the degree to which a fundamentally religious idea has anchored the entire project of Euro-conquest here (and indeed, around the globe). That idea is Christian in derivation, absolute in its effect, and foundational for the whole colonial edifice. Its essential presumption, conjured out of thin air, was the supremacy of Christianity to all native practice thereby designated and denigrated as "heathen." Its explicit assertion was the legal claim of Euro-sovereignty wherever land might be "discovered" to be unclaimed by any other "Christian" power. And its clear consequence was ruthless takeover.

Newcomb's particular contribution is archeological. He digs relentlessly under the murk of American exceptionalism to uncover and decode the root-stock of doctrinal concepts—long since buried under technical legalese and popular ideology—that simply assert, without warrant, sovereign European rights to own the land and grant or revoke, at will, native occupancy and "use." As he painstakingly lays bare, those concepts trace their genealogy to a basic theological equation of Euro-Christians with the Hebrew peoples of biblical fame. These latter were understood to have invaded and decimated Canaan in the second millennium BCE on the basis of a vaunted "divine" promise to nomad Abraham that the spine of hill-country running through Judea and Samaria would be given to his seed in perpetuity. Without question the biblical binary "Hebrew/Canaanite" became the archetypal root-structure organizing European approach to the conquest of the Americas, translated into their own discourse as a primal "Christian/heathen" differentiation (as well as the more broadly secular "European/Indian" and more generally cultural "civilized/savage" designations) (Newcomb 2008, xvi, 37–50). In the equation, brute conquest, as indeed coerced assimilation, was justified as divinely mandated. And Euro-Christian expansion haloed itself as "salvific" and supreme.

At the deepest level, this writing takes Newcomb's polemic as the necessary "Genesis" for all subsequent "American" theology, throwing down a gauntlet of such thorough-going challenge, as to require a profound break with the very premise of modernity and indeed of this particular country's assumed right to exist. Obviously, embracing Newcomb's claim would require a profound rethinking of the nation's founding, and radical confession and change on the part of churches. While the nation-state thus far shows little willingness to engage the way the "doctrine of Christian discovery" has illegitimately anchored the imagination of US sovereignty or the entire prospect of US property law, more and more church bodies *are* beginning to confess the reality of the history and repudiate the premise of the doctrine officially. My particular focus in what follows does not seek to rehearse that work, but rather affirms its utter necessity, as the US equivalent of the political theology emerging in Germany following World War II that took as its impossible mandate the question of how to do theology after Auschwitz. The equivalent here might be phrased, "How do theology after Sand Creek (or the Trail of Tears or Wounded Knee)?" where the particular named debacle stands not simply on its own, but represents the entire regime of genocidal Christian conquest in this hemisphere that revisionist research would now peg at somewhere around 150 million dead bodies (counting African deaths precipitated by the slave trade alongside native deaths by disease and deliberate policy) (Stannard 1992, ix–xv, 317–318).

My project stipulates Newcomb's argument, confesses imperial/colonial Christianity as one of the most destructive ideological formations the planet has seen, and then asks how the tradition, as now embraced by more than a billion people globally, can be read "against itself" to begin to open up a different "Christian" response to indigenous cultures across the planet. I seek neither to disavow Christianity wholesale nor to try to rehabilitate its orthodoxy as somehow coopted and misused by empire. Rather I want to probe its varied configurations as yet carrying—buried, within some of its writings and ritual practices, like a recessive mytheme or a hidden transcript—traces and memories of the indigenous cultures it "metabolized" or reinvented. Arguing such is not to posit a supposedly pristine *Ur*-christianity that somehow became corrupted and warped, but rather to take seriously its origins as a resistance movement, inevitably reproducing (even while wrestling against) elements of the domination structure against which it was reacting in its very attempts to open new social space for eclipsed practices and repressed traditions.

More particularly, I want to dig into the topsoil of Christian enculturation around the globe, seeking to uncover the seeds and roots, tendrils and sprouts of older indigenous cultures, conquered and/or evangelized by one or another version of expansionist Christian conviction, that have remained rhizomically alive and at least partially resistive to imperial routinization, harboring memory of older possibilities for living sustainably in given ecologies. In particular, the work here is beholden both to ancient folk tradition and more recent theorization going by the name of anarcho-primitivism. It is animated by the conviction that the entire trajectory of civilization—the 10,000-year-old expansionist project of settled mono-crop agriculture issuing in the industrial and digital "revolutions"—has brought us to the threshold of collapse (global warming, peaking oil, population overshoot, species extinction, ocean acidification, topsoil erosion and desiccation, aquifer depletion, watershed destruction, rapid disappearance of long-standing human cultures and languages, etc.). Whatever the possibilities for using state-of-the-art technology to change course and draw back from the brink of catastrophe, certainly the sociology and mythology of older modes of organizing our species-life on the planet offer salient witness to some of the necessary cognitive and affective alteration required (if not indeed, the only prospect of "salvation" we have available). And to the degree Christianity has been understood and organized historically as part of various regimes of imperial conquest and reengineering of local cultures and ecologies, there is much to answer for, much to denounce and repudiate, and much to reinvestigate and reimagine. It is especially in service of this latter conviction that I write.

The effort here will sample the history of Christian development and formation—beginning with the oldest biblical stories up through quite recent amalgamations of the tradition with various indigenous cultures—to uncover and lift up "little tradition" versions of the kind of practices that became exemplary in Jesus' Palestinian peasant movement or show up as creative adaptations in various folk responses to being evangelized elsewhere around the globe. It will probe such under the rubric of messianism, seeking to profile subaltern christologies, indigenous epiphanies, animist theologies, and vernacular prophecies as features of collective initiatives that push back behind imperial routinizations of Christian tradition to more sustainable lifeways. "Composted"[1] inside imperial Christian formations are traces and memories of older orientations, based not on enslavement, surplus product accumulation, and tribute taking but on the complex symbiotics and reciprocities of hunter-gatherer, pastoral nomad, and subsistence agriculture lifestyles. It is these traces—enlivened in and "riffed upon" by various messianic movements rebelling against imperial enslavement—that will exercise our imagination here. As such, exactly what might constitute "messianism" will be part of the critical issue. And in the mix, the Jesus movement of the first century will offer insight not as fetishized norm but merely instructive version—one among many—itself congealing certain older creative practices that gain significance *alongside of and in cooperation with* other indigenous practices, predating Christian contact, that imperial Christianity only partially metabolizes and refracts as it expands by way of evangelism and conquest.

What Messianisms Memorialize

But first it is important to establish a kind of thought-horizon within which my (admittedly heuristic and idiosyncratic) use of the term "messianism" will signify. Specifically I am concerned to represent (indeed "construct") this category in relationship to popular memory of more just and sustainable forms of social order. Messianisms invoke and partially embody an alternative to domination and enslavement. They emerge historically, I suggest, in the context of urban-controlled systems of mono-crop agriculture that are in the process of materializing their expansionist ambitions by taking over less specialized and more sustainable lifeways. In ideal-typical terms, there are three such orders that show up in various combinations and permutations (given their own histories and ecologies) that remain enough counter to imperial logics to warrant reference as "alternative."

These are rooted first of all in the *hunting-gathering* formation of our species, dating from its earliest advent on the planet that encoded its foraging orientation into our DNA during our two-million-year span of Pleistocene existence as *homo habilis/ergaster, homo erectus,* and *homo sapiens.* Even today (though probably not for much longer, given the resource-interests of beleaguered national governments and globalizing corporations), a few such hunter-gatherer groups remain in existence, albeit engulfed in and compromised by the products and media penetrating their once pristine life worlds (the fate of "uncontacted tribes" grows increasingly dire, as organizations like Survival for Tribal Peoples regularly reports). While the research on hunter-gatherer communities remains the subject of debate, there is strong evidence that at least a good percentage of such groups elaborated lifestyles that for centuries (if not millennia) lived in sustainable mutuality with their ecosystems and did not practice anything like warfare on other groups (Wells 2010, 193–195, 208). John Gowdy's anthropological anthology of forager structures (*Limited Wants, Unlimited Means*) both highlights the debate and underscores the profile of such communities as what Marshal Sahlins once famously christened "The Original Affluent Societies" (Gowdy 1998, xv–xxxi; 5ff).

These "band societies" typically curtailed impulses to destructive over-reach in various ritual practices that maintained the community of humans as symbiotic members of a broad spectrum of diverse life forms (Reichel-Dolmatoff 1976, 308, 314). At the same time, they inhabited that diversity (and its geologic and aquatic surroundings) mythically and culturally as a kind of kinship system—if not indeed as a "second skin." Death was understood as the passage of community elders into transfigured status as living elements of the local ecology (e.g., the sprouting of corn or rootage of cassava as effectively the continuation of "ancestors") and birth as the transformation of ancestral plants and animals back into human form. Life was lived in face-to-face groups of 150 people or less,[2] exhibiting levels of social cooperation and even in many cases gender parity beyond what we have seen in most of our (supposedly) progressive modern liberal societies (Leacock 1998, 139; Wells 2010, 118–119; Woodcock 1998 87).[3] "Work" activity often took up only 3–4 hours per day and served a "gift economy" approach to resource management (Gowdy 1998, xxi). The wide sharing of tools and shelter, and immediate consumption of game and food, left large amounts of time free for rest, play, ritual pursuits, and social interaction.

And it is no surprise then that European colonists again and again expressed astonishment at the peace and gentleness and generosity observed on first contact, even among groups that combined hunting and gathering with low-tech agriculture (Columbus gushes over the Taino life he encounters on the island of Haiti as a veritable paradise on earth; Thomas More finds visions of utopia filling his head upon hearing the reports) (Stannard 1992, 63; Weatherford 1988, 122). Of course, post-1492 and post-European expansion around the globe, the desire to take over such "Edens of sustainability" also quickly gave rise to a huge and continuous "disinformation campaign," designed to legitimize the never-yet-halted conquest and plunder by pillorying indigenous life as hopelessly "backward" and "savage" (Weatherford 1988, 127; Hobbes,).⁴ And it is this latter denigration rather than the former fascination that most of us in the West inherit as our default picture of indigenous life around the globe.

But it is deeply tendentious. While by no means all hunter-gatherers managed to elaborate relatively sustainable, nonaggressive social forms of existence, they nonetheless remain critical "to think with," as offering counterevidence that our species is doomed (by "original sin" or some other endemic flaw) to either war or ecocide.⁵ Gaining perspective on this most formative of earlier lifestyles is crucial for grasping the kinds of impulses a messianic politics seeks to realize. It is in many ways the evolutionary baseline from which our dreams of "Eden" spring—more nearly and more often approximating such in actual social and ecological relations than the violence-laden hierarchies we have developed in the last 5,000 years. Some scholars would even argue that our DNA "frequency" was effectively "set" on a forager orientation through the long trek of our ancestry across the succession of ice ages and warming periods that have shaped our existence on the planet (anarcho-primitivist scholars will even argue that we are a species now living "out of our ecological niche") (Jensen 2008, 4; Shepard 1982, 4, 6, 9, 130).

In the *long durée* of our emergence as a species, however, management of both plant and animal life—as indeed of our own social relations—eventually became more dominating and controlling. Early humans were effectively hybrid creatures, "living and moving and having their being" as "grass-people," allied with perennials that provided the grazing bounty for the game humans relied upon for their own sustenance (Eisenberg 1999, 4–8). Symbiosis implied adaptation to the slow pulsations of Pleistocene climate change as well as to the seasonal cycles of life on the steppe—moving with the grasses as they extended their reach during ice ages or gave way to woodlands during interglacial periods when the temperatures rose. Over time, our Mesolithic cousins even learned to perpetuate the savanna-like conditions favorable to big game during the more stressful warming periods (when dense forests crowded out the open grasses), by initiating controlled burns to halt the takeover of trees. But some 10,000 years ago, a more radical shift occurred (probably initially by accident) as we discovered the possibility of switching our primal plant-alliance to annuals reproducing by means of seeds rather than underground runners and roots. With the invention of cultivation, the flux of hunting fortunes and population numbers attending glacial advance and retreat was decisively interrupted. The advent of *agriculture* meant we no longer needed to run plant nutrients through four-legged middlemen, but could go straight for the "green" (Eisenberg 1999, 5–6).

In learning to prepare seed-beds and clear out competitor plants, a "weed-human" covenant began to emerge to the advantage of both species. Whether in the form of wheat, oats, or maize, the annual grasses that soon became domesticated staples were essentially wild weeds, now controlled in cultivated beds, securing a growth-wave of our species (and of those grains) that has not ceased its planetary takeover of other ecological niches and cultural lifeways ever since. Hunter-gatherer comity with the wild began to face into the winds of a genocidal spread of new seed: the invasive human-annual alliance that goes by the name of *mono-crop agriculture.* In some places—most notably among the Levantine Natufians—an arboreal-human experiment also evolved, working out a symbiosis between olive, almond, and acorn trees and hill-dwelling Mediterraneans (Eisenberg 1999, 7). (Indeed, the Genesis stories may well reflect this human/fruit-tree mutualism as an early vision of paradise). But it was really the model of clear-cut colonization and grain-cultivation that became the new exhibit for how to be "human" on the planet—and "the rest," as they say, "is history."[6]

Except now ten millennia later, the blowback from wild nature on our ruthlessly expansionist project of domesticating and reengineering many of the life-forms on the globe, including our own,[7] is serving notice that the project is patently unsustainable and likely apocalyptic.[8] "More and more" and "better and better" in service of increasingly potent regimes of dominating control not only represents perfection of the impulse to enslave. It may well take us off the edge of the planet altogether.[9] And thus the need to turn back to older ways and wisdoms and at least listen for values and models that might suggest new forms of more sustainable hybridity in our time—if not actually try to recover some of the extant cultural forms and social orientations!

But even within this turn to agriculture (memorialized as it is in Genesis 3 as "fall" and not as in modern liberal thought as a progressive "revolution"), there are seeds of such values worthy of attention. Many cultures over long periods developed hybrid forms of life in which horticultural cultivation, mixed-crop gardening, and even swidden (slash and burn) practices (usually in woodland areas)were carried out alongside animal husbandry and foraging. The versions of interest here as our second alternative to imperial domination are those that remained largely "subsistence" in orientation, focused largely on mixed crop production for family or village use, and not exchange in a local market (though again, purity of form is not the primary consideration). Historically, *subsistence agriculture* developed in a cultural context of profoundly ritualized and mythologized concourse with plant and animal life, in which human communities elaborated collective identities as peoples living out a kind of hyphenated existence in mutuality with their primary floral symbionts. Humans were not "individuals"—either as single beings or as communities. They were ensembles of organic alliances, and much of their energy consumption was focused on maintaining (ritually) some kind of equilibrium with the local stocks of plant (and animal) life. They understood themselves as "seed-people": children of the maize, *agave*-offspring, rice-beings, and so on.[10]

And just here, it is *apropos* to detour for a second to highlight what the biblical tradition in broad brush may represent. Eisenberg's *The Ecology of Eden* outlines the development with intrigue (Eisenberg 1999, 69, 76–79). The slopes of Canaanite hill country are the first to host the experiments with domestication of plants that becomes agriculture writ large. Indeed, it is quite probably the unique positioning of Canaan as the nexus between three great continents—including the one that mothered all of us (Africa)—that prompted the experimentation. Canaan was "edge territory" ecologically, a zone of promiscuous contact between very different continental ecologies as well as a conduit for peoples migrating out and trading back across its slender pathways. At the end of Pleistocene glaciation, the mountain heights of Lebanon, Syria, and Armenia, which had hosted refuge species (trees, grasses, quadrupeds, and humans) fleeing the advancing drought as the waters locked up in ice, trickled these same species back down to the lower hills, as temperatures warmed. The hills themselves offered a cornucopia of diversity, their slanted terrain condensing microclimates and microecologies, accordionlike, into small areas of contact (fairly begging human cooperation with their possibilities of selection). Here rose for the first time both farming and transhumant parading of livestock up and down the slopes.

But this was also an advent of domestication yet clear on the source of its fecundation. Memory of such was carried in myth—the world's oldest that we know of—enshrining the "northern," cedar-clad mountains as World-Pole, abode of the storm- and cloud gods, whose rains refurbished the watersheds necessary to life.[11] Codified in these archetypal poetics is recognition that it is the *wild* fastness of the heights from whence the rudiments of life proceed—things genetic as well as nutrient, cross-pollinating fowl as well as annual cultivar. Divinity is the image of an uncontrollable liquidity, generated in domains not regularly trucked by human beings. The World-Mountain regularly flushes soil and seed from its bosom into the riparian veins that gift the hills below with mix and the valleys with "fat." Those hills become the site of both primitive cultivation of plant sustenance and early human settlement. And in this prospect, both the peoples and the stories that attain centerfold interest in the biblical tradition are versions of this Canaanite template, riffing on much older memories and practices, whose basic orientation anchors Israel's own—even as animus intensifies between Hebrew and Canaanite in actual historical encounter (Eisenberg 1999, 86, 90).

Where the contrast is most profound, however, is not among hill-dwelling squabblers, but with their later descendants, who, by the sixth millennium BCE, have arrived at the Mesopotamian floodplains and begun the vast irrigation projects necessary to render the marshes and dunes around the two great rivers hospitable to large-scale settlement. Over time, by ingenuity instructed by the meandering river channels themselves, swamp and desert are laced with canals to support the developing city life. And the forgetting occasioned by distance begins to convert wild largesse into an imagination of elite provision. It is here that agriculture develops both its technique and its tower. Out of sight of the mountain origins that inundate the plains with silt and flood and all things living, gouging new courses by axe and bent backs of growing hordes of laborers, Mesopotamian rulers begin to adapt Canaanite myth into a story of urban origination. The World-Mountain is now built of baked brick, its "peaks" the host site of hanging gardens, its gods, the elites themselves, though masked under lip-service paid to deities who structure heaven itself into a hierarchy. Laborers are reimagined as themselves merely a form of "crop"; *bedouin* nomads dismissed as quasi-human "savages"; hunter-gatherers no longer even known as a possibility (Eisenberg 1999, 83). And thus is born the vocation of the city as the new world-pole, its sacred tower-Temple as the source of all things necessary, and its image of royal ostentation as the new meaning of the divine.

It is worth noting in this perspective that the eclipse of the Wild as the original sacrality, and its replacement with an increasingly transcendental "divine," is in one sense, a projection of the city structure itself. It reflects the growing distance between urban elites—epitomized in priestly royalty managing affairs in Temple heights above the buzz of the main thoroughfares—and the rest of the populace, laboring the surrounding fields into food. Increasingly absent from the apex of that urban power is any real contact with wildness and in consequence, the correlative evacuation of the organic otherness of plants and animals (and mountains and storms and headwaters) from the substance of the sacred. What is available for ritualization is rather the techno-sophistication of urban planning as the real focus of celebration, and divinity as a now increasingly abstract "form" whose transcendent emptiness is filled in with the narrative content of elite city power (kingship)—effecting a transferal of "awe" from thunderous nature to bellicose *urbs*. Likewise, as myth is written down by the early *literati* retainers of these emergent city rulers, it is reoriented away from memorializing an original "agreement" to remember the wild genesis of things and toward providing under pinning for that new mode of human power (Prechtel, in Jenson, 2001).

And in this evolutionary/historical context, the biblical tradition is then remarkable as a strain of "edge literature." Caught up in the incessant struggle between imperial floodplains and subsistence highlands, it ends up codifying, in its written form, *both* Israel's own turn toward urbanized monarchy (under David in Jerusalem) *and* the continual effort of various tribes and clans (and prophetic bands) to step free from the control of empire by way of renegade networks and contrast communities. The bible is thus arguably the world's first resistance tract, itself embodying an unresolved argument between hierarchy and symbiosis.

What is key for our purposes, in all of this, is recognition of an older form of agricultural lifeway lived over a significant period of time in roughly sustainable interaction with a local ecology.[12] In such, the very identity of the human community is memorialized as a mode of organic reciprocity rather than human supremacy—so intertwined with a respected and honored form of "otherkind," as to be unthinkable apart from such. What is central in primal agriculture is some measure of continued "hallowing" of the wild—a carefully tended relationship with the local ecology mediated by myth and ritual in which plant life, in particular, is regularly "offered" respect (through dances, songs, beads, other human artifacts, etc.; Prechtel, in Jenson, 2001). This mnemonic practice recognizes that the conscription and domestication of certain plants as "food for humans" (in farming) is at cost to the wild prodigality of the land itself and is thus a deep gift of the divine in nature that enjoins a return gifting. Such a mode of cultivation also stands forth as an alternative to imperial hubris and aggrandizement, though often enough, subsistence agriculture was engulfed within expansionist mono-cropping, and reinvented as a form of peasant or tenant farming, underpinning and making possible the prodigious accumulation and wasteful ostentation that in history books gets labeled "civilization."

The third social form among our three ideal-typical alternatives is represented by the folk who reacted against the enslavements of settled agriculture by exiting such communities altogether. Historically, *pastoral nomadism* emerged in most places on the planet as a response *to* the oppression and enervation of peasant life (except perhaps among peoples such as the Sami of northern Europe, whose foraging relationship with reindeer herds led, over time, to a certain kind of cooperative venture between the two species). Herding developed alongside agriculture as its compliment and trading partner—diary and meat and skins exchanged regularly for grains and spices and vegetables. But the skills exercised in spending large amounts of time away from village or town life, wandering the steppe or semi-arid scrub lands in forays ranging from hours to months at a time (depending on needs for summer pasturage or winter shelter), maintained a possibility of independence that occasioned the first "radical social movement" in humanity's brief tenure on the planet. "Going feral" with one's flocks became the prototype of social revolt—a staple of dissent from agricultural routine and taxation that in various times and places occasioned a definitive "break" with settled life altogether. It gave rise to equestrian *kazaks* in Central Asia and camel-riding *bedouin* in the deserts, goat- and horse-herding Moguls fleeing the containment of China's Great Wall in the east and Maasai with their cattle on the southern savannas of the Mother Continent, Celtic sheepherders in Nordic hill country, and Diné wanderers into the American southwest. Regularly defamed by imperial authorities as "outlaw," feared in towns as "renegade" and "barbaric," nomad herders everywhere ran afoul of sedentary protocol. By no means themselves exemplars of "saintliness" or high moral achievement, pastoralists nonetheless beg attention as collectively offering testament to the requirements of counter-imperial aspirations. Whoever would exit the imperial "Matrix," must know an alternative economics and be ready for retaliation. Pastoral nomadism—whether herding goats, cattle and sheep, or horses, llamas, and yak—offers prospect for sedentary humans to reintegrate with some aspects of a wildlands economy and reinvigorate a more animist cosmology and sensibility.

Herders are the first folk to wax "primitivist," to forsake the siren song of security for a proud independence—on the run, if necessary, but under no one's royal thumb. And while most of the displacements that human history has witnessed have been in the direction of greater social complexity and technological distance from "nature" (farmers displace hunter-gatherers, "civilized" peoples incorporate primitive farmers, industrial regimes subjugate everyone else), pastoral nomadism represents the one recurrent reversion from that vector of change. Certainly herder life often proved ecologically destructive in the long run and in various places itself gives rise to imperial conquest (think Genghis Khan). But apart from ecologically necessary "returns" like the Chatham Islands Moriori who reverted to foraging once they left the Maori farming culture on New Zealand from which they had originally come,[13] pastoralism stands as the archetype of exiting empire for the sake of freedom. Nor does it represent only an artifact from history. The work and writings of Sanctuary Movement Cofounder Jim Corbett and the practices of the Saguaro-Juniper Covenant Community he founded in Tuscon, AZ, offer a deep exploration of modern possibilities of such a reversion, seeking to "hallow" the San Pedro River basin and return Covenant members to a sustainable lifestyle of symbiosis with the desert, "apprenticed to" and mediated by herds of cattle and goats as their effective "teachers" (as we revisit later in this chapter).

While none of the these three lifeways everywhere and always achieved benign orders of existence, on average—ecologically and socially—*hunting and gathering, subsistence farming,* and early, small-scale *pastoralist reversion to nomadic wandering* represent social architectures distinctly less destructive than mono-crop agriculture. The latter's thrust toward expansionist conquest, urbanizing appropriation, and social and ideological domination and enslavement has generally been far more vicious in both scale and logic—and usually at the expense of the former three modes of existence. On the other hand, within the cultural forms of these latter three are practices and values pointing toward a different ordering of human aspiration. Materially less developed than settled agriculture's urbanizing concentrations and technomilitarist organization, each of the three nonetheless exhibits complex elaborations of cosmology. Animist codes of relationship to the ecological surround offer testament to life lived within an embraced limit and habituated to at least a measure of respect for and mutuality with plant and animal "partners." Articulated across the divide of human and other life forms, spiritual sensibilities were arguably even more incarnational than Christian notions of such. The spirit-world in such cultures was not accessed transcendentally and hierarchically as much as materially and ecstatically. Mosquitoes among the Sami as whales among the Inupiat or oaks for the Celts and vines for the Amazonian Shipabo were not merely totemistic "kin" but actual shamanic presences relied upon for guidance and protection. And indeed, not all was idyllic and alluring in such a life; certain spaces and features and events (typhoons, tsunamis, volcanic eruptions, predation by large game, etc.) were mythically remembered and ritualistically reserved as "terroristic" in their "revelatory" power (Deloria 1999, 250–260). But even these geologic or animistic encounters with something like the *Mysterium Tremendum* were rendered socially and spiritually useful in serving as a rebuke to human hubris and marking a limit on the impulse to exploit. And it is in relationship to this entire panoply of less aggrandizing values and more profoundly mutualistic "wisdoms" from earlier in our planetary venture that my category of messianism will construct its meanings and vision.

Messianism Broadly Speaking

Historically, messianism (as I am using the term) could be said to designate any number of largely antiurban "people's traditions," appearing well after the establishment of settled agriculture in the eighth millennium BCE as a counterpoint to the system of extraction presided over by local kings (operating through bureaucratic structures of retainers appropriating surplus product from peasants, whose spoils were the subject of continuous struggle between the royal house and the local aristocratic class). It emerges out of unresolved impulses at the intersection of imperial aggression (whether military or socioeconomic) and some version of foraging, herding or subsistence farming. It has rupture and contradiction as its soil and embodies nostalgia for—and creative reworking of—the values and greater sustainability of these latter lifeways. And while the "spiritualities"[14] of these more indigenous social orders generally do not organize their insights around a need "to be saved,"[15] messianism itself will often articulate such a concern—embodying some of those insights and values as a dangerous memory of an "other way" to live. Messianism thus is not originally part of these older ways, as not needed by them. It is largely a reaction to settled agriculture's invasive militancy and rapacious hierarchy. Among native communities in this country, for instance, something like the prophetism of Pauite medicine man Wovoka and the collective rite of "ghost dancing" that he initiated only appears after white decimation of indigenous cultures is far advanced—and it arises as a visionary rite projecting salvation *from* whites and their Christianity and return *to* a more balanced and traditional way of living in and on their lands. (Even when it is not merely recalling older forms of living but projecting a more hopeful and "new" future, that future is typically composed of reconfigured elements of the past.[16])

Salvation emerges as a typically messianic concern primarily as a *response to* and *critique of* imperial aggression, even if consciously framed in more existentialist and spiritist terms. It seeks to open a space of reimagination within and underneath the repressive structures "reducing"[17] more indigenous lifeways to subservience and domesticity, even where memory of these alternatives appears only in murky dreamscapes or inchoate longings. What we need to be saved *from* in such an orientation is imperial pretension to conquer, control, and enslave an entire planet of resources and life forms. Indeed, it may well be that in our time we are facing need for a messianically dialectical retrieval on the largest scale imaginable. Our ten-thousand-year agro-industrial quest to accumulate, reengineer, and commodify everything in sight stands as evolutionary "anti-thesis" to the "thesis" of hunter-gatherer (and to lesser degrees, subsistence agricultural and pastoral nomadic) "live-and-let-live" symbioses. (Indeed, we typically style the advent of agriculture and industry as "revolutions.") Today, however, perhaps the deepest contradiction of our planetary emergence begins to appear with apocalyptic clarity: we are a prodigal species, thus far genetically "wired" to engage life emotionally and meaningfully in small scale, face-to-face communities now trying to survive in a monstrously globalized hierarchy. What we now need is a revolution in the other direction. As 96-year-old Detroit activist Grace Lee Boggs regularly intones, for the first time ever, we (who inhabit the "developed" side of the world divide) face a "progressive" demand for the *giving up of* continuing material aggrandizement if our species is to remain viable on the planet (Boggs and Kurashige, 42, 45, 71–73). This effectively amounts to a creative "negation of the negation" of technoexpansionist-development and a synthetic retrieval and reintegration of indigenous "wisdom ways," incorporating such into newly hybrid and more culturally diverse modes of being human. Far from fetishizing growth as we now do, these latter would focus on active embrace of *limitation*, recreating relations of *reciprocity* (socially and ecologically) and working out *sustainable* patterns of dwelling within a finite biosphere.

To anticipate, for a moment, some of the focus of chapter 3 by borrowing a major trope of the Jesus movement, messianism, as we have thus far suggested, could perhaps be likened to an invasive species like mustard,[18] responding to the environmental disturbance caused by the age of agriculture, seeking, in long-range ecosystemic terms, its own succession in climax forest. Pioneer weeds are rapid propagators, quickly infesting broken soil with wild proliferation, that nonetheless in the long run—unless they somehow ally with tougher, more aggressive species—create the conditions for their own demise in more durable and stable forms of biodiversity. Historically, mono-crop agriculture has been precisely that kind of alliance between pioneer weeds and a tougher expansionist species—in this case annuals like wheat, oats, or maize and human beings—wherein our role as the more aggressive partner has been one of keeping the ecological niche open for the more vulnerable pioneer (Eisenberg 1999, 8). (We clear the fields, plant the desired weeds, and keep out invaders.)

Within this trope, however, messianism appears as a *renegade* invasive, bearing recessive traits, that steps into the figurative and literal breech caused by mono-cropping *to act against and begin repair of a* prior invasion (settled agriculture). It opens up, inside the latter's disturbed relations, atavistic memories of other ways of being, less disturbed, more viable—both by invoking images of those ways and by partially embodying them. Certainly such a messianism is a form of lived *artistry*, symbolically recalling older possibilities that have been eclipsed by settled agriculture with its deskilling and specialization (which make even imagining something else hard). *But it is also material,* rekindling, in imagination and in fact (in some kind of practice), one or another form of alliance with perennials or herds or even a multiplicity of annuals (not mono-cropping) whose evolutionary career was less destructive and whose prospect for justice and sustainability is more tenable. But it also has—and this is the real rub—as its deep ecology aim, its own demise in questing for a level of stable diversity far beyond its own frenzied opportunism. This vision of messianism is provisional and tactical; it does not focus on its own expansionist triumph but on an "ecosystemic regeneration"[19] whose true destiny is wild biological and multicultural (and multispiritual) *plurality*. What if Christianity had been envisioned and lived *this way*?

But in any case, the particular use of the term here will key off of the work by Horsley and Hanson, entitled *Bandits, Prophets, and Messiahs:*

Popular Movements at the Time of Jesus, in which a typology of such collective uprisings is developed ranging from social bandits and messiahs to oracular and eschatological prophets (Horsley and Hanson 1985, 246–247, 251–252). In their continuum, messianism represents generally a more economically organized and politically savvy development out of merely rebellious social banditry, and prophetic movements give focus and articulation to the energies of riots and shamanistic "spirit-possession" troops (I Sam10:1–13). For our purposes, I use the term in an admittedly idiosyncratic and heuristic manner, both to defamiliarize and disturb our thoroughly domesticated notions of "christology" (that have been enervated and warped in appropriating, and being appropriated by, the Roman "emperor cult"), and to provoke more creative imagination of the stakes at issue in various modalities of political resistance.

Messianism in this view arises fundamentally as *revolt,* usually under the charisma of what is thought of (from the imperial point of view) as a kind of "social bandit," galvanizing a following provisionally organized into an alternative economy of reciprocity. This following lives roughly "outlaw" on the land, renegade from urban centers of power, and guerrilla in action, before being persecuted and crushed by the royal authority and supporting armies. Typically encoded in the symbology of such a movement—and lived out to one degree or another—is memory of less hierarchical modes of social organization, whether hunter-gatherer, pastoral nomad, or horticultural (subsistence agriculture), whose alternative vision of living had been kept alive (at least fractionally) inside various folk wisdoms and vernacular media (songs, proverbs, rituals, mythologies, etc.). The key element in such a profile is the instinct for a roughly egalitarian sharing of resources in band-sized groupings of 150 or less—perhaps coordinated across a larger alliance of such local communities—whose experience of reciprocity is intimately linked historically with an ecological symbiotics, codified in religious imagery, and reinforced in ritual practice.

As such, messianism is here understood as *revisionist* and *restorative,* harking back to older models for being human, articulated across a kind of social rupture provoked by and provoking continuous struggle between subsistence-living peasantry and avarice-driven elites. It is also *performative.*[20] While focused around a given leader, such a messianism is best comprehended as a popular movement, mobilizing memory and resources, imagery and affect, that have long been "composted" and safeguarded among "the people" in forms sometimes explicit, but more often inchoate and unconscious. A given messiah-figure is then not some kind of "lone ranger" genius, but a social dramatist of the "little tradition." This is someone able to speak and act, posture and prophesy, conjure shamanically and gesture archetypically, out of a shared subtext of "dangerous memory," invoking ancient intuitions of a different time, when economy was more nearly shared and the natural ecology embraced as a second skin or body, hallowed in symbol and engaged as a kind of spiritual/physical "mother."

In this construction of messianism, provisional organization of the originally outlaw band (whether violent or nonviolent in tactics) into a recapitulation of such a communal symbiotics is successful enough to attract a wider following. Inevitably, it also attracts the attention of the authorities, whose tolerance for such alternatives normally proves to be inversely proportional to the movement's economic savvy and symbolic sharpness, and whose redress for such is usually quite vicious. What is then at stake in sussing out a messianic event within a given social order is the radicalness of its alternative economics, its "soil wisdom" in surviving on the land or in the wild (whether its mode is foraging, herding, subsistence growing, or some combination of the three), its invocation of older symbols in marking out new meaning with ancient images, its artistry in articulating a vernacular pedagogy for its members and recruits, and its "guerrilla savvy" in surviving under the radar of political authorities.[21] Typically operating clandestinely in public by way of coded communication, such a messianism will also maintain underground spaces where "hidden transcripts" can be (relatively) safely aired.[22] And it will seek to develop supportive alliances among sympathetic population sectors whose cooperation becomes necessary to maintain the covert character of the movement long enough, potentially, to relearn survival skills effective in moving toward greater self-sufficiency.[23]

Messianism and the Urban

Obviously, the argument as outlined constructs messianism as in some ways a counter-urban phenomenon. In the history of Israel, as we rehearse it in the next two chapters, most of the critical energy focused on will erupt from the countryside and speak and act against the organization of power exemplified in the city. Whether looking at Abel as pastoral nomad victim of agriculturalist Cain's wrath (who becomes the first city-builder),[24] Moses leading an escaped slave movement earning its chops in desert foraging, early Israel as primitive farming cooperative in the Canaanite highlands, or prophetic bombast directing its ire against royal predation on little people, the tradition carries a clear antiurban tinge. Both John the Baptist and Jesus the prophet will eschew urban work, concentrating their organizing among peasant villages and out-of-the-way places, and entering the city (in Jesus' case) only to disrupt and "exorcise" privileged institutional spaces like the Capernaum synagogue or the Jerusalem Temple. But the strain of resistance I emphasize is not merely out of deference to biblical precedent. As should already be obvious, the argument is substantive. As I read the city—out of more than 30 years of activist involvement and artistic engagement in Detroit's urban core—the issue is structural. (And it is worth adding that I nonetheless love what Motown has wrought in my own soul. Even as I argue negatively about city potency, I live inside its struggles and act within its possibilities. Convinced of its current unsustainability, I nonetheless remain passionately committed to its people and their pain and creativity.)

Thus far in human evolution, cities have functioned as concentrations of resources forcibly gathered from elsewhere. The city, in essence, has been a force of violent appropriation of carrying capacity from its various "surrounds." Structurally, it emerges out of the increased population numbers made possible by settled agriculture's mono-cropping productivity. Historically, in many places city centers coalesce around sacred shrines, presided over by priestly elites, creating the discourses and public liturgies necessary to secure the extractive order (one or another version of "sacred ideology" or "scripture" enacted via Temple/shrine ritual). Former hunting and gathering peoples are taken over and "reduced" to peasant small farmers as the need for arable land to feed a growing population results in expansionist policies on the part of ruling elites. The cities that arise from nascent hierarchies operate as emergent structures of concentration—in effect, putting food under lock and key after forcing peasant growers to give up between 30 and 60 percent (or more) of their product in rent, taxes. and tithes (the Genesis accounts of Joseph serving as Pharaoh's top executive, implementing a ruthless "food as weapon" policy on the Egyptian populace, is a classic example; Gen 41:14–57; 47:13–26). And of course, behind the collection brokers stand the ruling class armies, trained in tactics, disciplined in organization, and outfitted with state-of-the-art weapons technology.

All of which is to say, the city is fundamentally an apparatus of violence, even if its everyday operations proceed by seeming cooperation. The terms of struggle between peasant farmers and elite rulers center on perceptions of "subsistence"—peasants seeking to secure a modicum of resources above and beyond the bare minimum as a hedge against misfortune (bad crop years, sickness, accidents, and storms) and for festive occasions, and the elites seeking to extract all but the amount necessary for the peasants to continue to reproduce their labor input. Over time, the reach of such metropolitan centers becomes vastly wider and immensely more complicated—embroiled in competition with rival centers, faced with recurrent peasant revolts or sabotage and struggling with outbreaks of famine, as elite price manipulation jacks up costs and rural-dwellers flee to the cities out of desperation. These latter create conditions ripe for outbreaks of plague and disease that cull the population, foment die offs, and then allow the cycle to begin all over again.[25]

With the advent of the industrial "revolution," the centers of manufacturing production are "gerrymandered" into their command position by ruthless colonial policy, gutting native infrastructure around the globe while transferring indigenous technologies and skills to the metropolitan centers. The modern metropole gains ascendency by carefully relegating peripheries to dependent roles of raw materials production that, only one generation down the line, have effectively erased popular skill sets capable of doing anything other than extractive labor.[26] From that point forward many Global South countries become client states of northern interests, locked into an international role of providing only one or two raw materials (coffee, bananas, copper, oil, etc.) for the manufacturing operations monopolized by Euro-American concerns (even with the current outsourcing of such production "south-wards," financial return does not follow. And the globalization of economic production and marketing for 500 years now has been buttressed by almost ceaseless military intervention (more than 550 times in scarcely two centuries for the USA alone[27]), guaranteeing Euro-States and their offshoots (such as the United States, Canada, and Australia) an almost unassailable hegemony in the resulting global flows of raw goods and finished products.

Today's debacles are merely more of the same, with the marketing of debt (under IMF and World Bank patronage and "economic hit man" finagling of Third World ruling classes) assuming primary status after the overproduction crisis of global capital in the 1970s, and casino-finance emerging as the new apparatus to continue the old game. Metropolitan life in current conditions can only be adequately analyzed in its incredible structures of planetary "reach." But once so analyzed, the verdict is as has been for five-thousand years: cities are parasitical formations, eviscerating their peripheries continually, while ever-more stridently inflating privileged appetites for status products and ostentatious lifestyles, and enforcing their insatiable demands on immiserated labor forces with draconian militancy and virtual impunity. But the real-life effects are now global crises in environmental viability and social infrastructure everywhere, attended by a growing "sea" of garbage and indestructible waste products (plastics, nuclear materials, chemical effluent, etc.).

While such an evaluation of planetary urbanization appears bleak to the point of apocalypse (Mike Davis' *Planet of Slums*, for instance, gives a shocking read of the phenomenon, simply in terms of the vast numbers of urban poor literally living "in shit" because of unavailable sewage treatment), it must be faced (Davis 2006, 137–142). I would simply offer here, that messianisms of various kinds effect important ruptures in the otherwise enervating ideologies that mask the reality (and promise only "trivial pursuit" preoccupation and somnambulist denial). The city perhaps could become something other than it has been in history—but only by radical break with how its predatory appetites have thus far functioned. The last chapter in this work actually takes up this possibility as it is currently emerging in my own beloved mess of a polis called "Detroit." "Poster-child" of rampant deindustrialization and urban blight, recurrently "murder capital" of the country, Detroit nonetheless is also laboratory—a kind of "wild west" incubator zone for the question of whether a city can reinvent itself as roughly sustainable within its own boundaries (at least with respect to food). I conclude my sampling of messianic signs by posing Detroit as potentially an *urban* icon of such—a post-industrial core of 139 square miles, hosting open space of sufficient size to engulf a Boston or a San Francisco, struggling toward a new kind of hybridity wherein the city "incorporates" large tracts of reemergent wildness into its vision and practice. But in the immediate prospect, our messianic discernment will remain focused on historically rural-based uprisings, challenging urban hierarchy and predation with irrepressible memory and insurgent beauty, before being crushed or bought off.

Messianism *in Nuce*

In sum then, in what follows, I use the range of the term thus: *messianism* will normally designate the kind of social movement just profiled earlier; *messiah* will indicate one of its more charismatic leaders; and the *messianic* will refer to its symbolic production, both by way of the artistic signs (gestures, codes, stories, songs, proverbs, etc.) it mobilizes and in the way such media are "read."[28] In the event, it will become clear that the term references not only a broad range of concerns, but especially emphasizes this latter mode of reading. At stake is not only savvy discernment of "artful signs" lionizing an exemplary leader but also committed appreciation for the character of the social movement animated by such artistry. And it is this assertion that is the key for this writing. It is possible, for instance, to read messianic signs—like say, the gospels' portrayal of the prophet of Nazareth—as indicating that Jesus is in some vaunted sense *the* "messiah," but do so outside of any clear awareness of, or respect for, what the movement (he led) itself embodied, or the fact that the term "messiah" gets used in relationship to all kinds of creative rebellions on the political horizon of first century Palestine. And doing so leads almost inevitably into the kind of messianic reification we have witnessed in the history of Christianity: Jesus repackaged in an imperial theology as individual "Slum God," doing drag for a day among poor wayward humans to bedazzle our blindness with spirit-spectacle and Holy-Ghost-titillation, before returning to the great suburb-in-the-sky to sip wine with the Father and give a thumbs up or thumbs down on our wormlike struggles to believe in the bird-like possibilities of "ascension" or "heavenly communication" of such a "God-Man" figure. The fact that he was a "creature of a movement" (no matter what we may believe about his origins—eternal or other-wise), who learned his own role from another movement (led by John the Baptist) to which he apprenticed himself, gets entirely lost in the mix. And with it—any reality for those of us locked into history and nature as the entire theater of our thinking and acting. Preeminently, this work is a *reading* of the Jesus-event *as movement*—recognizable as such in relationship to many other such movements throughout history and intelligible only to the degree we take such "movement history" seriously.

Historical examples of such movements (or their facsimiles) abound. From escaped slaves wandering the Sinai under Moses to the "retrib-alising" *'apiru* fleeing seaboard cities and organizing in the Canaanite highlands of the late second millennium BCE; from the peasant move-ments of John and Jesus in first century Palestine to the desert-going monastics of Egypt in the fourth century; from various Buddhisms emerging as contrast communities in their respective Asian social orders over millennia to Muhammed's *bedouin*-following, challenging Quraysh control of Mecca; from New World *marronage* among escaped slaves beginning already in 1512 to Wovoka's Ghost Dance uprising among genocidally assaulted Native Americans in the late nineteenth century, from the Diggers of the seventeenth century England planting the commons to the spread of what Vadana Shiva calls "forest satyagrahas" in twentieth century India, issuing in the recent "tree-chaining" actions of Chipko women resisting agribusiness incursions into their forests (Shiva 2010, 66–67), etc.—all to one degree or another could be comprehended as culturally specific forms of messianism, memorialized in various forms of creative artifice.

Of course, speaking this way goes counter to so much of the Christian tradition's focus on the person of Jesus (once the "preacher became the preached," quite soon after his death). It raises, as a prime consideration, the question of enculturation. What symbols, whose titles, which privileged categories with what focus will structure imagination of our understanding of "the messianic?" Even within the biblical tradition itself, the struggle emerges. Most of global Christianity today, one way or another, emphasizes Jesus as agent of "salvation," figures such as primarily a question of eternal destination of "souls," and articulates the way into that afterlife through epistolary texts like Rom 10: 9, where the focus is on "believing and confessing" his "lordship." An entirely different economy of wholeness might have been teased from the biblical corpus, however, had a parable like Mt 25:31–46 become the privileged focus. In this latter, eternal life is decided entirely by mundane response to other human beings in need (the "least of these"), quite apart from any recognition of "Jesus" anywhere in the scene (neither group— "sheep" nor "goats"—perceives "the Son of Man" inside the "hungry, thirsty, naked, sick, imprisoned, or alien"). What might it mean for care given to poor people and strangers, by itself alone, to leverage entry into eternity? Certainly the 1,700-year-long career of Christianity as predominantly an acolyte to empire would have looked quite different. It is imperative to emphasize that the choice to lift up one or the other of these (Rom 10:9 or Mt 25:31–46) as *the* privileged image of salvation is itself a choice *we bring to* the scriptures, not something in the scriptures themselves.[29] It is fundamentally the question, "How do we read?"

Needless to say, here, I am proposing a reading that does not privilege a person demanding obsequious recitation of the magic code and handshake, but rather a movement whose "messianic" profile as a challenge to domination is wide open to all kinds of cultural codifications and artistic depictions and religious namings of that political phenomenon. My interest is not in who is lip-synching the right formula, but who is daring to remember and organize an alternative possibility. I trust "divinity" is at work everywhere under the surface of global cultures in raising up such collective witnesses—as ubiquitously and prosaically as mustard rampaging through Palestinian fields in the first century or chicory singing blue-notes through sidewalk cracks in midsummer Detroit! Like Jesus the Jew before Caiaphas the priest in his day, the issue is "agitating among the people" (Lk 23:2, 14) and threatening to "dismantle the Temple" (Mk 14:58), not mouthing the right formula.

In what follows, however, we will not limit ourselves only to public forms of contestation but also seek rather to open perspective on the will-to-resist in more cryptic modalities of creative expression that flash against the grain of imperial constraint. Even the most shadowy forms of insurgence can be glossed as figures of messianic hope. Ezekiel, we might remember, in the biblical corpus, locked away in the bowels of Babylon in the mid-sixth century BCE, having fallen out in a trance-dream while gathered with the elders-in-exile, recounts being addressed, in that vision, "son of man to son of man" (Ezek 8:1–9:6). He writes of having been plucked up, in the hand of his Spirit-interlocutor, by a lock of his hair and wafted on a shaman-journey back to the homeland, there to witness—amidst the depths of colonial violence—another son of man "with a writing case at his side," who is ordered to mark the foreheads of those who only so much as *sigh over* the agony being inflicted there. It will be a sign granting strange sanctuary—a certain "untouchability"—in the violence to come (Ezek 9:6). And it is in recall of such writing, memorializing the merest "breathing against" injustice—haunted by dead bodies and gathered up in the artful sign of "anointing"—that this writing goes forth.

CHAPTER 2

Ancestral Invocation: Messianic Traces from Abel to Isaiah

And therein lies the frightening aspect of haunting: you can be grasped and hurtled into the maelstrom of the powerful and material forces that lay claim to you whether you claim them as yours or not. (Gordon 1997, 166)

A voice cries: "In the wilderness prepare the way . . . " (Is 40:3)

In seeking to open up the question of vernacular christologies, much of what is at stake is an issue of "reading." The next chapter camps out on a moment when Jesus is represented by the gospel writer Luke as having pointedly thrown down the challenge, "how do you read?" as an interpretive gauntlet to a scribal spy, sent to do surveillance on his activity. In that challenge, as we see, lies much of the substance of what is meant by christology. Jesus himself, as any good classical christological treatise will point out, apparently sat loose to the title "messiah" ("christ"). This is especially evident in the *Ur*-text of the tradition. Mark's gospel, at one level, is a nuanced negotiation of what the term *christos* potentially entails—a designation as "anointed" that invokes the deep past of Israel's appointment of various kinds of leadership and a popular culture use, in first century Palestine, for the more sophisticated forms of social banditry that coalesce into social movements of peasant resistance to the dominant powers of the day (Horsley and Hanson 1985, 246, 251–252). Mark's Jesus ducks the term when an over-eager inner circle of followers too loosely begins naming him such—presumably in full awareness of the political dangers entailed (Mk 8:27–33). Messiahs in general—not just Jesus in particular—tended to end up as the highlighted villains in imperial morality plays, staged at the spectral crossroads for the colonial populace at large, whose denouement was a bloody and dead body. Being a "christ" figure had a very short vocational arc.

But of course, this "social banditry" significance of first century Palestinian folk employments of the term was quickly eclipsed in the cultural shift of its use from the Jewish outback of Galilee to city-state centers of the Roman Empire in subsequent centuries. Much of the guild discipline of christology has focused for two millennia on the person of Jesus, filtered through the terminologies and debates characteristic of Greek philosophy and Roman law, generating entire libraries spanning multiple centuries and dozens of cultures in sussing out the supposedly precise ontological composition of the man from Nazareth as the Christ incarnate, downplaying if not entirely obfuscating his depiction as a criminalized agitator.

For our purposes, however, the primary question is one of *effect*. The issue is not so much conformity to the gospel picture of Jesus of Nazareth as an icon of individual human embodiment of divine interventionist intention. It is rather the unleashing within any given sociopolitical order of an impulse to resist inappropriate death with defiant or surreptitious creativity, whether carried out under an explicit invocation of the name of Jesus or not. Again, the term "messianism" in first century Palestine was not monopolized by the figure of Jesus of Nazareth, and according to our best exegetical lights, was not even his own preferred self-designation (that honor goes to the term "Son of Man," or as Ched Myers reframes for our age, "The Human One"—a reference whose precise resonance we touch on below). Mark and the other gospel writers fill out the chain of associations opened up by the term "messiah" from its particular cultural repertoire of more than one-thousand years of Jewish use. They do so in a set of carefully sequenced and creatively layered narrative "tropes," whose thread of significance they "spin" for their different audiences according to their own set of presuppositions and aims (in their respective editorial assemblages of the discrete memories of Jesus' life and ministry handed down by way of oral traditioning for more than three decades). Which is to say, they do art on memory!

The gospel writers are taking up the dangerous recall of a torture victim, whose body has been entombed, but whose living essence, however we choose to interpret the texts of resurrection, has refused to stay put inside the grave. In the words of Mark Taylor, himself redeploying Avery Gordon, they have created a "seething presence" inside an explosive "artful form" (Gordon 1997, 175; M. Taylor 2011, 14). Theirs is the provocative evocation of a body living through violent death with such symbolic force that it strikes the present like a clanging bell. The gospels present both the undead horror of a savagely dismembered past and the insistent question of something yet to be done—an "emergent politics" demanding a "material practice." Gordon's own language was animated by the restive gravity of Argentinian women writing about their "forcibly disappeared" friends and family members after that country's "Dirty War" from 1976 to 1983, especially as those disappearances were liturgized in the public square every week for years by *Las Madres de Plaza de Mayo,* parading pictures and names of their "absented" ones. Taylor underscores that the issue here is not aesthetic efficacy alone, but the up-take of eruptive artful symbols in active social movements, whose public force channels the writhing energies of an open wound into a political push-back on the order of forgetting and whitewash.

And at this level, it is then not enough merely to cherish in worship the gospel depictions of a messianic *desaparecido* ("disappeared" one) who is brought back to life in the practices and preaching of his followers. We are rather bound also to ask about the artful animation of his own resistance to the powers that be, *before* his death. What seething presences carried in which artful images galvanized his messianic practice? Indeed, what we seek to track in this writing is the trace of such subversive memories of the "undead dead" wherever their force ruptures the surface of silent conformity to oppressive order. What renegade sounds or outlaw images detonated the local cultural symbolics of first century Galilee with enough charge to mobilize social movement around their artful representation? Whence Jesus' own provocation?

This chapter thus opens up a question of what might be called "incipient- or proto messianisms" exhibited in Jesus' own teaching. It does so by exploring the tradition of memory in which the prophet from Palestine stood, *before* he himself was enshrined as christology's normative and singular icon (at once memorialized *and forgotten* under its advertisements after his movement is coopted and inverted by imperial wealth and power beginning with Constantine). Here the Abel story emerges as emblem of indigenous disappearance, whose continuously shed blood echoes across the history as the unrequited cry by which all settled agricultural and city-building activity is to be judged. Here also Abraham is offered as feral progenitor and exemplary ancestor of the new experiment in being a people that only comes to fruition centuries later under renegade Moses. The latter shows forth as the quintessential champion of the tradition, initiating a motley crew of escaped Hebrew slaves into a *cimarron* lifestyle in Sinai whose Sabbath-Jubilee tenets of practice are set up as constitutive for the centuries-long retribalization struggle in the highland zones of Canaan, battling continuously to remain outside the oppressive city-state systems of the Mediterranean seaboard. And from the time after Israel itself goes monarchical under Saul and the tragic history of royal domination galvanizes the counter-tradition of prophetic contestation—we find recourse to that tradition's earliest "hope" in herder David's guerilla resistance, its archetype in the Elijah stories, its apogee in the Jubilee figurings of Isaiah, and its later apocalyptic trope in the likes of a Daniel catching vision of a coming Mortal One within whose "reign" the oppressed will find vindication, and the release promised under the Jubilee sign.

Abel's Soil

Therefore also the Wisdom of God said, 'I will send them prophets and apostles, some of whom they will kill and persecute,' that the blood of all the prophets, shed from the foundations of the world, may be required of this generation, from the blood of Abel to the blood of Zechariah, who perished between the altar and sanctuary. Yes, I tell you it shall be required of this generation. (Lk 11:46–51)

By faith Abel offered to God a more acceptable sacrifice than Cain, through which he received approval as righteous, God bearing witness by accepting his gifts; he died, but through his faith he is still speaking... (Heb 11:4)

In the origin myth of Israel, the great ancestral narratives of Genesis, Abel stands as a peculiar footnote, a "disappeared one," whose voiceless absence is invoked by Yahweh to the face of his killer, Cain, and made a vortex of soundless witness. "Where is your brother Abel?" resounds no less sharply than the earlier query of those texts seeking out a closeted Adam after he had eaten from the wrong tree—and does so with a good deal more "thunder"! Especially telling, in the ensuing tradition, is the name of this voiceless shepherd, in the curse-litany offered by the synoptic Jesus of all those slain across the entire panorama of history, whose blood—still speaking, though completely without word—will be required "of that generation" (Mt 23:29–39; Lk 11:46–51). In such an incantation, Abel is made primal in what we might characterize as a kind of prophetic "hit-list" of those whose rent flesh and torn life upwells ceaselessly as a messianic energy of seething animation for ever-renewed movements of social redress and political change. If we feel bound to maintain a certain primacy for the testimony borne to Jesus of Galilee (when styling certain representations as "christological" or "messianic"), then here in Luke's rendition (as also in Matthew if we care to buttress the claim) is the very Wisdom of God speaking by way of Jesus' own tongue, underscoring the roll in which he is to be enlisted by his own refusal not to speak. He names Abel as ancestor of the first rank, whose blood-cry he now inhabits and channels. And John of the Apocalypse will go even further and invoke this "red pool of testament" as the very substance, the real meaning and cost, of all the commodities so loved and hoarded inside Babylon, whose bloody "under-story" of conquered resources and disappeared indigenous and oppressed labor will ring down the ultimate calamity on that urbane celebrity as the archetype and final end of all urban reality throughout time (Rev 18:11–24).[1] There is much here to be entertained that can but be glossed in this writing.

Abel ghosts the kaleidoscope from Genesis to Revelation as the haunt that refuses to leave, the subaltern of ages, the unjustly slain and disappeared "field-hand," whose nonspeech and otherness—underneath the text of history, beneath the floor of every civilized achievement—the biblical tradition lifts up as unforgettable and unforgotten. His name itself signifies his own throbbing absence: a mere *hebel*, a "vapor," a "breath," "unsubstantialness" incarnate, as notes scholar Theodore Hiebert in his eco-exegesis of the primeval texts called *The Yahwist's Landscape* (Hiebert 1996, 182). Only a fragment of Abel's body will make it into the speech of history—but that speaking will itself become a kind of crescendo. Abel's blood cries from the ground, echoes in sonic percussion like a deep drum-pound whose reverb becomes the pulse of contrast to every temptation to forget. As we see in our cursory run-through of the tradition in this chapter, that screech of spilled plasma finds enshrinement in an entire menagerie of narrative artistry, running from Exodus to Malachi, ululating in law codes and prophetic groans alike. And it becomes definitive of the event of deliverance from Egypt that will anchor the vision it memorializes for subsequent millennia (Exod 2:23–25).

There is, however, another hint worth attention. As biblical scholarship has well attested, Jesus' own preferred nomenclature is the apocalyptic title "Son of Man," most likely referencing Daniel's vision of one coming to champion the vindication of those suffering the predatory rule of the "fourth beast" in his alarming glimpse behind the veil of history (Dan 7:13–14, 21–22). In Hebrew, this reference is literally to a *Kibor Enash*, "One like the Offspring of a Mortal" (a "Vulnerable One," that is—*enash* means something like "wound-able," "defenseless") who will nonetheless receive the "kingdom" and secure justice. What is suggestive is the way the invocation calls up the replacement line of Abel in its word-association, invoking the genealogy going back to Eve through Seth, whose first-born son is Enosh, "the Assailable One." "Seth" himself, in the Genesis story, is "compensation" for the loss of Abel, named such (*"shet"*) by Eve, as "another" child, replacing "the one slain by Cain," and emerges in the text as the new counterpoint to the older brother (Gen 4:25–26). What seems to be subtly implied is a telling divergence, epitomized by the two genealogical lines descending from the Great Mother. The one leading from Cain through Enoch is noted for erecting the machinery of the city and launching metal-working technology—inhabiting, we might say, a kind of "full metal jacket" of invincibility and organized urban power, coercing resources from the surrounding peasantry (Gen 4:17–22). Its logic points toward the "achievements" and catastrophe of Babel (Gen 11). The other is an entire tradition of "kill-able offspring," erupting from the great absence of Abel, replaced by Seth, projecting his son Enosh as Enoch's direct counterpart—the epitome of those living vulnerably on the land, whose only recourse to defense, the cryptic commentary of Genesis intones, is a matter of "calling on the name of YHWH" ("Yahweh" or "God"; Gen 4:25–26).[2] And it is telling then, as already indicated, that when Jesus (in Luke and Matthew's telling) rehearses the history of violence whose "murderous sons" he charges the elites of his day as having become, he begins with Abel's disappearance, not Adam's eating (Mt 23:29–36; Lk 11:45–52). This is the line he consciously inhabits, whose ancestral memory he invokes and whose constantly reproduced experience of violation he carries. And indeed, in the epistle to the Hebrews, this line of citation will be rounded off in shorthand form by bringing Abel's shed blood right alongside Jesus' own as the archetypal witness of the subaltern subtext of history, in which the latter's voluntary "offering" overturns the horror and gives artful ("gracious") representation to the former in ongoing struggles for justice (Heb 12:24). Voiceless Abel, says the Hebrew-whooper, is "speaking still" (Heb 11:4).

But there is a paradox here. Abel is no challenging word-slinger, belching forth poetic bombast. In what sense can he be "read" and invoked as "prophetic"? To catch the full significance of what may be at stake here, we need to probe a bit more into the kind of struggle that the story of Abel's annihilation emphasizes. The issue is, arguably, not individual "sin," but social and political conflict centered in a different orientation to the land and different relationship to labor. Abel represents pastoral-nomadism over-against Cain's agricultural lifestyle. But the relationship between these two forms of social existence is complex. Hiebert analyzes the history of over-simplistic interpretation of the two at great and convincing length in his work, arguing that the herder activity in question in the primeval history of Genesis is not simply counter-posed to cultivation, as its economic (and moral) opposite, but is actually part of that very lifestyle. The J-strand in particular, he will insist, privileges the dry-soil, subsistence farming characteristic of the more humid highland zones of Canaan, in which field crops are grown with the assistance of "helper" animals loosely described as "cattle," while nutritional need for protein is supplied by the meat and dairy of herds of sheep and goats, grazed on semi-arid lands surrounding the tilled and cultivated plots of wheat and barley, figs and olives, and the grape vineyards anchored in Noah's story (Hiebert 1996, 33, 37, 41, 45, 52, 60). For J, writing immediately after the period (1200–1000 BCE) when iron technology was first broadly introduced into that rocky Canaanite hill-culture, YHWH is envisioned as the Great Divine Patron of subsistence farming, creating *adam* from *adamah*—red-hued-soil-creature scraped together from the red-hued soil of tillage. The favored deity of his text is a kind of Storm-God-Divinity of Rain and Seed whose very "life-breath" we are invited to find echoing in that great eponymous ancestor of old and his son Cain (Hiebert 1996, 64–66, 67–68, 74). The reference to Abel, on the other hand—invoking the younger son-brother of the older males of the family and pastoral-nomad "servant" to the main vocational line of subsistence farming—anchors memory of an archetypal conflict whose precise motivational outbreak in the Cain-Abel story we are not told, but whose bloody outcome we are given, in stark terms. In the story as we have it, when his own plant-based cereal offering is refused, Cain apes Abel's acceptable blood-offering by making Abel's own blood his (Cain's) late "send-up" for the nostrils of the deity.

There is much here that begs deep pondering, but can only be hinted for further exploration. The profound dislocation remarked in the Garden etiology (Genesis 2:4–3:2) is between humans and plants—more specifically Adam's relationship with fruited trees and the soils from which they grow. The fault is one of transgressing a limit, coercing forbidden fruit in quest of knowledge. The possible reading here is a turn toward technique and calculus, reengineering soils and trees in a project of control whose subsequent history of grand achievements and now potentially catastrophic destructiveness we "know" all too well.[3] The subsequent curse falls on the ground, planted originally by YHWH, whose flora previously (in the text) has grown in wild fecundity, but whose nurturance and cultivation subsequently will require Adam's labor and sweat and will yield (presumably in its more concentrated intake of carbohydrates and resulting larger fetuses) harder births for Eve's line. Cain reaps and furthers the consequences—and is ultimately banished from farming altogether to become a "fugitive and wanderer" and finally a city-builder (Gen 4:12–13, 17).[4] Abel, on the other hand, traffics in animals, off to the side of the broken relationship between humans and tillable soil that now bears a curse, and occupies a subsidiary niche, apprenticed to the land by way of his herds, living marginal to the main settlements, more subject to chance encounters with predators (I Sam 17: 34–37) and the nuances of nature unaltered by technology.

Exactly how to interpret the primal murder remains uncertain, but the undercurrent of a conflict between lifeways haunts the text. While Hiebert is quite right to deconstruct the simplistic and inaccurate opposition predicated by earlier exegesis—between a *bedouin*-like pastoral-nomadism and the settled agriculture of Canaanite city-states—and clarify the more accurate picture of a mixed agriculture-herder economy of the highlands requiring both tillage and shepherding, subsequent biblical tradition tends to underscore the outsider cast and suspect civility of herder life. In David's early struggles as a renegade, on the run from Saul, cover and support is found among various shepherd bands, whose outback lifestyle David had shared as a youth and whose familiarity with "living on the land" granted him advantage and local knowledge sufficient to resist discovery and arrest (I Sam 24:1–25:17; 17:34–37). While shepherding will be taken up in subsequent popular parlance and prophetic proverb alike as a trope for royal leadership (Ezek 34:1–31), this is a typical move of domination systems appropriating terminology and reference from a subordinated sector of society to popularize ruling class hegemony for mass "consumption," casting the ruling function in terms of a lifeway whose actual vicissitudes and struggles elites in no way share. Kingship exercised from palatial estates in urban centers is in actuality nothing like shepherding in the wilderness. The P-writings, riffing on J and E from the vantage point of life in exile in Babylon, will call onto the surface of the tradition the subtext of herding, emphasizing the pastoral nomad side of the experiences of the earliest ancestors (Abraham, Isaac, and Jacob) that the J-document tended to eclipse in J's emphasis on his own contemporary economy of subsistence farming. By the time of Jesus, herding is clearly a suspect activity, one of three "unclean" vocations (alongside tax collecting and prostitution) by priestly standards, closely associated in dominant discourse with thieving and social banditry (thus the ironic "bite" of Luke's assertion that shepherds are the first to perceive the "good news" in the dark of night in a *wadi* outside Bethlehem and the polemic "throw down" of Jesus' self-reference as "good shepherd" in John) (Lk 2:8–15; Jh 10:1–18). The latent difference from farming harbored in the herder tradition is profoundly teased out in a more contemporary witness. In our own time, sanctuary movement leader Jim Corbett has become posthumously legendary for his deep exploration of pastoral nomadism in the Sonoran desert region of Arizona, teaching himself survival skills outlined in his book, *Goatwalking,* as a necessary adjunct to prophetic critique of political policy in late twentieth century USA. Corbett argues that the effectiveness of a political critique embodied in a given social movement (like the new "underground railroad" of church sanctuary networks he helped work out for El Salvadoran refugees in the 1980s) ultimately requires knowing that one can live entirely independent of the empire economically, if need be, if such critiques are not finally to be undercut by fear. His subsequent writing about wildland herding of cattle, published posthumously in 2005 (under the title *Sanctuary for All Life: The Cowbalah of Jim Corbett*), is now carried forth by a covenant community of followers, living out the land ethic he practiced and prescribed. His challenge gives nuanced pause before Hiebert's perhaps too facile assimilation of herding to subsistence farming in ancient Canaan.

Corbett agrees that "pastoral peoples are typically familiar with and to some degree dependent upon peasant and city ways," but claims that their identity is rooted historically in the actuality of having gone "feral" (referencing domesticated creatures who have begun to return to a wild state) (Corbett 2005, 108, 119–121). They are capable, in the pinch of emergency, of "escaping from civilization" and "surviving in desert wilderness where peasants would starve"—a capacity Corbett himself replicated in his sanctuary work, "disappearing" into the Sonoran desert to intercept El Salvadoran refugees before they got close to the urban settings of Nogales or Tucson and the dangers of discovery and arrest by INS ("Immigration and Naturalization Service"; Corbett 2005, 108). Certainly Corbett lived an urban life, dependent on agriculture for most of his existence. But at moment's notice, he could exit and wander for weeks (or even longer) at a time, independent of imperial constraints, a "maroon," as he says, embracing other maroons (from the Spanish *cimarron,* for domesticated animals that have gone wild, or slaves who have escaped into the outback) needing shelter and sanctuary (Corbett 2005, 108, 120; 1991, 4). And this practical experience, I would deem decisive for nuancing Hiebert's claims about the dependence of pastoral nomads on subsistence agriculture. Pastoral nomadism in this frame, stands (practically, if not usually in evolutionary chronology) somewhere between hunter-gatherer lifestyle in the wild and the settled village life of peasant-based agriculture, ruled from city-centers by rapacious elites.

For Corbett the key is the deep question of what it means, finally, to be human and live sustainably on the planet. His own embrace of the Jewish and Christian tradition as a Quaker-practitioner, avows an explicit repudiation of the tradition wherever it sets the bible up as idolatry, locking down meaning in a credal formulation that locks human beings away from land practices that are symbiotic and sacralizing (Corbett 2005, 212–213). On the contrary, Corbett reads the tradition as a hallowing way—from Abraham to Jesus, enjoining prophetic critique of the kind of imperial enslavements that begin with land and wildlife, run through farm animals and laborers, and end with slaves and the urban poor (Corbett 2005, 118). Its key "institution" in this compass, is Sabbath, rooted in the foraging practice of "living off the land," instituted by pastoral nomad Moses in the Sinai desert setting that he had earlier learned to "read" as *his* bible (Corbett 2005, 220). Under tutelage to his herd, the desert here became his primal pedagogue—a schoolhouse of the outback, initiating him in wildland ways sufficient to lead and sustain a band of escaped slaves, when the time came, outside the confinements and provisions of empire.

Sabbath here merges as a full-blown program of reschooling for feral slaves and imperial maroons. Though their destiny will indeed be subsistence farming in Canaanite highlands (although interestingly its promise is of pastoral nomad sustenance like "milk and honey"), their formative experience and identity will be anchored in the *manna*-memory of the hot sands, gathering enough for a day at a time, in good hunter-gatherer fashion,[5] unlearning the political economy of grain-hoarding and "food as weapon" policy that required their enslavement and hard labor in Egypt (Exod 16: 1–36; Gen 47:13–26; Exod 1:1–2:24). Early on, that Sinai experience of foraging came to be elaborated in a continuum of confession and practice that enjoined release of "captive" land, of "chattel" labor, and of "cattle" domesticates to a wild condition every seven days, seven years, and seven-times-seven years (in the "Grand Culmination" of Sabbaths known as Jubilee). This was reinforced annually by a round of festivals giving ritual "flesh" to the memory. Required was a seven-day sojourn under flimsy ramadas ("booths") in the seventh month celebration of Sukkot, as well as the necessity of "eating on the run" during Passover's recapitulation of Hebrew "marronage" from Egypt, itself followed forty nine (seven times seven) days later by the Pentecost commemoration of the Sinai revelation (Corbett

2005, 221–223). Corbett finds the confessional centrality of such a "rewilding" memory powerfully epitomized in the Deuteronomy 26: 5 liturgical outcry about Abraham, "*Arami 'oved 'avi*"—an "Aramean *cimarron*[6] (was) my father"—whose weight and bite we consider in the next section (a "going stray" that Jacob will replicate in his relations with Laban the Aramean in Gen 31) (Corbett 1991, 4; 2005, 221–222). At stake in such a "school-house of the sevens" was the struggle to keep Israel rooted in its original exit from Egypt, on the way to becoming a people committed to ending "the earth's human bondage and idolatry" (Corbett 2005, 220). The issue is not precisely a lifestyle as pastoral nomad, but rather a regularized revisitation of the paradigmatic Sinai experience of foraging on the land, eating the "what is it?" of *manna* that grows without either sowing or reaping (as Jesus will later invoke in the anti-imperial story of the birds of the air and lilies of the field in Mt 6:25–33). For Corbett, something like this Sabbath-celebration is the primal condition of freedom. The regularly engaged practice of "release to the wild"—of land, of plants, of animals, of humans—enjoined practical remembering and recreated existential respect.

Corbett's texts are rich and teeming with insight and provocation, but for our purposes perhaps nowhere more so than in his notion of a goat-human or cow-human partnership of "pastoral symbiotics," as the only way practically to reenter relationship to the land as "holy" once empire has established its grip (Corbett 1991, 4, 8, 85, 88). (And indeed across the globe, pastoral- and equine-nomadism is now recognized historically as largely a reaction to empire—choices engaged by formerly oppressed and enslaved peoples to escape their chains by adopting wandering ways, away from city life, configuring grazing routes in large figure-eight rhythms correlated with seasons, mythologized in relationship to the constellations, and memorialized in song cycles) (Corbett 1991, 4, 8, 85, 88). Corbett is strident: his own writings cannot be embraced as "teaching": the only real teaching available that does not lead right back into surreptitious idolatry and enslavement must come from the land itself as teacher, mediated by way of "otherkind" (goats or cows, in his experience, but not limited to such) (Corbett 1991, 24, 28–29, 39; 2005, 85, 86). The choice is conquest or Sabbath. The only way back into sustainable communion is by committed apprenticeship to a herd or other wildlife species.

And the necessary "discipleship" in relationship to the herd (as oneself a "member" thereof, living and moving with the animals) is exactly what any management paradigm (including range land management) is not. The prime concern here is redemption of any and all chattel relations (wives, concubines, children, servants, slaves, cattle, etc.) by way of land redemption. "If the cow-human symbiosis can outgrow the master-slave relation," Corbett says, "it could be a decisive opening for other interspecies partnerships and might also suggest ways to outgrow alienated livelihood relations that have succeeded chattel slavery, such as wage and market slaveries" (Corbett 2005, 86). What he specifies is a *haggadah* practice of "walking," in whatever tradition one finds oneself moving (Buddhist, Taoist, Sufi, Hindu, Celtic, O'Odham, Apache, etc.), that exits abstraction and enters upon a "specific way in a particular land by a cocreative community," given over to hallowing that land as holy and learning its rhythms as constitutive of "God" and human being alike (Corbett 2005, 88).

And it is just such a notion of an *interspecies mediation* of genuine human dwelling on the land that intrigues from a christological perspective. Anselm in the midst of feudal Brittany formulated the classical understanding of a "God-man" (sic) union, erecting feudal status relationships into his model of an eternal and asymmetrical economy of honor-obligation and debt-satisfaction. But that classical formula partakes of and pertuates an older Neo-Platonic notion of ontological hierarchy rooted in a city-state political practice and domination structure that has contributed to the ever-increasing removal of human self-understanding from its real-life economy intertwined with plants and other animals. Corbett's *cow-human* or *goat-human* model of a return *out of* imperial-urban alienation and *into* lived reciprocity with land and biosphere is suggestive for a refiguring of christology along the lines of an eco-ontological exchange that is rooted in actual commensuality and sustainable codwelling. Even Hiebert's articulation of the J narrative as quintessentially a subsistence agriculture vision, hints at a peculiar dependence on (even tutelage to) the land: the term for tillage (*'ăbōd*, "cultivation") he notes as deeply shadowed by its root meaning of "servitude to a greater power," elsewhere used of the stance of a servant to his master, one people to another, or Israel toward YHWH in worship (Hiebert 1996, 65–66; Gen 12:16; 27:40; Exod 4:23; 7:16, 26). The hint, even in J's emphasis on cultivation, is that human relationship to divinity is profoundly practical and collaborative, requiring mediation in relationship to land and other living beings (plants, in the case of J's narrative).

Later exploration in this text will exemplify the ways indigenous communities have appropriated Christianity precisely by means of such an "interspecial" reconstitution of Jesus as "Christ" for their context (as "Jesus-Yage plant" or "Jesus-Signifying Monkey," as we shall see).

Here, however, it is enough to underscore the way the invocation of Abel functions within the tradition as an emblem of a shepherding lifestyle that is held up as the provocation in the Genesis narrative for the primal scene of political murder and underlies the ancient liturgical reiteration in Deuteronomy of the identity of the "faithful" as a *cimarron* people who are interspecially educated and constituted (a symbiotics[7] with other life forms that Adam presumably "knew" in connection with trees, before his attempted gerrymandering of the relationship resulted in banishment). And indeed, it is this name and lifestyle that even already "ghosts" the earliest instances of anointing, in which a stone might be set up as an altar-marker and witness between houses and flocks (Gen 28:17; 31:43–54).

Abram's Trees

Again, the tact I am taking here is neither inclusively comprehensive nor broadly thematic, but rather suggestive, seeking to strike fire with textual traces of messianic flint. The elusive subject is subaltern: vernacular moments of gestures creatively resisting domination, depicted with craft and art, potent for subsequent movement uptake and elaboration. The goal is to occasion a "christic" reading, a Little Tradition musing on the possibilities of "Something Other" than mere capitulation to imperial constraint or elite appropriation.

The so-called primeval history of Genesis 1–11 is functionally so much anticipatory context for the opening act of the epic of the patriarchs/matriarchs (Abraham and Sarah, Isaac and Rebekah, Jacob and Leah, and Rachel and sons). With Abram, the spark has already been struck in noting the ancient Deuteronomic (26:5) confession of the primal father as *cimarron*—one who late in life set out from the security of the city for (literally) greener pastures and became a feral "stray" from his father's house (Gen 20:13). He is a "lost one"—as some translations would gloss *'oved*—but only from the point of view of urban terror before nomadic freedom. For one schooled in the wandering ways, however, becoming *'oved* is merely the first step away from enslavement and subjugation (as Buber clearly saw in his book on Moses, noting that Cossacks similarly called themselves *kazaks* not to denote supposed "lostness" but a free status as "undomesticated adventurer" or "masterless guerilla"; Buber 1958, 25–29). This is Abram as primal "Hebrew" (*'Ivri* as Abram hails himself in Gen 14:13), traced back to meanings associated with the name of his ancestor, *Eber* (Gen 10:21), as one who "crosses over" (the Euphrates, in exiting his homeland), or in keeping with Ugaritic parallels, as one of the *'Apiru* or outlaw renegades who have lost standing with their community of origin and struck out on their own. The *Ur*-command of the tradition here is for Abram to leave the city of Haran, walking away from "country, kin, and ancestral home," to a place he is to be shown (on the way).

Moving along the uplands spine of Canaan stretching roughly north–south, he finally comes to the "place" (*maqom* or "sanctuary") at Shechem, "to the oaks of Moreh" (Gen 12:7). While scholars have wrestled inconclusively with whether the terminology here is best grasped literally as "oaks of oracle" ("the trees that teach") or in a folk aphorism (based on word-sounds) as "oaks of seeing" (trees of revelation), the point here is that it is oaks (*'elon*, from which we likely get the Hebrew word, *'el*, "deity") that anchor divine appearance (Hiebert 1996, 109). Abraham will build an altar; call the name; give an offering. This will also be the case later, after similarly marking out a mountain east of Bethel with an altar and offering (and a trek to Egypt to escape famine), when Abram moves his tent to the oaks of Mamre, following a dispute-resolving clarification of grazing rights between himself and Lot (Gen 12:8–13:18). Here too, the association may be the sonic play between the place name (Mamre) and the verb *ra'a,* "to see" (Hiebert 1996, 109). At Beersheba, Abram-now-become-Abraham will get into the tree-planting business, concluding a water-rights treaty with Abimelech by cultivating a tamarisk as a site of divine naming, destined later to become the place of theophany and altar-building for Isaac (Gen 21:33; 26:23–25). And Jacob likewise will get in on this project of naming—in the wake of experiencing a sudden natural disclosure—in his case, on the part of a rock, subsequently "anointed" and set up as designating a "house" of God (*Beth-'el*) (Gen 28:10–22).

While Hiebert is likely on the mark in delineating the broader focus here as a J-narrative concern to trace the etiology of the land claims presumed by the Davidic kingdom of his (the Yahwist's) own time (which is to say, to legitimate the claims of an agricultural society to its land-base), underneath that ideological layering there still appear intriguing traces of a schooling of nomadic ancestors by ecological phenomenon themselves, "outside" the artifice of urban architecture. It is trees, mountains, waters (rivers and springs), and rocks that carry the weight of revelation and occasion a diversity of divine appellations (*'ēl 'ôlam, 'ēl shaddāi, 'ēl 'elyôn, beth-'ēl,* etc.), lifting up the landscape as primal map of the ancestral history, perhaps not all that different from the way Australian hunter-gatherers or various Native American tribes or indeed nomadic cultures across the globe have memorialized their sacral experience by coding the natural phenomenon in story, buttressed by offerings and ritual returns of substance to the holy. These are instincts that find their deepest roots in land-practices that hallow the wild as revelatory, mark off certain precincts as forbidden terrains of dread encounter (virtually every one of these theophanies is couched in the language of fear where any details of the experience are given), and demand give-backs to the divine.

"Anointing," in its earliest instance here (Gen 28:18), convenes all of this compost of meaning—a marking out of a piece of wild nature as aura-ed with dread significance, provoking creative naming, mythological coding, and ritualized honoring from the economy of one's substance. Hiebert is right to emphasize that the "ancestors in Canaan" are depicted by J in such a way that they reinforce the primacy of subsistence highlands agriculture as the lifeway that supplies the framework within which YHWH is presented as a kind of Divine Guarantor, giving rain and nurturing seed. But behind and underneath that agricultural frame lies also the memory of a herder way[8] that enables mobility and exiting from situations of constraint—in Abram's case from Ur (and Haran), and indeed later from Canaan itself in a time of famine (Gen 12:10–16)—and remembers multiple names for wild holiness associated with multiple sites of encounter. For instance, after engaging in a raid to recover his kinsman Lot (and his household), who had been kidnapped during the rebellion of subservient kings in the War of the Valley of Siddim, Abram honors the requirements of the local royal cult of "God Most High," but refuses any of the goods offered by the king of Sodom, lest he afterward be deemed beholden to such for having been "made rich" through participation in the network of urban-based extraction (Gen 14:1–24). This is a nomad impulse, hypersenstitive to the dangers of envelopment in the shackles of settled life, a sharp refusal of shared plunder and the soft emollients of patronage-obligation that would cut the nerve of fierce independence and freedom.

Likewise different from urban impulses to extort is the central practice with which Abraham is associated in the synoptic tradition of Jesus' teaching (indeed, the only practice for which Abraham's name is ever invoked by Jesus). And here too, the ways of Sodom supply contrastive relief. In Matthew and Luke, Jesus solicits Abraham (along with Isaac and Jacob) as host of the messianic table "in the kingdom," to which will assemble all manner of unexpected folk ("strangers") from "east and west, north and south," while those more commonly expected to be the guests (the "sons of the kingdom") are excluded (Mt 8:11–12; Lk 13:28–29). This cryptic reference to "Abrahamic hospitality" is notoriously fleshed out in Luke's gospel in terms of the parable of Lazarus and the Rich Man, in which the honored guest of the father of the faith at the messianic banquet is a disenfranchised son of the tradition, reduced to begging, suffering malnutrition and hunger, and dying early. This is in marked contrast to the rich gourmand of the story, dressed in finest linen and feasting sumptuously, who ends up tormented in Hades, still trying to finesse his self-importance into special treatment (featuring Lazarus as "water boy" for the rich man) and into a special dream-visitation granting insider information for his relatives (Lk 16:19–31). Exegete William Herzog teases out the political context and real-life implications. Lazarus represents, in the folk typology of parabolic storytelling, a typical figure of first century Palestine—a younger son of a family caught in the debt-trap managed by fat-cat landlords who preyed on peasant households needing loans after bad crop years. Whenever such a loan could not be repaid (as was often the case), the family was forced to sign over claim to their ancestral plot to the creditor. The father and older sons were then often rehired as tenant farmers on what had been their own land, serving at the mercy of the landlord. And younger sons were frequently pushed into seasonal day-laboring (during planting and harvesting) and begging for the remainder of the year—a circumstance where life-expectancy was typically 5–7 years, before being claimed by an early and painful death in the throes of disease and deprivation (Herzog 1994, 114–130).

The sharp polemic here, pillorying the presumptions of wealth, builds on the "street rep" of Abraham as quintessential icon of table-welcoming hospitality. It is rooted in the Genesis story where the tent-dwelling old man, faced with three strangers (angels in disguise as it turns out) suddenly appearing in the Mamre oak shade, instantly offers food and rest, kills the calf, and serves as butler (Gen 18:1–8). Sharp relief is supplied for this encounter by the unfolding of the "angelic" visitation toward its intelligence-gathering objective. The mission of the three is one of gathering information on nearby Sodom in response to a growing outcry about the city's harsh reception and violent abuse of strangers. The angels here will continue their disguise as political "aliens" in testing Sodom's hospitality practices in action (we might think of Sanctuary Movement tactics in 1985 publicly "shepherding" two El Salvadorans across the border to create a test case challenging INS/US government legal commitments to its own policy regarding

asylum seekers) (Gen 18:16–19:29; Corbett 1995, 174 ff.). This ready
extension of sanctuary to strangers is the epitome of the justice-keeping
to which Abraham and his household are called in perpetuity (Gen
18:19). And it will be precisely for such that Abraham will be invoked
in Jesus' own movement teaching.

In actuality the Genesis juxtaposition of Abrahamic hospitality and
Sodomic abuse draws a sharp line of contrast between pastoral nomad
and settled agricultural orientations. Herders the world-over must
count on open tents and tables as a form of reciprocally shared insurance against the vicissitudes of life "out on the land" (Hillel, 78–81).
The deep valuing of welcome typical of nomadic sensibility, amplified
by Abraham's own experience of having gone feral from the city and
wandering with his flocks in a land not his own, stands out in stark
relief, in the iconic story, against the cold opportunism and rapacious
nativism of urbanized populations, huddled in fear behind walls. The
same contrast is vividly signaled in the gospels. Stranger-welcome and
open commensality are central tenets of the messianic practices of Jesus'
movement. But it is exactly at the apex of his march on the city for his
fateful showdown with the powers-that-be that Jesus explicitly holds
Abraham aloft—in messianic proverb and emblematic parable alike (Lk
13:28, 16:1–30)—as the quintessence of a herder host. Underscored in
both riddle and story is Abraham's renown for a hospitable tent and
an open table, offering safe harbor for refugees that the metropolitan
powers otherwise treat as "illegal aliens" subject to seizure and violent
repudiation. And it should be no surprise, then, when engaged in a
high-stakes debate after arrival (inside the Temple precincts) with elite
representatives claiming Abraham as their ancestor, Jesus will defy
those leaders' genealogical claim on the basis of their continual readi-
ness to exclude and execute people like himself or the woman just then
caught in adultery (and draw down from them a charge of himself being
a "Samaritan and demon-possessed") (Jh 8:1–48). In quick succession
of polemics, Jesus will contrast himself, as "good shepherd," to the elites
cast as "thieves and robbers"—sharply inverting the urban stereotype
about herders as thieves and openly identifying the most consequen-
tial form of mugging in the Palestinian political economy (Jh 10:1–31).
This is clearly the Johannine version of naming the Temple as "plunder
central," the real "den of robbing" that is the core of Jesus' Temple-
action polemic in the synoptics[9] (Mk 11:15–19). And in consequence,
he will have to retreat, once again, to his own movement "haunt" out in
the wilderness (the epicenter of his strategizing and teaching, as we see
later) (Jh 10:40).

Moses' Bush

This same Lukan parable just examined—built around the reputation of Abraham as convener of the great messianic banquet of the time to come—concludes with a deft displacement. In Palestinian popular culture of the time, Abraham was claimed by the wealthy priestly-scribal-elder elites as patron saint of a well-heeled lifestyle (Mt 3:9, Jh 8:33–58), the one at the center of the tradition whose evident prosperity they could claim as license for their own (one who had held some 318 servant-slaves at the height of his power!) (Herzog 1994, 25–130). The parable indeed sets up Abraham as host, in typical herder largesse, of the great banquet, but then has his discourse direct the audience focus away from himself to Moses and the prophets. This is an Abraham who points toward those who turned away from hoarded wealth and political cachet to immerse themselves in solidarity with escaped slaves and oppressed peasants. Moses is one who grew up in the posh quarters of Pharaoh's palace, with all the advantages and access such implied, only to go "feral" himself, after seeking out affinity with his own bloodline in the slave-fields and then killing an Egyptian overseer who was abusing a Hebrew relative in the process. The prophetic-line Moses embodies as prototype references those in monarchical Israel who took up the cause of the 'am haartez ("people of the land") and other marginalized denizens. Their common vocation was visionary articulation: sharp polemic against all the royal policies and elite practices that resulted in impressed labor, stockpiled surplus and pirated substance (exorbitant taxation, rents, fees, etc.) squandered in ostentatious building projects and fat-cat lifestyles, and poignant invocation of an alternative way of living. In subtle but pointed polemic, this parabolic Abraham showcases the messianic banquet as a table of justice for the poor, and hails "prophet" Moses as exemplar of the tradition's central word.

For the gospels that word is clearly "Sabbath." Moses appears sparingly on Jesus' lips as a reference point, but in the laconic display that does appear, anchors synoptic vision for just treatment of excluded lepers, at-risk widows and other elderly dependents, and women facing patriarchal repudiation in their marriages (Mk 1:44, 7:10; Mt 19:7). When Moses is cited by Jesus' opponents—tendentiously as guarantor of patriarchal practices designed to keep family "wealth" in the family-line in Levirate marriage—Jesus will relativize this Sadducean attempt at entrapment by centering the Great Legislator squarely within the wilderness experience that most epitomizes his herder identity and schooling (Mk 12:18–27). Like Abraham, Moses has been taught by trees and grasses, and at the ripe age of eighty, after forty years of living quietly as a pastoral nomad with his father-in-law's flock in the Sinai, is suddenly accosted by the ecology itself. An unnameable presence speaks from the ineradicable bush (Dt 33:16 speaks candidly of the "one who *dwelt in* the bush"), a flaming foliage variously denoted in later tradition as "the Lord" or an "angel," (Acts 7:30, 35). The great "I AM" of the line of ancestry that is cited here is quintessentially a repudiation of all names, a use of language against language itself as the first idolatry. Far from acceding to Moses' request for clarity, the primal bush-experience rather underscored a divine refusal to be named that demanded, in subsequent Jewish invocation, the necessary interruption of what the eye read as "YHWH" with the generically substituted sound *adonai,* a kind of mental stutter-effect, that reminds there is no word that captures the teeming wildness and undomesticated everywhere-ness of this Reality. Corbett finds in this conceit an intractable *aporia* that thwarts all of our attempts to incarcerate sacrality in a formula or object (Corbett 2005, 84–87). This Voice is "the Wild" speaking, in whose schoolhouse Moses was enrolled for a four-decade-long rite-of-initiation and to which he returned with his band of renegade (*'hapiru* or "outlaw") slaves when it was their turn similarly to be debrided of imperial memories and resocialized into the radical egalitarianism of nomadic ways. And the first command given those feral slaves—pre-dating even the ten commandments that would outline the social identity that this new peoplehood was to embody—would be a demand "to gather," as any good forager band would, only enough for one day (Exod 16:1–36). They were eating what they could not even articulate (*manna* colloquially means something like, "what the hell is this?"), on the run, learning as they went. To mark the meaning of this means of economic living, they are told every six days to gather two days' worth—but not an iota more! And this practice would become the primal experience on top of which would be erected all the subsequent Sabbath injunctions to cease and release and trust and rest—whose keeping will be what "keeps" the people, in perpetuity (Ex 31:12–17)!

Corbett is again prescient here, as one who became a living testament to the herder ways that give rise historically to a Sabbath vocation. He imagines Moses struggling with the predicament—a people routinized in irrigation-agriculture's regime of accumulation and coercion in Egypt, called out to a radical independence and a covenant embodiment of an "other" way of being together as humans. This other way will find its core tenet in a focus on hallowing the land and its biota as a living community of sacral goodness (Corbett 1991, 81–86).

Four decades of "desert deconstruction" and "foraging initiation" may prove to be enough, in the short term, to reskill a new generation and weed out the older, compromised mindset. But what happens when the new group eventually resettles into agricultural ways in Canaan? How will they *not* become quickly recolonized in thought and practice by imperial protocols of hoarding and coercion, living sandwiched between the large-scale agricultural empires of Egypt and Mesopotamia?

The Mosaic disciplines of regular Sabbath-year and Jubilee-year "releases" (of land, labor, cattle, and debt) enjoin a cyclical return to the Sinai condition of living off the land. Practically, they mandate a radical leveling down of any incipient hierarchy that has grown up in the interim and return everyone, including "owners," to a forager mode of living, proscribing sowing for those years, and calling for cooperative gleaning of fallow fields. Ritually, the weekly *Shabat* and annual *Sukkot* festivals regularly reschool the body in just this conditionality, rendering the ideals "somatic." And at the heart of the entire prospect is the utterly simple and primordial calculus it serves. As Moses is depicted "throwing down" in the Deuteronomic version of a covenant-renewal ceremony, the choice is starkly clear: "See, I have set before you this day life and good, death and evil . . . therefore choose life, that you and your descendants may live" (Dt 30:15, 19). The entire regime of Sabbath-Jubilee is a Mosaic mechanism of remembering and reschooling. It requires the people regularly to turn aside out of their (dangerous) involvement in the more domesticated modalities of settled agriculture and reawaken themselves to what forgers and herders (and indeed, primitive farmers) "know" and live: a practical symbiosis with the environment that trusts to the "divine" goodness of the wild and commits to honoring its interdependence, hallowing its independence, and preserving its raw aliveness. And this symbiosis constitutes the primary revelation of "God" and the primary mode of living as "God's people."[10]

It should be no surprise then that where we get the most trenchant invocations of Moses in the gospel corpus, we find the central issue is precisely this regime of practice. In Jesus' high stakes public ripostes with the authorities scheming to get him to "misspeak" (so they can destroy his reputation among the people at the same time they execute his body), it is finally the question of Sabbath-Jubilee that emerges as the sharp axis of conflict. John gives four occasions on which charges of sabbatical violations erupt into heavy debate with the ruling elites. In John 5 the instance involves a Sabbath healing of a paralytic by the sheep-gate pool; in John 9 the *Shabbat* "crime" restores sight (by mud-anointing!) to a beggar who was blind from birth. John 7 recounts a sudden advent of the marked man of Galilee in the Temple precincts during the Feast of Booths, explicitly naming Sabbath as the ever-ripe moment not only for incising the "sign" of wholeness into the flesh (Mosaic circumcision) but also for actually making someone's *life* whole (for which he is quickly labeled as "demon possessed"). And John 6 is reportage on Jesus' own recapitulation of the *manna*-tradition, in which an entire crowd is reinducted into the wilderness memory of feeding in the desert, where abundant provision is underscored as the outcome of "unhoarding" food from peasant pockets (in an astonishing display of what today might be called "asset-based" organizing—building on resources already present in poor communities rather than pining for policies that grant a tiny bit of trickle-down from the state). In John's narration of these imbroglios, Moses' primary utility to Jesus is as the great authority on Sabbath release. Rightly reading the Sinai seer is the question. The heart of Jesus' "beef" with the Palestinian powers-that-be is over just deployment of this community-shaping tradition—the theological pivot of his entire movement and the *crux* of its denouement as outlaw, on the run, and irrepressible (Myers 2001, 23).

David's Bread

This latter claim comes clearly to the fore, when we turn to the two times Jesus invokes the messianic archetype par excellence in Israel, YHWH's premier "anointed one," David. Early in his movement, the Galilean prophet is traversing grain fields on a Sabbath day with a hungry band of followers (Mk 2:23–28). In full view of Pharisaic custodians of torah purity conventions, the disciples glean the grain, provoking instant reproof, charging them with violation of Sabbath proscriptions regarding sowing, reaping, and transport of crops (Myers 1988, 180). Jesus responds with sardonic riposte: "have you never read what David did?" And then he proceeds to lift up an iconic episode from the archetypal king's life *before* he has assumed that role. In the scenario Jesus quotes, the "hit" on David has just been ordered by king Saul: the young herder is outlaw, on the run as clandestinely "anointed" upstart, desperate for food and weapons, forced to mimic insanity to avoid arrest, and just then in the process of collecting his own "discipleship" band of disreputables (a motley crew of the distressed, the indebted and the discontented (I Sam 20:30–31, 21:1–10, 22:1–2). Hardly the conventional image of David triumphant! This vignette, from the very first years of Israel's choice to betray its calling and opt for life under the thumb of a ruler like the nations around about it (I Sam 8:4–22), leverages the great "messianic icon" (David) as warrant for Jesus' own practice of satisfying hunger as the real meaning of Sabbath traditions regarding release and rest. One episode further on in Mark's narration the old Mosaic polemic (highlighted earlier) will be thrown down in stark relief: "Is it right to do good or do harm on the Sabbath, to make life whole or to kill?" And immediately following this challenge the plotting on Jesus' life will begin (Mk 3:1–6). In the ground tactics of the first century Galilean "messiah," the quintessential tradition of Hebrew messiahship is mined only for a singular moment when hunger had trumped any notion of sacral taboo—precisely in the name of the deepest sacral demand *of* the tradition ("Sabbath-Jubilee")—and had done so in service of a renegade movement that gathered all the "unreleased ones" of the time. David's own "messiah-hood" at that moment was basically that of a former shepherd become social bandit, organizing oppressed malcontents in the outback and finding sanctuary among fellow pastoralists (I Sam 22:1–5; 25:1–26:1).

The only other time Jesus is represented lifting up the Davidic archetype is at the far end of his own confrontation with the powers. He has already marched on Jerusalem, cleared the Temple precincts of its low level operatives who were using Torah sanctions to further rearrange resources from peasant pockets into priestly coffers, convened a sit-down strike and hosted a day-long teach-in, and then in subsequent high-stakes encounters with elites on Temple grounds surrounded by peasant pilgrims, has finally gone on the offensive against their attempts to entrap him in actionable repartee (Mk 12:35–37). He pointedly repudiates scribal characterizations of David as "restorationist"—in whose name the Temple authorities seek to corral the crowds with (naïve) hopes of divine overthrow of Roman occupation and a renewed priestly scribal hegemony rooted in the Temple-State apparatus of control. Against such, Jesus invokes a different David—David-as-psalmic-lyricist[11]—to ventriloquize a "Christic" conundrum: "How can the Lord say to my Lord, sit at my right hand...?" (Ps 110:1). The import is a kind of renegade messianic repudiation of the royal "son of David" messianism articulated by scribal interest—rooted in the recognition that David himself sings of bowing before his own messianic offspring. Indeed, here again we have hints of a herder sensibility, a skill on the lyre, presumably developed while tending sheep in the wilderness, that becomes the calling card for David in Saul's court, precisely as the musical therapy (stringed instruments as the primal "vehicles" of shamanic trance developed by pastoral nomads out on the Asian steppes) capable of regularly "exorcizing" the evil spirit to which Saul falls prey after

David is surreptitiously anointed by Samuel (I Sam 16:11–23). What does not show up on the lips of the Palestinian upstart is anything from the actual reign of David. Rather we have David as renegade organizer and as lyrical prophet.

Elijah's Wind

Tellingly the messianic tradition finds its most typical employment in Israel's historical narratives as a mode of prophetic rebuke. The original anointing story (of Saul by Samuel) is ironically one of rebellion *against* the Mosaic vision (I Sam 8: 1–22), which gives rise to a chain-reaction of clandestinely desperate prophetic interventions, anointing new leaders against previously anointed figures whose power (almost inevitably) grows to resemble that first moment of betrayal.[12] As already touched upon in the Lazarus parable considered earlier, Moses himself is eventually drafted into this list of provocateurs (in virtue of his interventions in Egypt) and sometimes lumped together, in gospel reference, with "the prophets" in general. In one story in particular, however, that generalized reference coalesces into a single, towering figure. The Transfiguration tableau of a mountain-top "summit meeting" to prepare for Jesus' final showdown in Jerusalem pairs precursor Moses with "wild man" Elijah, the very epitome of prophecy inside Israel itself. Here is the tradition's irrepressible "one-two punch," headlining the vocation to truth-telling in the face of oppressive power (Mk 9:1–13). And Jesus' own decision to march on Jerusalem will be warranted by his "cloud consultation" with these two forerunner upstarts. But not surprisingly then, the name "Elijah" also emerges as a kind of "floating trope of contestation," in Jesus' teaching, woven into movement consciousness by him as the ancestral example par excellence, whose spirit is embodied most immediately in the activities of John the Baptist. In the popular culture of the day, the name is recurrently used by outsiders to the movement to try to focus their understanding of who *Jesus* might be ("Are you Elijah?" ask the authorities in Jh 1:21; "some say you are Elijah" report the disciples when Jesus asks them what is being said about him "out on the street," Mk 8: 28). But Jesus himself will redirect the image away from his own persona to that of the Baptist, cryptically implying that John has come under the sign and in the mode of Elijah, possessed by his energies and orientation, and indeed, taking up his peculiar "mantle" of clothing (camel's hair and leather) quite explicitly (Mt 11:1–19; II Kg 1:8; Mk 1:6).

In invoking John, Jesus will immediately remind the crowds of their having just recently "gone out"—in a kind of radicalized Sukkot return to wilderness practices—to listen to this Baptizer character who wandered the arid wadis east of Jerusalem, living off of "wild honey and locusts" (Mk 1:6) and preaching a reinstitution of the Sabbath/Jubilee vision (proclaiming "release" of sin/debt—the two words are one and the same in Aramaic—and calling for sharing of all food and clothing; Lk 3:3, 11) (Myers 2001, 24). Jesus depicts his forerunner as haunted by the memory of Israel's Sinai formation, foraging for his own living out in the trans-Jordan desert, "dowsing" for ancient grief under the sands, trod long before by Moses and crew before entering Canaan, and drinking in its message as his vocation (Mt 11:17–18; 2:18). He is explicitly contrasted with those living in king's houses (Mt 11:8; Lk 7:25). If the crowds will accept it, "he is Elijah who is to come" (Mt 11:14).

This prophetic invocation—painted onto the Baptizer like a carnival mask—is the quintessential wilderness cipher. It takes on its gospel flavor in virtue of the wildlands vocation that the "original" Elijah, realized after fleeing his home dwelling among the Gilead "settlers" (what his nickname as "Tishbite" references). Once having gone "underground" ("hidden himself") by the brook Cherith, east of the Jordan, Elijah's word emerges as a feral power—at one with his nomadic reputation as a rider of the desert *ruah*-winds (I Kgs 18:12), haunting the outback in flight from the various kings who sought his arrest and execution (I Kgs 17:3; 19:1–18). There he learns to trust ravens[13] for food (I Kgs 17:6, 19: 5–8) and read the subtle intonations of mountain silence[14] as revelation (I Kgs 19: 11–13). And from there he makes regular raids city-ward in "terrorist" campaigns of "assault," conjuring storms as blessing (I Kgs 18: 17, 41–45) and lightning as defense (I Kgs 18:38; II Kgs 1:10–12)—as indigenous folk have often done in their struggles with imperial aggression, seeking to counter royal oppression with ancient "eco-technologies" of "weather magic."[15] In the process, Elijah becomes the quintessential figure of the antiurban animus-to-come that will continuously challenge royal domination and elite exploitation throughout the four-hundred-year debacle of Israel's flirtation with monarchical aspiration. His spirit will portend, among others, shepherd *nabi* pronouncements like that of Amos, ferreting out oppressive wages and unfair prices inside a simple agricultural product like a basket of summer fruit ("Amos, what do you see?" Amos 1:1, 8:1–6). Or the anguished love howls of a Hosea for an exploited woman of the night—reading his own connubial-pain as augury of the country, announcing the necessity to return to the wild where the mysterious

"I AM" could once again be heard in tenderness, and the covenant with beasts and birds and creeping things be reestablished in abolishing the implements of war (Hos 1:2, 14, 16–20).

This Elijah is not merely an individual *persona*, but the voice of a place from which prophecy is spoken toward the city and its rapacity like a blast of wildlands memory. He is also precursor of the power of the local watershed to anchor and augur vocation. Elisha in the near term, and John and Jesus in time to come, will inherit a "mantle of Spirit" confirmed in the enveloping waters of the Jordan that at once "drowns" (in "baptism") everything connected with empire (like Pharaoh's army) and opens up dry land like a revisited "Exodus" (a new-old way based on Sabbath-Jubilee reciprocity and herder hospitality for strangers) (II Kgs 2:6–16; Mk 1:9–13; Myers 1988, 129). Indeed, in Luke's depiction of Jesus' inaugural address at Nazareth—marking out the newly emergent "home boy" as a "Jubilee Messiah" who proclaims the great release year on the spot in the sermon's conclusion (quoting Isaiah's "acceptable year of the lord")—it is an Elijah-Elisha story that underscores the stakes. It focuses the meaning of Jesus' quotation by lifting up episodes of feeding for alien widows and healing for alien lepers (Lk 4:16–30). It also results in immediate death-threats on Jesus' life.

Daniel's Cloud

If the Elijah allusions anchor the Jesus movement in "one who comes before," allusions to Daniel similarly anchor it in "one who will come after." Jesus dances in and out of a messianic frame that is actually a continuum of reference across time, a set of folk-ciphers giving sharp color and layered depth to his words and actions. Though explicit invocation of the name "Daniel" occurs only once in the gospel corpus (in connection with the desolating sacrilege of Mt 24:15), the specter of Daniel's *Kibor Enash* (one like a "Son of Man" or "Human One") ghosts the text like a haint from the future who is pushing continuously on the veil of time from the far side. Jesus appears to live his ministry as if already channeling this future figure like a familiar ancestor from the past, troubling the living community by conjuring its currents of ungrieved violence and promising vindication for the "disappeared." His Galilean messianism is thus one whose details are filled in from a past that is still future (Elijah whose inconclusive disappearance ignites expectation of his coming back) and a future that is already past (the Human One-to-come whose triumph is already verified in what is unfolding). As previously discussed, the *Kibor Enash* may subtly echo the replacement line arising from the void left by Abel's murder. Within such a reading, Daniel could be said to have envisioned a kind of "New Abel," coming with the clouds, stepping into the dock before the Ancient of Days to receive vindication. This is a collective figuration embodying the oppressed "people of the saints of the Most High," worn out by the wars that the beast of the fourth kingdom has made upon them, whose witness compels judgment in the heavenly court at the utter nadir of events. What is pictured as the result is a sudden inversion of the meaning of events and an unanticipated transference of "rule" and "glory" ("beauty") to these suffering ones (Dan 7:9–27).

If Daniel is, in one sense, the major prophet least explicitly invoked, he is also the one most thoroughly internalized in the gospel writings, especially in terms of Mark's use of the *Kibor Enash* vision. Here is Jesus' most often invoked messianic trope, deployed continuously to critique the operative messianisms of his opponents and his followers alike in the great challenge "to see" which the gospels effectively narrate. The imperial colonization of Palestine by a Roman-Jewish condominium of power (Myers 1988, 391) inevitably inveigled the Torah into its ongoing struggle for legitimacy. Scripture became a mine-field with parties on various sides gerrymandering texts into a valorization of violent force as alone worthy of aspiration. Mark, in particular, in his writing, is parrying both the Roman-Temple-State hegemony and the counter-hegemony of the Zealot-Sicarii-fourth Philosophy comity that briefly overthrew Roman control by means of a tumultuous revolt from 66–70 CE. Messianisms are thick on the scene, in this short interlude of militant hope, offering variant "readings" of unfolding events in the midst of revolutionary upheaval. In this particular ideological mix, Mark depicts a Jesus laboring to speak at multiple levels to different audiences—seeking, on the one hand, to "conscientize" the peasant crowds (by means of highly polemic public confrontations of the elites in teaching and symbolic action), while at the same time auguring deeply into the false hopes and misperceptions of his own inner circle in order to prepare them for what is to come.

The Markan narrative carefully walks the reader into the pivotal confrontation in chapter 8, in which Jesus queries his circle with a personal riff on the burning bush. At stake is the core pedagogy of the movement. All the usual suspects of imminent expectation are on the table—"John the Baptist" revived, "Elijah" returned, "one of the prophets" reincarnate, and finally through Peter's boldness, the category of "messiah" itself, directly attributed to the Narazene for the first time. Jesus silences the identification like a demon and quickly eclipses that category with yet another reference to the Human One who is now cast in explicitly apocalyptic terms (Mk 1:25; 3:12; Myers 1988, 242). In this first "passion prediction,"[16] Jesus frames the coming of the *Kibor Enash* as necessarily (*dei* in Greek) engaging suffering rather than triumph (Myers 1988, 244). Contra Peter's implicit invocation equating "Messiah" with "royal accession and restoration of Israel's collective honor," this Human One will be "rejected" (*apodokimasthēnai* in Greek, like a "court case weighed and then thrown out") by the authorities and killed (and rise again only after having perished) (Mk 8:31). By the second prediction, Peter has backpedaled into calling Jesus "Rabbi"—elsewhere in Mark an appellation associated with doubt about Jesus' teaching in favor of the dominant ideology of triumph and take over (Mk 9:5, 11:21, 14:25; Myers 1988, 250). With the rest of the inner circle, he reverts back to scribal assertions that Elijah must (*dei*) come *before* the messiah, in good apocalyptic fashion, in order to restore relationships, avert judgment, and *avoid* a curse upon the land (Mk 9:11; Mal 4:5–6). Jesus' response is seeming agreement. But he then immediately upends those expectations in asking why suffering is predicted for the Human One "in what is written" and simultaneously hints that perhaps Elijah has indeed appeared and "had things done to him"—as it was "written" of him. Myers reads this as a cagey (and preparatory) "what if"—"What if Elijah has already come . . . and been repudiated rather than welcomed by the ruling elites and subsequently murdered by them?" (Mk 9:11–13; Myers 1988, 253). Since domination systems typically meet prophetic resistance with a politically predictable ("necessary") "script of suffering" (arrest, jail, torture, and death), can it then go any differently for the Human One-to-come? (And of course hanging in the air, unsaid, is the same implication for predecessors . . . and followers.)

Again and again, Jesus evades the triumphalist cultural categories constantly being "hung" on him (by opponents and followers alike) in favor of cryptic solicitation of this militantly nonviolent Danielic figure, who appears suddenly at the heart of catastrophe and violent repression to invert understanding of who is actually triumphing over whom. In the seer's writings, the archetypal "scene" is the royal court; the accused are vulnerable "saints" or innocent marginalized ones; and the dominant political assessment is imperial condemnation and execution. But the "apocalyptic revelation" is that it is actually *empire* that is being judged, and *principalities and powers* overcome—precisely in that courtroom vision of seeming loss! And this becomes the hermeneutic key to Jesus' movement teaching and action!

Critical, in a situation of seemingly calamitous defeat, is keeping sight unclouded by fear in order to "see" clearly, and with deep dignity, who is actually overcoming whom in the harsh theater of imperial judgment. It is this crucial insight rooted in the *Kibor Enash* that will find its apogee in the passion narratives, in which once again the combat myth of apocalyptic (between the Powers and the Innocents) will be convened around mundane and horrific political events, to overturn despair and pull back the veil for "watching eyes" (Mk 13: 35, 37). Myers' work, in particular, makes this hovering of apocalyptic myth over political mess trenchant (Myers 1988, 389–391). It shows up as the interpretive backdrop at each pivotal turn in the gospels. The rending of heavens and veils and glistening of clothes, the descent of doves and clouds and darkness, and the haunting specter of Elijah over the scenes of disclosure, underscore the three synoptic moments of "baptism," "transfiguration," and "crucifixion" as decisively apocalyptic in their import.

But especially telling, in the unfolding sequence of these three glimpses behind the veil of political delusion, is Mark's hint about the "place" of the divine voice heralding the "Beloved Son" for this Palestinian theater of struggle. What originally "rends the heavens" over the waters of Jordan out in the wilderness, and emanates from a Sinai-like thundercloud over the Mount of Transfiguration in the Galilee outback (ghosted by the shades of Moses and Elijah), is nowhere to be heard over the terror of Golgotha ... *except* in the cry of the Vulnerable One himself, giving voice to ruptured flesh and spilled blood, back "up" toward the leaden sky. Jesus has appeared to the bystanders here to have bellowed for intervention by Elijah "to come and take him down" (Mk 15: 33–36). But they have misread the moment. Elijah is nowhere at hand. This is rather a shout that has pilloried *Elohim* (*"Eloi, Eloi, lama sabachthani"* in the retained Aramaic), a great groan of abandonment that has put divinity itself at issue. And it is not merely Jesus' own.

Here at the utter end of things is unexpected uptake of the narrative's beginning: "a voice crying in the wilderness," says Mark—pointedly sidestepping Malachi's insistence on the Temple as the place of advent (Mk 1:3). But just how far back does the apocalyptic veil peel ... how deep does the haunting go? (How do we read? How are we read?) Whence this "genesis" cry ... ? This is the groundswell of unrequited disappearance coursing from primal Abel, through contemporary John, into the visceral core and out the grimacing lips of Jesus. It was the cry primordial in ancient Israel—echoing from the spilled blood of herders (Gen 4:10). It was enshrined in the Exodus narrative as the signal expression galvanizing divine action on behalf of oppressed slaves (Ex 2:23–25; 3:7). It was memorialized in Israel's legal codes as the special "weapon of the weak" (especially widows and orphans and strangers and the poor in general; Ex 22:21–27; Dt 15: 9). It shows up as the animating energy of prophetic outcry against monarchy (Is 5:7; 40:6; Jer 8:18–9:11; etc.) and the final denouement of messianic engagement with the powers that be (Mk 15:33–36). And it is most decipherable in its most decisive meaning especially by way of the mortal *Kibor Enash* of Daniel's vision. As a groan from the ground of Genesis, breaking out again and again like an ancestral murmur, this upwelling is raw in its figuring of political murder, but also juridically final in constituting and convening the court of justice for both ancient covenant people and heavenly "divine" council. It first comes to gospel narration by way of the other prophetic influence so determinative for Jesus' movement.

Isaiah's Branch

The beginning of the gospel of the Messiah, according to Mark, is actually not Jesus, or even John the Baptist, but ancient desert moan, given momentous voice by the prophet Isaiah, in the devastation of exile. More accurately the prophetic herald of this wilderness haunt is a denizen of the Isaiah school of prophecy known in scholarly circles as deutero-Isaiah (II Isaiah, 40:1–55:13) or even trito-Isaiah (Isaiah, 56:1–66:24)—an Isaiah figure carrying forward the tradition of political critique anchored by the mid-eighth BCE poet of the southern kingdom (who verified Hezekiah's defiance of Assyrian overlordship and announced the downfall of Sennacherib). Even though this entire corpus of Isaiah writings pre-dates Daniel (itself written in veiled critique of Antiochus IV Epiphanies' reign over Israel 175–164 BCE), we position its messianic influence last in the line-up here, as the voice most immediately invoked by the earliest gospel writer (Mark) to stage his own artistic figuring of the Jesus movement.

The wilderness cry, thrust onto our readerly eyes from verse two, forward, in Mark's creation, is a bit of cryptic polemic for the savvy inquirer. Where the evangelist first feints toward Malachi's expectation (which in that last prophet's rendition reads, "Behold I send my messenger to prepare the way before me, and the Lord whom you seek *will suddenly come to his temple*," Mal 3:1), Mark suddenly breaks off the Malachi focus on the Temple and slips in Isaiah's bombast, "the voice of one crying in the wilderness" (Is 40:3). This is like a slap on the cheek of sleepwalking! The favored locus of the coming is polemically figured.

Not the height of royal architectural achievement bleeding peasants dry with the demand for taxes and special levies, but a wildlands track, is the favored place, discernible only with a nomad's ken.

The Isaiah vision of return (from exile) articulated in 40:1–31 is actually a herder riff on the exilic experience of Babylonian processional magnificence. Isaiah's ancient words subtly signify on the Babylonian royal hanging gardens and glittering god-statues and sensuous onslaught of music and dance and high-fashion celebrated in the ritual round of imperial Temple-State glorification (cf. also Is 35:5–10; 41:17–20; 43:19–21; 52:7–12). Against such, his prophetic promise is not nostalgia for Israel's own royal pomp in the heyday of the Solomonic Temple complex, but rather a new wilderness exodus, once again learning rudiments of rest and release from rough places (Is 40:4) and renewed strength from eagle-wings and ways (Is 40:31). The gospel is thus framed in what has been core from the tradition's beginnings. It is a "way" (as the nascent movement will come to be called) learned from wildland living, in tutelage to herds, listening for bush-speech and mountain-moan. And it is led by YHWH as "shepherd" (Is 40:11)—a designation whose various after-images will shadow the good news narratives (ranging from synoptic concerns for the beleaguered peasantry as "shepherdless sheep" to the Johannine Jesus's inversion of the shepherd stereotype as "thief," as mentioned earlier).

When we turn to Jesus' own appeals to this compelling precursor, we find Isaiah-eloquence nurturing messianic wit like an underground river. While direct citation by the Palestinian prophet of the older seer's name is infrequent, Isaiah-insight shows itself prevalent as a paradigm with which Jesus can think through his own situation. Certainly it grants the Galilean organizer a rich poetic template requisite for galvanizing high hope from hard peasant struggle. The Isaiah school in its entirety will supply Jesus potent portraits to assert the Sabbath-Jubilee continuum of release (from labor, debts, illness, blindness, captivity, etc.) as the trenchant demand of the hour. This emphasis shows up not only in Luke's stylization of the messiah as a living, walking embodiment of "Jubilee Liberation" in his inaugural address in Nazareth, but also throughout his subsequent actions and teaching (Lk 4:18–30/Is 61:1–2a; Lk 6:20–26/Is 29:18–21; Lk 7:18–23/Is 35:5–6; Lk 11:3–4/ Is 58:5–6). It will likewise ghost Mark's text at key moments of challenge (Mk 4:1–21/Is 55:10–13; Mk 6:30–44/Is 49:9–10; Mk 8:1–10/Is 55:1–2; Mk 10:17–30/Is 58:7–14). The Isaiah vision of Sabbath release and Jubilee reversal is held up as the very premise for the Jerusalem Temple's existence (as a place of rest and refuge for every manner of alien and outcast, Mk 11:17/Is 56:7ff). It supplies the core demand of festal celebration (food and drink and harvest freely offered, Jh 7:38/ Is 41:17–18; 44:3; 55:1; 58:11). And it becomes the primal measure of Israel's "failure" (Israel's betrayal of a Sabbath-Jubilee lifestyle, Mk 12:1–12/Is 5:1–7). But for our purposes it is especially Isaiah's contribution to questions of pedagogy that commands focus.

The early Isaiah grants to the later messiah pedagogical provocation writ large. This is particularly the case in the face of a sharp need for effective ideology critique when Jesus is up against scribal and Pharisaic charges of "uncleanness" connected with his practices of exorcism and table fellowship. In each case, the peasant provocateur from Nazareth invokes an Isaiah conundrum (Mk 3:19b-4:34/Is 6:1–13; 7:1–23/Is 29:9–21). Twice in the extant writings of the latter, the question of ideological captivity had exercised prophetic consternation. In Is 6:9–10, the seer was given a mission to name and incite—and incite *by* naming—people's *misperception* ("see and see, but do not perceive; hear and hear but do not understand"). He was to make "hearts fat, ears heavy, and eyes closed" (thus forestalling a too quick turn to healing). And in Is 29: 9–14, the prophet had called down stupor on a leadership given over to blind fabrications and rote recitation of counsel that only dissimulated and hid the reality of exploitation. In both cases, the prophetic confrontation thickened murk into miasma over the top of a tender hope. It ramified ruling class delusion—dilating its hubris and false certainty of seeing—while simultaneously laboring to create the conditions for a different kind of vision at the bottom levels of society (among the poor, the lame, the deaf, and the blind) (Is 29:18–21; 9:1–2).

The bifurcated focus coded a harsh dialectic in seemingly simplistic vernacular. What Isaiah projected was the amplification of ideological contradiction to its point of boomerang. His hope was for the emergence of another kind of mentality, one that gave up on easy resolutions and dared see clearly how dire the circumstance had become and how damming were the politics that presided. The Temple-State of his time would not—and should not—survive! Despite its presumption of pomp and glory, it would end harshly, like a felled oak, whose trunk is burned once it is cut down (Is 6:13).[17] But then from its naked stump—a "holy" surprise! Seed germinating, like a clear-cut field once again on its way to becoming a forest (Is 6:13; 29:17; 14:3–8; 41:19–20; cf. Mk 4:1–34)!

Here is the Isaiah-vocation stretched over a three-century-long travail, continuously excoriating the sight that "sees, but does not observe" while elevating the eye that is blind but *does* see (Is 42:14–25; 43:8). From this latter "wisdom," like a sapling from a root, would emerge a new hope. A new leader would come, judging *not* by sight, but "with justice for the meek" (Is 11: 3–4; 35: 5; 42: 6). Such an evocative image of "messianic branching" (from the residue of destruction) would become Isaiah's great contribution to the subsequent movement. And pedagogically, his koan-like work of elaborating obfuscation between ruling class literacy and the "little tradition" sagacity of the peasants would become exemplary. It will serve Jesus as the motive force and inner potency of his own parabolic style of teaching.

In occupied first century Palestine, in which peasant labor was made to supply elite prosperity through manipulation of torah codes of purity and debt, messianic intervention necessarily focused on the way spiritual ideology leveraged economic rapacity. Parables become the primary mechanism by which Jesus counters attacks upon his teaching, using the twisty logic of riddles to open up space for mental struggle inside a discourse otherwise closing out reflection.

The strategy will become especially clear in Mark's gospel. Quickly in opening his Galilee campaign of "direct action" in that narrative, Jesus will "occupy" the Capernaum synagogue with his little troop of recruits (Mk 1:21–27; Myers 137). His teaching there (and throughout the region's villages) will stir "unclean spirits" from their lairs in the broken souls of displaced peasants and precipitate a struggle to exorcize them before they name him (and coopt his action into service of the "politics of holiness" controlling public expression) (Mk 1:23–26; 1:34; 3:11–12; Borg 1994, 6). Just as quickly, Jesus will find himself labeled "unclean" by scribal elites for daring to consort with lepers and for leading hungry followers to glean grain from uncut fields in supposed violation of the Sabbath (Mk 1:40–45; 2:23–27). Indeed throughout this early campaign, the question of interpretation of the Sabbath-Jubilee tradition of release will anchor much of his verbal combat with the authorities (2:1–12; 2:14–17; 2:23–28; 3:1–6). Back in Capernaum after his first circuit, it immediately draws down a charge of channeling Beelzebul, arch-prince of Canaanite pollution from times past (Mk 3:22). And it results in the "hit" on his life ordered by a conspiracy of the elites (the hastily "contracted" Pharisee-Herodian agreement to kill him; Mk 3:6).

His immediate response is parables (Mk 3:23; 4:1–34; 7:14–23)—instant asides to the peasant crowds to huddle close for folk analysis, seeking to sidestep the binary logic of the spiritual forces he is up against. If either epithet—the send up as "holy" by the departing demons (Mk 1:24, 34; 3:11–12) or the later claim of "possession" thrown down by the scribes who have come to do surveillance on him

(Mk 3:22, 30)—"lands" on him, the game is over. He would then be locked into one end or the other of the hegemonic discourse (either as exemplar of scribal "cleanness" or as paragon of suspect "pollution"). The parables instead engage the charges in a slowed-down process of reflection, keeping alive—for those "with ears to hear"—the uncertainty necessary to engage the painful struggle to unhook from hegemony (Mk 4:33–34). "Decolonizing" is always a matter of hard wrestling, kneading lumps of deception into "food for thought" (Mk 3:23–27). It takes time ("time" had indeed been a primary concern for his precursor, Is 6:11; 29:17), holding back easy conclusions long enough to provoke deep questions.

These "little tradition puzzles" of Jesus function like folk riddles have through the ages, offering a thought-cauldron for cooking up alternative reason. They set up a kind of obstacle course for the understanding, layering the dominant logic in a small labyrinth of thinking, repelling easy resolution(Mk 4:10–13). Rather, they threw grit into the grind of order and began the "binding" that alone would allow Jesus eventually "to plunder the strong man's house" and free his "goods"[18] (his "exorcism" of low level operatives of the priestly scribal pipeline of extortion, in his action of clearing the Temple; Mk 3:27; 11:1–19; cf. Is 49: 24–26; 42: 21–25; Myers 1988, 166).

In first century Palestine, we might say, parables opened a kind of "Jubilee of the mind," a space of release from the operative assumptions, broadcast by the powers, in order that a different hope might sprout. Indeed (as we see in chapter 3), crafting artful images useful to this messianic movement required juxtaposing the harsh reality of the Temple-State political economy with the "dark" wisdom of rootwork (contrasting, as had Isaiah, "the kingdom" as a renewed Davidic power bloc with "the kingdom" as wild seed working a field into a forest: Mk 3:24; 11: 10; 12: 35–37 versus Mk 3:27, 4:11, 26–32; 11:23; 13:1–2; cf. Is 6: 1–10). Parables cleared a little safe zone in the thicket of misinformation, a psychic space for mental vision-quest, where the strictures of imperial "seeing" could be short-circuited in favor of germinating insight from blindness and developing what anthropologist James Scott calls "hidden transcripts" of resistance (Is 11:1–5; 42:20; 43:8; 4:11–12, 21–25; 8:21–26; 10:46–52; Scott 1990, xii–xiii, 8–9, 1, 37–39, etc.). Like Isaiah comprehending stumps as seed banks, they likened the kingdom to a weed and anticipated that even a tiny grain of mustard could branch out into a huge tree (Mk 4:30–32; Crossan 1991, 278; Myers 1988, 179–181).

In a word—looping back to the inner city Detroit street-riddles the Introduction unpacked—parabolic vignettes did the same kind of work in first century Palestine as Tyre Guyton's garbage art does in urbanized postmodernity. They opened out a kind of "Heidelberg of the head," interrupting blighted expectation and recycling everyday struggle inside artful puzzles whose gradual decoding gave glimpses of another possibility. They composted survival into vitality and poverty into a reciprocity hinting at the messianic banquet to come (Lk 11:5–8, Herzog 1994, 213–214).

CHAPTER 3

Parabolic Incantation: Movement Messianism and the Jubilee Jesus

The myths of the ancient Near East are the oldest myths we know of. They come from the part of the world from which at least two great waves – farming and civilization – moved outward to fill the world, and they are the record of humankind's first attempts to make sense of those waves. (Eisenberg 1999, 69)

With what can we compare the kingdom of God, or what parable shall we use for it? It is like a grain of mustard seed . . . (Mk 4:30–31)

Thus to sum up so far, what we see in Jesus' own messianism are invocations of precursor figures in whose example he anchors his movement. In a moment of bombastic confrontation, Jesus ventriloquizes speechless Abel as the disappeared pastoralist whose blood-cry initiates the primal outbreak of prophetic protest against indigenous disappearance that will reverberate across the entire face of biblical history. He periodically lifts up Cimarron Abraham as the primal emblem of a herder hospitality whose welcoming table under the teaching trees stands in stark contrast to Sodom's urban terrorism and serves as example for the movement. And he regularly calls renegade Moses to the witness stand as the great innovator of Sabbath-discipline—a rigorous round of sabbatical rest and Jubilee release originally designed to keep an *hapiru* horde of escaped slaves from settling too comfortably into Canaanite agricultural patterns by requiring "Israel" continuously to revisit its earlier Sinai schooling in wildlands sacrality and nomadic freedom. Each of these ancestral appeals is rooted in values and practices associated with the earliest form of social resistance on the planet—the historic choice of dominated peoples to flee imperial constraints managed from urban centers by taking up flocks and going feral. Saying such is not to argue that pastoral nomadism was everywhere and all the time a mode of resistance. Hiebert is right: it was and is, in most places, most of the time, collaborationist, issuing from and cooperating with peasant-based farming settlements. But within its basic practice and mindset there remains alive both a preference and a possibility: the freedom of spending large amounts of time away from village or town in a mobile vocation, "conversing" with a herd and attending carefully to environmental cues and warnings, and the skill-set and means (along with the "peace of mind" such a possibility confers) to exit settled life at moment's notice, if necessary.

It is the wild, not the city, that will host this new messianic advent (Mk 1:1–3)—precisely because the untamed spaces of wandering *have always been* the place of both deepest pedagogy and most reliable regeneration for the social movement known as "Israel."[1] The retribalization movement in the Canaanite highlands that amalgamated escaped slaves from Egypt and outlaw peasants from the coastal cities under that theomorphic name, idealized the experience of wildlands wandering in Sinai, even as it confessed "YHWH" as a Rain-and-Soil deity, who would guarantee its dry-farming highlands lifestyle (Corbett 2005, 228; Hiebert 1996, 65, 138). And when Israel had itself gone monarchical and grown oppressive, the prophetic movement galvanized in response would recurrently invoke the memory (as we have glossed by way of Elijah, Daniel, and Isaiah). And it will not be different for the Jesus-led movement of Galilean peasant resistance to Roman military incursion, Herodian land expropriation, or Temple-State tax domination in the first century.[2] Jesus' own messianic alternative will mainstream Sabbath-Jubilee as its fundamental practice and offer peasant-followers the prospect of a hundredfold abundance of care-giving kin-relations and freely circulating material assets such as lands and fields (Mk 4:8; 10:29–30). It will not thereby enjoin recourse to nomadic pastoralism *per se*. But it will highlight values and recall traditions whose power is rooted in wildlands symbiotics and insist these are central to the struggle for justice in an otherwise settled lifestyle.

In this chapter, we shift from asking after what Jesus himself marked out as worthy of consideration and emulation (as "messianic traces" he relied on to shape his movement) to begin querying the boundaries within which he himself becomes the newly minted and archetypal representation of "anointing" (though never actually physically christened with poured oil, as far as we know). In doing so, we attend not only to the central teachings and practices of his own movement or interesting hints the texts offer under the guise of seeming metaphor (the real "kingdom" as wild mustard seed, the real messiah as a good "shepherd," real economics as merely "daily" bread, etc.) but also to two moments when a certain messianic excess begins to subvert the image of the messiah himself.

In one sense the gospels already reflect "Big Tradition" concerns. They are already answering to the needs of apologetics—of at least responding to, if not satisfying, a gaze and a threat from outside the communities trying to live what the text memorializes. Moving *from* adaptive and flexible tellings of messianic memories while on the run from authorities, *toward* a greater focus on the writing of such for the sake of cultural translation and wider dissemination, in its very execution, privileges one story over another. It begins to reduce complex nuances to a simplified party line. Affect and tone bow to denotation. But within that very emphasis, haunting after-images may jump up between the marks on the page. Possibilities for how the overtones and undertones of the story were heard during the oral phase are now relegated to brief flickerings at the edge of what must be taken in through the eye. But they do not entirely disappear. It is especially these little tradition nuances, a kind of "ghosting" attending certain details, that will tease our imagination as we gaze straight at the canonical representation. We will seek to divine a Jesus who has become subaltern to his own story. Or said in a form more in keeping with our emphasis in this writing, we conjure prodigal messianic possibilities from spirit flashes not quite managed by the canonical text.

Movement Power: The Messianic as a Little Tradition

But to catch sight of such shimmering, a habit of popular expectation must be broken. Messianic hopefulness must not be confused with royal power. The two are antithetical. Perhaps the sharpest polemic against such occurs near the end of Jesus' assault on business as usual in Matthew's parable of the unforgiving servant (Mt 18:23–35).[3] Biblical exegete Will Herzog decodes the pedagogy. What gets read in many mainstream contexts as an almost comedic story of hardhearted refusal to extend a mercy shown is actually a sharply messianic critique of popular messianism itself. Matthew has the Galilean Jesus, late in his advance upon Jerusalem and attended by discipleship fantasies of take-over, conjuring the impossible (Mt 18:23–35; Mk 10:32–45). Riffing on the very practices of Sabbath-Jubilee release ("forgiveness" and "release" are the same word in Greek; Myers 2001, 24) that he has mandated as entry requirement for his movement followers (Mk 1: 16–20; 10:17–31), he "riddles" an archetypal messianic scenario. An agrarian king, reckoning accounts with a retainer caught in an astronomical debt of ten thousand talents (the districts of Galilee and Peraea together yielded Herod Antipas only two hundred talents annually), "forgives" the entire amount! Here is the fantasy of every peasant smallholder locked into inescapable indebtedness, realized! The accession, at the very heart of power, of a royal representative who initiates Jubilee!

Horsley and Hanson detail the degree to which "the little tradition of the common people" heralded "royal pretenders and popular messianic movements" that incarnated the hopes of the people for a basic "restoration of social and economic justice" (Herzog 1994, 146; Horsley and Hanson 1985, 88–134, 122). Kingship in this tradition found its legitimacy only in popular acclamation of "charismatic figures of humble origin," whose heroic feats might awaken the people "to overthrow Herodian and Roman domination and to restore the traditional ideals of a free and egalitarian society" (Herzog 1994, 146; Horsley and Hanson 1985, 116). Recurrent waves of popular uprising from the time of Herod the Great (37–4 BCE) until the Jewish revolt (66–73 CE) had hailed such figures and hoped in their triumph, only to be disappointed time and again. And these traditions found particular resonance in the rural north, outside the immediate Hellenizing influence of Tiberias and Sepphoris, where the ancient lifeways of old "Israel" remained alive under the surface of the imposed "Great Tradition" of the Jerusalem Temple, brought north in the second century BCE Hasmonean "colonization" of Galilee.[4] The parable outline only barely abstracts from the actual situation on the ground in first century Palestine, in which Roman tribute-taking compounded by Herodian taxation and Jerusalem Temple tithe-extraction pushed increasing numbers of Galilean peasant families into severe economic stress and endless debt.

Yet the very infrastructure of tribute-taking, tax-collecting, and debt-manipulation that forms the necessary economic substrate of kingship does not keep the peasantry from projecting their hopes for deliverance on the position of a king. They simply want it filled by a people's champion, who will use the levers of power to redress injustice and restore a measure of equitable reciprocity. History is replete with the archetype of "royal messiahs," "czar-deliverers," "just kings," and "religious saviors," across wide-ranging cultures, whose image remains potent not merely in elite promulgation of ideologies of passive waiting (for a never-arriving reckoning), but as well in crafty invocations of such by upstart peasants, fashioning cover for themselves under a posture of loyalty to the reigning sovereign, from whose hand they seek redress of real grievances (Scott, 1990, 100–102). And occasionally, rulers will even find it advantageous to their power to "step into" such images and enact momentary releases of indebtedness or tax burdens (when the coffers are not facing bankruptcy), for the sake of enhancing their reputation (Herzog 1994, 148). But these are only respites that prove the rule. The parable here would seem to be aiming straight for this form of messianic hope.

Herzog's approach is uncompromising in insisting that gospel parables in general be taken as "political cartoons," typifying existential situations in sharply sardonic form, and not simply as the equivalent of theological fairy tales (which is how imperial Christianity has long cast them). Landowners and judges, banquet hosts and kings, are not stand-ins for God in these first century Palestinian stories. They are rather what they are—figures an agrarian society would instantly recognize as true to type. And the stories then lay out a familiar scenario—except (usually) for one detail or behavior that is anomalous and provocative. This anomalous "twist point" then emerges as the story-shard around which peasant reflection pivots and struggles and eventually must conclude with its own wisdom or construction of meaning.

Here the story lifts up a reality known only to the peasantry by hearsay—an exposé of the inner working of the court bureaucracy focused on royal values and retainer struggles, inside the patronage system, to gain greater power and ward off competition. The retainer class—some 5–7 percent of the population in such societies—typically lives by subterfuge and intrigue, engaged in continuous machinations to secure position and rebuff threat (largely from other retainers). The king is a typical agrarian ruler, reconciling accounts, faced with a patronage client who has apparently taken liberties with his right to collect the royal tribute (upon which the kingdom depends), which had been granted him on the basis of personal recognizance and proven competence, but is now being "called" or demanded of the retainer by the king in a reminder of the latter's monopoly of royal power. While the brevity of the parabolic form leaves much to imagination, the central focus is clearly on the continual calculation and subtle negotiation attendant on bureaucratic life in honor-shame cultures. "If it caught the attention of its audience," Herzog argues, "it might have been precisely because it purported to reveal a glimpse of the inner machinations of court life rather than presenting the usual way the royal court impacted villagers, namely, by means of the toll or tax collector" (Herzog 1994, 139).

The king—as a typical satrap of the day—operates above the law, both in originally resolving to send the retainer and his family into slavery, and in the reversal with which he answers the retainer's desperate plea for mercy. Even more than the debt, the king's honor and power are at stake. The severity of the penalty and the abundance of the forgiveness alike reiterate his potency as sovereign. The granted release, at another level, further "indebts" the retainer to the king's honor, binding him even more tightly in his trusted function to act on behalf of the king's overall interest. But the retainer miscalculates in his own response. Concerned for the court gossip about his own financial indiscretion and its surprising release (by the king) that will inevitably filter out and affect his image among competitor retainers (and the aristocracy at large), he can only obsess over the perception of weakness now ghosting his own high standing in the hierarchy, rendering him potentially vulnerable to predatory subterfuge. In seeking to counter such, he opts to inculcate fear and close out any tendency to seek advantage on the part of lower officials, by ruthlessly remanding the one indebted to him to prison (Mt 18:30). But the action only precipitates defection among some of his own clientele further down the bureaucratic ladder, who report his vindictiveness to "their lord," knowing the report will percolate up to "his lord," the king (Mt 18:31).

The reaction is swift—and, at one level, surprising. Herzog notes that the retainer was actually only demonstrating the same values that the king himself embodied in his office—uncompromising methods of extracting tribute, shrewd maneuvering inside the bureaucracy, quick seizure upon opportunity for advantage (Herzog 1994, 146). Nor is the issue one of causing upset among the cotillion of retainers—kings regularly manipulated the fortunes and positioning of court functionaries to keep them at each other's throats and out of the royal hair. Remanding the unforgiving servant to the torture chamber indicates a violation far more sacred. Honor itself has been impugned—the very substance of courtly legitimacy—the carefully crafted image of royal sagacity and dignity, now ridiculed by the retainer's action as a royal weakness that the retainer has "played" to his advantage and to the king's great shame. The retainer has failed to grasp that the intended calculation on the king's part was that such mercy would ripple out through the bureaucratic operations, extend release across the entire land, and redound to the king's repute throughout the kingdom. It was not a matter of personal beneficence shown to the retainer, but a subtly dramatic indication of policy change by the king, seeking to turn the retainer's malfeasance into a grand gesture of royal forgiveness, conducing to the good of the entire kingdom (Herzog 1994, 146–147). Here in a single act, the cycle of ruthless exploitation had been broken; a messianic intervention introduced!

But what happens, says the parable? The triumph of the system! Such release, initiated by no lesser a figure than the king himself, in net effect, can only result ultimately in an even more vicious routinization of the bureaucracy and its sustaining values. Jubilee release inside the typical patron-client hierarchy leads to . . . irremediable torture! Do not be confused. New wine cannot be put into old wine skins. Messianic abundance and kingly prerogative are an insoluble mixture. The latter does not operate in a vacuum, but inside a bureaucratic machinery that will inevitably iterate such mercy into an even more ruthless promulgation of its own predatory relations. As Herzog will jibe: "What if the messiah came and nothing changed?" (Herzog 1994, 146). Precisely!—at least at the level of the political hierarchy. (And indeed this *is* what happened to the degree Jesus' movement ultimately ended up inside the Roman bureaucracy by way of Constantine: "Christology" did not change the character of empire, but empire did change the perception of the messiah.) Kingship and messianism must part ways in the people's consciousness. Sabbath-release and Jubilee-liberation—as the very sum and substance of what messianic practice should look like—cannot be "imposed"—even by a supposedly messianic king. Within the settled agriculture configuration of social relations, concentrated in metropolitan centers and governed by royal powers and aristocractic prerogative, messianism will necessarily be marginal. It cannot be otherwise.

The "messianic" is not the image of a benevolent satrap presiding over an empire. It is rather a remembered subject of beauty and reciprocity circulated in a set of relations that seek greater social justice and are roughly symbiotic in environmental effect (messianic advents in prophetic representations often include restored ecologies; Is 29:17–21; 35:1–7). In a setting such as occupied Palestine in the first century—as indeed among other forms of messianic rebellion showing up in other contexts across the entire history of aristocratically dominated agricultural societies—messianism references a set of practices demanding a particular mode of relations. At best, such can be glimpsed for a moment of electrifying vision, in the achievements of various people's movements, before the window is violently slammed shut by imperial powers. If arguing thus seems less than hopeful to so many of our middle-class-deluded eyes, for peasantries and marginalized folk over the course of the last five-thousand years, this briefly realized vision has been almost the entire substance of "things hoped for." The realism is harsh, but accurate. Thus far, inside imperial histories, "the messianic" has been a briefly realized memory of human beings living proudly and compellingly "otherwise"—before being decimated, coopted, or disappeared *by* royal power. But even that memory itself is not secure. As Walter Benjamin has prophesied—and as the last two millennia of "Christianity" verify—the past itself is at risk. (Benjamin 1969, 255). And struggling over the messianic is thus a matter of struggling to keep social space open to the haunting of that memory for the sake of a present politics. Movements can accomplish such; bureaucracies cannot.

Movement Place: The Messianic as Shared Jeopardy among the Galilean Unclean

But it is also the case that this deep antipathy between a people's messianism and powerful kingship had begun to be established already with Jesus' earliest teaching. While Mark has Jesus beginning his ministry with an assertion that "the kingdom of God is at hand," his first teachings about such will ironically juxtapose harsh political critique with stark "kingdom comparisons" that are decidedly antiroyal, as we see later. This in part reflects the peculiarity of first century Galilee.[5] Its northern hill country populace sat uneasy to Herodian hegemony and Jerusalem "Temple-State" policy alike, hunkering down in clan-based village loyalties with not always hidden defiance expressed toward the absentee landlords holed up in Tiberias and Sepphoris.[6] (It is no accident that Jesus launched his movement in a region of growing economic disenfranchisement and political repression, where more and more of the restive population was being reduced to day laboring and begging.[7]) Against easy identifications of messianic hope with kingly power—an identification that is thoroughly deconstructed in the movement itself—Jesus will regularly invoke the cryptic "Son of Man" figure from Daniel whose *Kibor Enash* "penumbra" may hint memory of pastoralist Abel and his "replacement offspring" Enosh (as pointed out above) as well as of a coming "people's dominion" envisioned by the ancient seer. On the other hand, memory of various folk initiatives, preserved in the artful signs of vernacular idiom (oral stories, torah rulings, prophetic poetry, rustic riddles, etc.), will form the substance of his teaching, as we have sampled in the previous chapter. Throughout his ministry, Jesus will recurrently reference a kind of people's tradition that has preserved, within its popular imagery, an orientation not to hierarchical practices, but rather to freedom values peculiar to renegade herders, escaped slaves, highland subsistence farmers, and upstart bands of prophets. To once again become a practical movement in an occupied environment (such as first century Galilee), however—this dangerous memory-bank of debt-release and Jubilee-justice will need a galvanizing and public event.

As already hinted, in Mark's narrative, Jesus' inaugural action has him teaching provocatively in a Capernaum synagogue on the Sabbath, stirring up a hornets nest of opposition (Mk 1:21–28). An unclean spirit addresses him from its "perch" in a poor one, seeking quickly to gather the upstart rabbi under a label and dispose of him as "holy." The resulting exorcism, however, silences the certainty and opens the space to all manner of "questioning"—peasant wit suddenly licensed to speak in a space occupied and controlled by the scribal elite (Mk 1:27). Myers is prescient in unpacking the strange plural the spirit invokes in its protest: "have you come to destroy *us?*" (Myers 1988, 142). It is as if the scribal authorities are ventriloquized by the possessed individual, whose ruptured psyche has internalized their terms of denigration. In clearing the unclean spirit from the person, Jesus also begins to clear the discourse of uncleanness from the space. It is the scribal "principality" as a whole—the scribal use of the purity code to lock down voice and leverage resources—that has been served notice of its own uncleanness in the event. And it returns fire in short order. Just a few more actions forward in this Galilee campaign of organizing (by Mk 3:22), we are told that Jesus himself has been marked as possessed in his own exorcisms, publicly accused by these very scribal authorities of hosting no less than Beelzebul[8] and channeling the prince of demons (Mk 3:22). It is he, they charge, who really harbors the "unclean spirit" (not least because, immediately following the Capernaum synagogue encounter, he had dared embrace—literally and physically!—an unclean leper out in the countryside and then simply declared "uncleanness" clean!) (Mk 1: 40–45; 3:30).

The messianic response in kind—as highlighted in the previous chapter—is a form of parabolic haiku: pithy polemics, promulgated among the crowd that he calls to "lean in" close for some vernacular breakdown (Mk 3:23). He does not resist the charge, but "inhabits" it and amplifies its purchase. "How can Satan cast out Satan?" he queries. The emphasis so far in his ministry has been on unclean spirits haunting the broken souls of poor villagers (though with innuendo about complicity higher up[9]). And he is numbered among them (as subaltern, submerged in an "untouchable" condition). But quickly here his figuring shifts the focus. They have upped the ante by charging him with harboring "the Lord of the house" (one of the meanings of Beelzebul) and operating by way of a demonic "prince" (*archon*). If low-level demons have indeed fled (as in the synagogue action in Capernaum) then some higher power has obviously been brought into play (and this is an issue that commands much of our attention in the next two chapters). But Jesus is cagey here. He neither affirms nor denies the indictment, but slows down the logic and introduces another category, "Satan," which may or may not be synonymous with theirs. The counterquestion flips the reference. If an unclean spirit *could* regularly "attend synagogue" without stirring healing action from the synagogue authorities, who and what are *they* channeling? The next leg of the parable will infer a kingdom, divided against its own interests, that "cannot stand" (Mk 3:24). And then a house, similarly contested.[10] Here begins the twist.

Now what is in the cross-hairs is power—the kind of "principality" ruling through a king like Herod or a house like that of David anchoring the Temple-state system in Jerusalem. This constitutes a sudden inversion of sight, looking back upstream. The small fry are spawn of much bigger creatures. "Possession" readily reveals its most raw forms among those most beleaguered—it is easy to identify the demons when their hosts are homeless and unwashed. But of far greater consequence is the regime they reference.[11] Jesus circles back around to the real question again: "If Satan has risen up against Satan and is divided, he cannot stand, but is coming to an end." But now we have a different lens—the demonic insidiousness of bureaucratic power, oppressing peasants in hardening conditions of labor and debt (cf. Mt 11:28–30; 23:1–4, 23–32; Lk 6:17–26), pushing smallholders off of their heavily mortgaged land (Mt 20:1–15), younger sons into begging (Lk 16:19–31), daughters into prostitution (Mt 21:31–32), and elders into deepening hunger and early death (Mk 7:1–15; 12:38–44). The divisions are first of all those created by the elites themselves, using the purity and debt codes with scribal and Temple-State backing. These media control the product (telling peasants what must be tithed to the Temple, what sacrificed as "sin" offering, what forfeit as "unclean" because harvested or gleaned on the Sabbath, etc.). They legitimize the plunder that fat cat landowners are amassing and enjoying as "divine blessing" (through rent and loan re-payments). And they police the rights of access to festal abundance (the party tables of the rich) and public approval (the approbation of torah codes of supposed "righteousness").

But the shifting here is indeed "twisty" as in any good parable. The deep question certainly concerns identification of the culprit: will the real Satan please stand up!? Who is who in this zoo? Except now an end is in sight. It would seem clear that Satan cannot cast out Satan. But Satan *is* an agent of division. And division opens an opportunity that could unravel toward a desired outcome. In the parallelism of kingdoms and houses that the parable unfolds, the mind ricochets back up the line of analysis. Maybe these are destined to end—maybe their ending *would be the ending* of Satan. And indeed, when Jesus' teaching clinic next convenes immediately afterward, back out in the wilds around the lake (cf. Mk 2:13), he will direct the peasant crowds, Isaiah-like, not to Temples and pomp, but to the wisdom of seeds and soils, and a "kingdom" rooted in weeds and fruit! (Mk 4:1–34). Its primal image will be a wild mustard plant developing "messianic branches" (Mk 4:32; cf. Is 11:1–6) capable of offering refuge to all manner of creatures!

In the altercation at hand, however, Jesus concludes with an even more freighted figure from Isaiah (Mk 3:27; Is 49:24). The end is indeed coming...*But*. It requires intervention. "No one can enter a strong man's house and plunder his goods unless he first binds the strong man." Do not be confused, he implies. When we are speaking of spirits, the issue is plunder. The "goods" so mentioned here will appear only one other time in Mark's rendition—when Jesus occupies the Temple, clears out its functionaries, convenes a sit-down strike, and offers a teach-in (Mk 11:1–19; Myers, 166). In that action, he will literally "exorcise" the low level operatives in the priestly scribal pipeline of extortion, and shut down any transportation of their goods across the Temple mall. This will be an exorcism that "un-plunders" the take (as Is 49:24–26 had promised), and frees the space for those for whom it was originally intended (the refugees, the stigmatized, the outcasts, the "others," as Is 56:3–8 had envisioned[12]). It will also, however, occasion the prediction of a messianic apocalypse, with the house master coming as a night thief, breaking and entering into his own abode! (Mk 13: 32–37; see parallels in Mt 24:42–44; Lk 12:35–40).

But in this first salvo (Mark 3) with the local Galilean representatives of the Jerusalem power bloc (priest-scribes-elders), the riddle remains such. It will become clear only over time, as the conflict deepens and the shadows grow. Meanwhile, Jesus gets very direct (especially regarding the debt code). All manner of evil action and untoward utterance will be forgiven—a Jubilee inference of blanket "release"—except for one exception. That which utterly entraps! Mislabeling genuine deliverance as itself unclean, calling liberation its opposite in such a way that no real reflection is either given or allowed—blaspheming the spirit of what is, in fact, "holy"[13]—cannot be released because it is utterly closed in on itself. As Isaiah has taught Jesus, here reality has been turned upside down (Is 29:16). Wielding categories that totalize a reality as entirely "evil" leaves no room for discernment, but only invites whole-sale rejection. And if the predication is wrong—imprisons the user.

As already indicated, what is compelling in this brief probing of messianic polemics is a savvy pedagogy. Against dominant discourses of purity and debt, Jesus asserts little tradition *parabolais*. When faced early on with serious charges and death threats (Mk 3:6, 22), he immediately crafts riddles to sharpen the quarrel inside a strategically muddled comprehension. The tactic is symbolic codification (in parabolic form) for the sake of a gradual decoding (of actual political reality). These are stories and *mashalim* (comparisons) that feint toward the mythic in order to provoke insight into the deep murk and hard politics of first century Palestinian religious machinations, seeking to create a teachable "atmospherics" for those most suffering its consequences (Mk 4:1–34; 7:1–23). Finally it is an issue of who is killing who by means of economic coercion masked as spiritual devotion. And it marks the path of destiny for a marked messiah, as indeed for his movement writ large.

Movement Practice: The Messianic as Sabbath-Jubilee Reciprocity

As noted, in Mark 3:21–35, the inception of parabolic teaching in response to the charge of demonic possession had immediately deflected attention away from broken individuals among the crowds (or their itinerant healers like Jesus himself) to sharp interrogation of kingship and Temple as the host sites of real spiritual compromise. It continues at lake-edge in Mark 4:1–35 by lifting up peasant wisdom and highlighting lessons learned from soils and seeds. The venue here is in tandem with Jesus' having withdrawn to the "sea" in Mark 3:7–12, seeking refuge from the assassination plot hatched by the conspiracy of Pharisees and Herodians, bent on his destruction after he and his crew had committed the equivalent of civil disobedience over the issue of Sabbath-release (gleaning grain on the holy day and then entering a synagogue and healing a man with a withered hand; Mk 2:23–3:6).

Ched Myers, among other biblical exegetes, makes clear the centrality of the issue of Sabbath-Jubilee in Jesus' running battles with the authorities (Myers 2001, 23ff.). Jesus does not abrogate the Sabbath as much as issue a challenge about its spirit. He insists the tradition serves healing, not killing; making whole, not harming (Mk 3:1–6). It was "made for us"—and not us for it—in the sense of continuously "humanizing" us, calling us back from the brink of destructive hierarchies.

In early Mark the issue shows its face at every turn. The movement begins with Jesus calling a few local fishermen "to leave" their instruments of production—literally in Greek, "to release" or "Jubilee" their nets—in order to embark upon a prophetic vocation as "fishers of men" (Mk 1:16–20; cf. Jer 16:16; Ez 29:4; Amos 4:2). That call finds immediate fruition in the Capernaum Sabbath-action. By chapter 2, Jesus is shown responding to a paralytic that is brought to him, not immediately with healing as we would expect, but with an assertion that his "sins/debts" (the word is the same in Aramaic) are "released" (Myers 2001, 24). Immediately after that—and again "beside the sea"—he initiates a kind of "restorative justice" practice of table fellowship, reconciling peasants pushed into arrears on their Temple-tithe obligations (and thus labeled "sinners") with the low level enforcers of the Roman tribute system ("tax collectors") whose very predatory collecting had pushed the peasants into arrears in the first place (Myers 1988, 157; 2001, 25). As already indicated, the perspective taken here—influenced by Myers, Horsley, Herzog, and others—is that Sabbath-Jubilee forms the primary plank of Jesus' messianic platform—a movement practice of regular debt-release, neighbor-care, and "enemy-love," enjoined for Galilean peasant-followers who embrace his teaching and accept his organizing. This village movement was galvanized by covenant-renewal ceremonies (such as we see in the blessing-curses ritual of the so-called Sermon on the Plain/Sermon on the Mount in Lk 6:17–49 and Mt 5:1–7:28) reestablishing "Israel" as a peasant-run federation in the "liberated zone" of Galilean hill country (where, contrary to the situation in the Judean south, Jesus is relatively free to move, organize, and speak; cf. Jh 7:1–52).

And as noted in the previous chapter, in Luke the Sabbath-Jubilee theme is foregrounded explicitly, with Jesus being cast as a living emblem of the tradition, beginning with his inaugural address at Nazareth and continuing in a narrative that puts the ancient Sinai memory of manna-foraging and the immediate practice of debt-release at the center of the formulaic prayer that distills his teaching for his followers ("give us this day our *daily* bread and forgive us our sins as we forgive those who are *indebted* to us"; Lk 4:16–30; 11:1–4). Herzog deepens this impression with his own exegesis of the parabolic suffix to this prayer in Luke, in which peasant "shamelessness" in violating elite values (of ruthless "market calculation") is sharply underscored and celebrated.[14] The details of the story (the three borrowed loaves) strongly hint that village values of reciprocity and sharing—in this case readily offering bread to a midnight stranger with no hope of repayment—actually mimics Abrahamic hospitality and convenes a facsimile of the messianic banquet on the spot (Lk 11:5–8; Herzog 1994, 212–214).

As the ministry unfolds, Jesus will reenact the manna-memory in the wilderness feedings, freeing food from pockets in a kind of "bread-Jubilee" (Mk 6:30–44; 8:1–9; and parallels). Later—upon his approach to Jerusalem—an encounter with a rich young ruler who is unwilling to "release" and recirculate his assets (accumulated, the text hints, by fraudulent use of the courts; Mk 10:19), will provoke Jesus to a profound reiteration of the Sabbath-Jubilee promise for those daring to embrace the lifestyle (Mk 10:17–30). The "teachable moment" that suddenly materializes sharply underscores the prerequisite of "eternal life" (*this-worldly Jubilee practice* as the fulcrum for gaining "treasure in heaven") and one more time scandalizes his inner circle, still thinking "prosperity gospel" values. The demand is not for sacrifice, but sharing—a circulation of resources and relationships that "messianically" accrues to a hundredfold increase, like the seed-yield earlier promised the peasant crowds at lakeside (as we shall see later).

And once having entered Jerusalem, his public appearance will be "guerrilla-like." He commandeers a Passover pilgrimage to orchestrate a sudden epiphany of his movement within the crowded Temple confines, where he will exorcise the space and engage the authorities (Mk 11:1–12; 15–19). He will cite the Sabbath-vision of Is 56:1–8 as central to the Temple's purpose, name its actual operation as "thug central" (the *real* site of "mugging" in Palestine of the time), and then struggle, in the next day's confrontation, to expose the way torah-discourse had been made to license continuing plunder and oppression (keeping tenant farmers fearful, Roman tribute flowing, Sadducean wealth inside the family through Levirate proscription, and widows locked into giving away to the Temple anything they had not already lost through scribal legal wrangling: Mk 12:1–12, 13–17, 18–27, 38–44).

Whether asserted directly (as the precondition of discipleship practice), or implied through harsh critique of its opposite (predatory Temple taxes or fraudulent uses of Corban or the debt codes[15]), Sabbath-Jubilee appears everywhere in the gospels. Read with an eye informed by the central motifs of the Lk 11:1–4 "Disciples Prayer" (more commonly known now as the Lord's Prayer), the narrative sounds the theme of forgiveness/release like a ceaseless heartbeat. Debt-release, embrace of shared resources and trust that the small offerings of poor people will accrue to messianic abundance, form the core practices of the movement.

Movement Orientation: The Messianic as Wildlands Ancestry

But even having said as much, one particular emphasis yet remains unremarked. Sabbath-Jubilee entails not only continuous release in human-to-human relations but also profound respect for land-practices and a necessary engagement with wilderness sacrality for the sake of pedagogy. These too, show up as hints and traces—most notably perhaps, in Jesus' own vision-quest sojourn to begin his ministry (Mk 1:12–13 and parallels) and in subsequent "shock proverbs," enjoining an incredulous discipleship community to "consider the lilies of the field and the ravens of the air" as counter examples to the "sowing and reaping and stockpiling in barns" or "spinning and weaving and toiling" characteristic of imperial toil (Mt 6:25–33; Lk 12:22–31). Tellingly, the lilies example is explicitly counter-posed to Solomon's own courtly pageantry—a wildflower putting imperial extravagance to shame! Likewise, when confronted about his credentials for clearing the Temple, he will immediately invoke the baptism of John—pressing the authorities to disclose their "read" of his movement—sharply implying that it is watershed initiation alone under the hands of a feral-prophet-become-local-wild-man that constitutes his calling card at the door of empire. And when his own inner circle stands enthralled before the Temple's ostentation, he will announce its imminent collapse, juxtaposing to its repressive fiscal "militancy" and idolatrous cooperation with Rome an entire cacophony of natural response; sun, moon, stars, storm clouds, and winds as the countervailing witnesses, and a fig tree as the "prophetic messenger" (Mk 13:1–31). And indeed, in the final hour of his "passion," when even his most intrepid followers—women—stand "looking on from afar," it is cloud cover (midday darkness) and seismic activity (earth quaking and rocks splitting) that are represented as registering the event (Mk 15:33; Mt 27: 51–52).

But nowhere is the piquancy sharper than in Jesus' lake-side reinitiation school, directing the renegade crowds of Galilee away from royal fetishism (Mk 3:21–27) and toward "dirt wisdom" (Mk 4:1–34). As already indicated earlier, the Galilee watershed serves as outback refuge for the Nazareth prophet after the plots begin and the surveillance tightens (Mk 3:7–12). The peasant multitude that comes out for counsel and healing is directed by parable to consider the soils and seeds with which they struggle daily. And in Mark, this serves as the first moment of sustained pedagogy, building on the campaign of village organizing centered in Sabbath-Jubilee actions of release (that initiated his movement in reconstituted relationships cutting across various divides

of stigma and blood; Mk 1:16–20; 1:35–3:19; 3:31–35), framed by the
continuing questions of uncleanness and demon possession (Mk 1:21–
28—3:20–31). But the focus of the teaching is wild prodigality.

Context is key here. The deep back story to these seed parables is
the ancient history of the Canaanite highlands as host environment in
the eighth millennium BCE to the earliest human experimentation with
annuals, shifting our age-old (hunter-gatherer) alliance with perennial
grasses to pioneer weeds, whose beds and pollination we first began to
prepare. As already mentioned (in chapter 1), this early primitive farming ritualized its past by maintaining a clear memory of its source. The
Lebano-Syrian ranges of World-Mountain fastness—from whence the
lifeblood of water coursed downstream through the Jordan banks—was
mythically held aloft as the great "god home" and *axis mundi* for these
hills lower down. Here clearly, ancient story hinted ecological fact: a
"divinely" *wild* arboretum, full of cedar scents and storm mists, was
indeed the true source of this life, regularly fecundating the lower highlands with genes and energy flows, silt and nutrient, purified air and
vitalized soil (Eisenberg 1999, 75).

In those lower Canaanite hills, the old farming cycle "tragedy" of
annual vegetal demise memorialized this deep truth in oneiric myth.
The mountain-dwelling storm-deity Baal "died" annually by going
underground in seed planting and then miraculously returned from the
dead, in a sprouting abundance each fall, through the agency of earth-
goddess Anat (or Astarte or Asherah). As a resurgent vitality battling for
life against the salt and chaos of Yamm and Mot,[16] this storm-lord loses
the fight, down in the hills, in every summer's heat until he is freed
and revitalized by his sister/consort in the harvest's winnowing, and
returns as life-granting rain back up on his home mount. While certainly Ugaritic versions of this oldest of cultivar memorializations were
themselves subdued by later Israelite preference for the Exodus god,
it is patent that the mountain-patron of Moses, thunder-haunt of the
Sinai heights, emerges as the hybrid conjunction of these powers, once
the people are settled in the highlands of Canaan. YHWH-Elohim,
securing rains and granting fertility for the ex-slaves-become-Canaan-
ite-smallholders is a Hebrew recasting of this Baal/Anat potency (again,
Israelite uniqueness is actually just a peculiar version of "Canaanite"
heritage).[17]

None of our gods and goddesses are ever creations *ex nihilo*. They
are rather haints from the underside of successive waves of migration or
struggle, packed into verse, steeped in story fragments, squeezing their
ancestral juice into new veins. But what is of interest for this figuring

is the subsequent contest between these highland powers and the river valley empires that issued from them: historically, Mesopotamia will sideswipe Canaanite memory of the World-Pole for its own purposes (Eisenberg 1999, 77). As discussed in chapter 1, this becomes a twice-told tale—imperial writ framing ancient wit in an ideology conducive to the city. The Gilgamesh rewrite of this Canaanite struggle offers a mythic enactment of a historic battle—deep highlands memory of the *wild* mountain as the deep womb of things human, recast as a triumph of the floodplains *tower* and its *technology* over the trees and the soils (and their peoples) further west. On the actual ground itself, multiple millennia of Mesopotamian-Egyptian arm-wrestling over the tiny land-bridge between their imperial domains overruns those hills and their heights with metropolitan manners and clear-cutting appetites (reinforced by taxes and blood-letting)—while Canaan-Israel labors under the debt and fights for breath in between the bouts! In the end, the city subdues the mountain as new World-Center and home of the gods, and Canaan is recast as acolyte to empire.

And then late comes first century Jesus, carpenter-apprentice to the need for repaired farm implements in the hills of Galilee, telling his tales of seed-fortunes to soil-crusted peasants, climaxing his criticism with a little sliver of vision about insurgent mustard and its wily thrust toward becoming a tree. And in the mix, Sabbath-Jubilee[18] will appear as a window into a different kind of past, looking back through the seed-sowing to the promise of regrown cedar and rain-fed river.[19] The point of naming such a possible genealogy is the secret about siding with the wild over the city. The emphasis is hidden in story. But such a tale—told by a hill on the edge of a lake, favoring trees and seeds over scribes and Romans—figures suggestively. This is an understanding of YHWH-Elohim more likely grasped on a mountain than in a Temple, more likely "heard" from a bush than from a priest . . . even for peasants under the rule of Caesar!

Movement Identity: The Messianic as a Seed-Community

But there is a strange ambivalence in the telling. "Release/forgiveness" has been the great promise—as well as that alone which Jesus can*not* extend to those who insist on dismissing him as "possessed" (Mk 3:28–30). When the scribal informers depart after the main teaching event, those "about him" (the crowds and the twelve) ask for clarification. Release is again the fulcrum—the practice that must be safe-guarded from those who would otherwise use their intelligence-gathering "infiltration" to warp the movement (they may indeed "see, but must not perceive; hear, but not understand"; Mk 4:10–12). The ensuing commentary (Mk 4:13–20) maps out the way soil condition determines seed destiny— but does so in a way that seems to conflate peoples and soils, seeds and stories. What is sown is expressly "the word." But in the suggestiveness common to folk riddle, at a second level, "the ones being sown *with*" the word are themselves also "the ones *by* the way, *on* the rocky ground, *among* the thorns, *on* the good soil—as if they, too, are seed. And it is a "word" given only in *story* form ("without parables he did not speak to them"; Mk 4:34)—and only through people who, in a sense, "become" the story: (Prechtel, 2012, 13). To catch the full import here, the entirety of this parable sequence begs reading as a whole pedagogy—a simple agricultural story about sowing, decoded by extended "insider" commentary, ironically asserting that the teaching is actually for any "with ears to hear" (Mk 4:21–22).

But this insider explanation (that Mark implies includes the crowds, but not the scribal "spies" of 3:22), sharply cautions about what *is*, in fact, "heard" (Mk 4:21–25). Myers makes a strong case that Jesus is not advocating (as so many commentaries would have it) but *countering* the two "pop culture" proverbs that he quotes in his explanation. They are examples of the way that common sense clichés so often encode danger- ous ideology (Mk 4:24–25; Myers, 1988, 178). "Take heed what you hear" is thus not approbation, but warning. And the two sayings—"the measure you give will be the measure you get back" and "to the one who has, will more be given; from the one who has not, even what that one has will be taken away"—are actually held up as *negative* recita- tions, reinforcing destructive elite values! In countering the counsel of the first one to calculate "returns" carefully (to "measure," in market terms), Jesus will immediately juxtapose a parable of one who sows, and then sleeps and rises, day by day, *not knowing* (not "measuring") how the earth produces so prolifically, but who trusts in its "soil magic" anyway (Mk 4:26–29). And against the ironically clear identification, in the second saying, codifying how the predatory elites, in fact, do "get their take" (in effect, "the rich get richer" precisely by continu- ally taking what little the poor do have), Jesus offers the "kingdom as mustard seed" parable (Mk 4:30–32). And here, Mark's version hints deep subversion—perhaps the most scandalous antiimperial parable in Jesus' arsenal.

As narrated in his gospel, there is no human sowing explicitly identi- fied in this parable. Rather, the seed itself appears as its own agent—a wild weed, virtually ineradicable according to rabbinic sources,[20] invading what breeches human agriculture has made in the local eco-system with its prodigal proliferation, a tiny potency of life that issues suddenly in huge branches like a tree.[21] The cultural context of Jewish familiarity with "the law and the prophets" supplies the startling inter-textual "riff": Ezekiel and Daniel both talk of imperial powers in their day in the image of mighty cedars, whose destiny is sudden demise, falling to the forest floor to become a "dance platform" for the birds formerly dwelling in the branches (Ez 17:1–24; 31:1–18; Dan 4:1–37). And Isaiah echoes his "branch-messianism" (Is 11:1–6), wherein the stumps of fields, clear-cut for royal building projects, refuse to stay stripped and "agricultural," but issue in root-sprouts aspiring to full-blown boughs, granting shade and protection to all manner of creatures (Mk 4:32). This is sly polemic indeed that wild seed constitutes the real "kingdom," offering "messianic refuge" that imperial might supposedly claims to provide but ultimately fails to deliver!

And as always, the issue is one of reading—taking care what we see, how we hear. Read from our postmodern, hyperindustrial, hi-tech sen-sibility and experience, we tend to dismiss these agricultural parables as quaint figures, supposedly rendering sophisticated theology palatable for benighted peasant minds. But read from within a Jewish peasant mindset, harboring the archetypal memory of manna-foraging in Sinai and not completely cut off from a heritage of pastoral nomad "anarchy," the little stories signify starkly. Peasant agriculture is normally a fairly brutal system of urban extraction from rural infrastructure. Palestine in the first century was no different. But peasant recourse to the cycles of subsistence-growing kept hands and hearts close to the soil and its vital-ity. Back behind and underneath the enslavements of city-state powers and imperial formations was a lifestyle lived in no small reciprocity with the rhythm of seasons and the symbiosis of seeds and persons. And old memory of having once been "plant people"!

Indigenous cultures the planet over have normally codified their closeness to the soil in mythic representations that engender a profound sense of ecstatic identification. People *are* seeds and vice versa. Soil is the body of a living—and divine—being, harboring bones and souls of ancestors. Flora and fauna are not just food and vocabulary, but teach-ers and family. Where we read metaphor, people close to the earth read life. The spirit-world for soil folk is not primarily transcendent, but every day and earthly. Communication across the human/divine divide is profoundly material and vital—not separate from concourse with plant-spirits and animal *personas*. It is not accidental that Moses was stopped in his tracks by an "arboreal apparition," or Jesus driven to the wilds by a bird epiphany (Luke will even call the dove that alights on Jesus and drives him into the wilderness "the holy spirit come down in bodily form"; Lk 3:22). In the earliest torah-testimony, YHWH's own reality remained mountain-bound and cloud thick with the kind of "terrifying beauty" that an indigenous scholar like Vine Deloria would call, in his Native American apologetics, "land revelation." (Deloria 1999, 250–260). Subsistence agriculture is indeed the entry point for imperial control. But the reality of an older soil-based spirituality and seed-based subjectivity is not entirely eclipsed in the imposition of metropolitan rule and harsh technique.

What we have then in the lake-side initiation is a subtle but sharp contrast. Peasants are directed to seeds and soils, yielding the kind of messianic abundance (a hundredfold increase in an environment where tenfold increases were considered extraordinary) that would break tenant-farming dependency and enable autonomy (Myers 1988, 176–177). But the projected economic practice points toward the necessity of recovering older memory and a social choice. The abundance promised requires Sabbath practice for its realization (a realization that *does* materialize later in the movement in terms of a hundredfold increase in family relations and shared land; Mk 10: 28–30; Acts 2:42–47; 4:32–5:11). The two negative proverbs intrude market calculus into this otherwise organic picture. The conflict emphasized is one where production is motivated either by the logic of accumulation for the sake of gain or by appreciation for the wild power of natural processes; either coercion of soils benefiting elites at the expense of peasants or cooperation with soil power, in wonder at natural prodigality and abundance. Scarcity or sufficiency! But peasant embrace of such a messianic vision—in hopes of release from the toils of tenancy labor for masters—requires a clear break with dominant culture consciousness.[22] And through the last two parables, it is as if the soil itself subtly weighs in with a witness to its own prolific beauty, over against the way elite manipulation of cultivation in service of market efficiencies entirely coopts wild exuberance into a harsh and violent discipline of extraction (the subject of the next chapter). The barest hint of a question emerges. Just how large is the real Subject of this messianism? A restored humanity alone? Or an entire ecosystem?

Here is a subtle divining for a much older orientation toward living that is yet tangible under the layers of imperial control. It is conjured by parable, and promises wondrous release. But it champions a (seemingly) ridiculous synergy of things small—seeds and people, sowing and soil, stories and trust. And typical of folk culture—how such might lead to a material difference remains wrapped in riddle. Its fragile hope for a different future depends on a movement that itself acts like a seed of subsistence, sowing its possibilities in a husk of dying into the dust of history (as the immediate denouement of Jesus' own particular initiative will demonstrate). But the witness is clear. Such "seeds" remain everywhere at work and contain a potency of memory that is patient in seeking conditions that might allow something other than merely more of the imperial same. And this—even beyond the boundaries of movement "orthodoxy" committed to preserving such memory! In rounding out the suggestiveness of this perspective, we circle back to the question of possession and attend to eruptions of the messianic that surprise hard core followers and even the "messiah" himself.

Movement Spirit: The Messianic as Possession-Battle

Seed-parables and soil-stories are Jesus' response to the charge of possession. Discernment of spirits requires taking account of relationship to plant-communities and "ground" rules. Even in the theater of healing exorcisms, we face questions of political loyalty and indigenous sensibility. Very often in situations of imperial domination, peasant resistance can only be carried out in "occult" forms of communication. Folk revolt resorts to hidden transcript and symbolic rebuke, "conserving" the passions of dissent in coded gestures and oblique references. While spirit-possession and trance behavior have a long genealogy in traditional cultures, they become a peculiar "art of resistance" under imperial duress. And this too, is a central concern of movement action, though the full ramifications of such only become clear in the following two chapters. Here it is enough to hint the way soil-sensibility shows up in possession activity and, simultaneously, the way what might be called "possession-dramaturgy" mediates political struggle.

As we have seen, Jesus initiates his enterprise by storming a synagogue, provoking its leadership, exorcising its controlling "spirit," and opening that space to questioning and critique (Mk 1:21–28). When challenged later on, he argues that his power is that of "holy" spirit (Mk 3:29). But the claim hardly suffices to settle the question of which spiritual force he is channeling. The question remains lively across the three pivotal exorcisms (the Capernaum synagogue, the Gerasene graveyard, and the Jerusalem Temple) that organize synoptic narrative structure. Biblical exegete Richard Horsley offers background necessary to grasp the stakes. While noting that *ruah* in older Hebrew traditions references a kind of animate natural force of "wind/spirit," seizing hold of the people's militia in struggles for independence, and later designates the spirit of Yahweh seizing prophetic bands and individuals who are pillorying predatory kings and officials, Horsley emphasizes that "hostile alien forces" possessing people with invasive militancy only begin to appear with the gospel texts (Horsley 2011, 118).

The context of these latter writings, however, is that of actual historical conquest—first by Alexander the Great and his legacy of rule in the area (330 BCE and after), succeeded by Roman imperial repression starting in the first century BCE. Recurrent invasion and intense taxation become regular features of popular experience and provoke new kinds of reflection on such overwhelming incursions of irresistible power. The Book of Enoch (early second and late first centuries BCE) imagines a divine world structured in hierarchy that is itself engulfed in struggle, with rebellious heavenly powers ("star-god," "thunder-god," "lightning-god," "rain-god," "sun-god," "moon-god," "winter-god," etc.) mixing, in a new way, with humanity and "devouring the labor of the sons of men" (Horsley 2011, 119; I Enoch 6:1, 7). Daniel (second century BCE) rehearses similar struggles with imperial powers, whose theater of conflict must be engaged in the spirit-world, invoking figures like "warrior-god" Gabriel and "prince of Judah" patron Michael to contest the great "beasts" of Hellenic conquest channeling themselves through political agents such as Antiochus IV Epiphanies. The Dead Sea Scrolls (second and first centuries BCE) carry the battle myth further, articulating an ongoing war of the Sons of Light against the Sons of Darkness, whose near-term struggles on the Roman-occupied terrain of Palestine, require retreat to the caves of Qumran, there to train for the final encounter by way of ritual anticipation in military drills complete with trumpets and banners—all while possessed by the spirit of light as a protection against the prince of darkness (Horsley 2011, 120–121).

Against this background, gospel narratives of the spirit-battles of Jesus flicker with haunting significance. As already indicated, the opening volley of his Galilean Campaign (Mk 1:21–28) hints a much deeper battle. The plural "us" offered by the spirit in identifying itself suggests the battle is actually with the entire scribal regime (that effectively mediates Roman imperial might onto the local scene through Jewish cultural forms like the Torah and the synagogue). The "uncleanness" cast out is arguably that of the entire "discourse of purity" by which the comprador (colonial) class in Galilee articulated their control not just of the cultural space of the synagogue, but of production and marketing rights across the countryside (Mk 7:4; Myers 1988, 217–223).

The encounter with the demonic forces self-named as "Legion," narrated in Mk 5:1–20, gives unmistakable representation to the way imperial violence fractures community and psyche into a grotesque dance of damage. The demoniac that Jesus confronts in the graveyard, on his first visit to the "structurally adjusted" Decapolis ("Gentile-controlled" territory harboring significant numbers of Jewish residents) east of the Sea of Galilee, exhibits classic features of a locally "scapegoated" figure. Here is an archetypical collective "mechanism" where broader village experience of recurrent invasion and trauma is focused in a form of negative fetish—an individual made to bear the brunt of internalized colonial self-hatred ("stoning himself," in a typically Jewish form of punishment) that plays out the drama of domination for the rest of the community in the mode of projection and specter. This crazed grave-dweller has been made to function as a kind of "place-holder" for imperial violence. But once the demoniac-surrogate is exorcized, and the compromising economic accommodation to an "unclean" Gentile vocation (swine herding) is sent plunging "over the cliff," the village reaction is a cautionary tale for the reader. Unable to reimagine themselves outside the system of imperial dependence, they "beg" Jesus to depart the area just as the "Roman-legion-like" infestation of spirits "begged" a new home in a "troop" (the Greek term is actually one for military organization) of pigs. Whether referencing an actual historical exorcism or not, the sketch is a clear political "send up" of imperial occupation, promising it a destiny of drowning similar to that of Pharaoh's army in the Exodus liberation of slaves.

In between these two defining episodes of political exorcism, we are presented with the "legal" response of the Jerusalem authorities.[23] The official charge of channeling Beelzebul that issues from the synagogue drama (Mk 3:22) is met (as we have seen) not with denial by Jesus, but rather with aphoristic rejoinder. He quickly "captures" the accusation in a parabolic "net,"[24] sequestering its assumption in a sharp-tongued layering of questions—interrogating the meaning of "Satan casting out Satan," or of a "house" (like the Temple-State rooted in memory of David) or a "kingdom" (like Herod's) being "divided against itself"—and concludes with the assertion that the "goods" of a strong man can only be plundered once the strong man has been "bound" (not, it is interesting to note, "cast out") (Mk 3:23–27).

This exchange (of scribal charge and parabolic countercharge) effectively maps a geopolitics of spiritual battle. Already in the first verses of Mark the lines had been drawn: the story would feature a messiah of the *wild* (as in the quote from Isaiah in Mk 1:3 affirms), not a Temple advent (such as the interrupted Malachi reference in verse 2 hints)! In this chapter, the opposition is played out anew. In effect, Jesus is accused of mobilizing an old "Power" of the subsistence farming high country (the rain-god Baal)[25]; his counter-parables clearly suggest that the urban imperial formations of the Temple-State and the kingdom of Herod are in fact "Principalities" of Satan. But the Beelzebul indictment is not without a kind of after-life in the text. In the organizing campaign that follows, Jesus indeed twice gives evidence of having control over the storm-powers of the area (in the subsequent sea-crossings of the Galilean lake in Mk 4:35–41; 6:45–52). And once he has turned his face toward the march on Jerusalem, his major gesture of initiation for his inner circle has him taking them on a Sabbath-trek ("after six days," as the episode begins in Mk 9:2) up a high mountain where their visionary experience provokes a Sukkot-like response from Peter (let's build booths!) until they are overshadowed by a (storm) cloud that "speaks" to them (Mk 9:2–8). This indeed seems to be a revisitation of early Israel's initiation into wildlands "revelation"—kept alive for Israel in Sabbath practice and Tabernacles ritual as we have seen—culminating in a reappearance of the Rain-God Power of the heights (of both Sinai and Canaan) to hatch strategy for the coming confrontation in the city.

Interestingly, John's quite different version and vocabulary of events will also hint Jesus mobilizing this "wild-power" of what indigenous cultures would understand as weather magic,[26] brought to bear in Jerusalem itself. In the fourth gospel's version of Jesus' last Temple appearance before his arrest, what is foregrounded is not his occupy-action as in the synoptics (that action had taken place in chapter 2 in John), but a Voice of "Thunder" for the "sake of the crowd" (that confirms his resolve to continue the confrontation despite "the troubling in his soul"). It is almost as if he is bringing right up into the Temple environs, something of that ancient Baal-like storm-potency of the hill country, throwing down a wild gauntlet to the official claim that it is the Temple that guarantees "timely rains and bountiful harvests" (Jh 12:27–32; Herzog 1994, 220–221).[27] In joining the Passover procession to Jerusalem, Jesus has just offered up his seed teaching on his own death, casting his work in terms common to subsistence agriculture "plant peoples" (Jh 12:20–26). And his plant invocation is met with a ratifying "sign" of coming rain—"outside of" and implicitly *against* Temple claims to adjudicate land blessings! John's mention that others of the crowd characterize the sound as an "angel having spoken," confirms that we are in the realm of "the powers," but a power here clearly associated with natural phenomenon.

And just for good measure, in Luke's reframing of the Beelzebul accusation—where Jesus indicates that it is by the "Finger of God" that he casts out demons—he elaborates (compared to Mark's version) that taking over the strong man's "palace" entails taking away the latter's "armor" in order to divide his spoil (Lk 11:14–23).[28] Here again, the strategy emphasized is not one of exorcizing or even of entirely disarming the strong man's agency. It is rather one of dismantling the "panoply" (*panoplian*) of his defenses in order to "redistribute" (*diadidosin*) his "arms" (*skula* as it literally says in the Greek). The image here imagines a kind of decomposition and downsizing of the imperial stockpile of defensive and offensive technologies (various "militancies" of powers spiritual and material), returning them to more diverse and distributed (i.e., "natural") operations. (The significance of this "downsizing" of the "principalities and powers" and relocalization of their spiritual force is taken up in the following two chapters.) And the "Finger of God" reference, admitting of a relatively old genealogy (as the force by which Moses conjured the plague of gnats[29] in a manner that could not be replicated by Egyptian magicians, and then subsequently as the force by which Moses' stone tablets were inscribed on the mountain; Ex 8:19, 31;18; Dt 9:10), may reflect vernacular memory of an ecologically based numinosity, somewhat comparable to Jacob's invocation of the "Fear of Isaac" (Gen 31:42, 53).

In any case, patent, in these texts, is the idea that Jesus counters spiritual power with spiritual power. Stevan Davies' *Jesus the Healer* makes the argument explicitly and relatively conclusively (even if his work needs supplementing by the research of critical medical anthropology, clarifying the connection between imperial domination and spiritual possession). Jesus' name became known "because of these powers at work in him" (Mk 6:14–15). "These powers," Davies underscores, are ones that popular culture of the time hypothesized as representing someone other than Jesus himself—as a reappearance of "John the Baptist" or "Elijah" or "one of the prophets" (Davies 1995, 94). The vernacular "take" on Jesus' works of power was that he operated by way of possession: in the episodes of exorcistic healing for which he became instantly famous, he was "mounted" by, and channeled, someone else (what in many indigenous cultures would be understood as a "familiar" spirit, a natural power "married" or embraced as an ally—in this case, the *ruah*-storm-wind of ancient Jewish memory). For the crowds that followed him—as indeed for an alarmed Herod—the question was not *whether* he was possessed. But by whom! The irrefutable conclusion for Davies is that Jesus healed and exorcized by way of trance, hosting, as his spirit-familiar, not John the Baptist or Elijah, but the "holy spirit" (or "ghost").[30] Davies will even go so far as to read Jesus' parables not as instruction, but as primarily "induction techniques," seeking to trigger an empowering capacity of trance in their hearers by occasioning a moment of shock or confusion (Davies 1995, 130, 134). The perception of Jesus working healing by way of possession powers will haunt his conflict with the authorities to the bitter end.

As already indicated, the import of this argument only becomes fully clear in the next two chapters. But by hinting that the Beelzebul charge has more subtext and resonance than typically meets the eye in biblical exegesis, I am not implying Jesus may have been possessed by such a power, but rather that his own possession ushered him across the threshold of the spirit-world to engage "the powers" on their own terrain. I am suggesting that this theater of struggle involved different deployments of spiritual force—a facility with "nature spirits" over against the same natural powers forced out of niche and "unnaturally" assembled to do imperial work as "principalities" inside the city (the focus of the next chapter). However we understand the narrative function of stories like walking on water, taming storms, disappearing into the hills, interpreting thunder, and so on, Jesus is depicted in a mode immediately comprehensible as "shamanic." He is "familiar" with such natural forces as waters and storms and able to move among them with potency. And he does so in a battle committed to interrupting and "binding" the way such powers have been grotesquely corralled into service of empire, and to dispersing and redistributing their force on a smaller scale. The Moses-Jesus tradition clearly privileges, at its core, the idea of a Storm-Deity whose natural abode is wild mountain height rather than technologized metropolitan center, and whose name—whether invoked as "Yahweh" or "Elohim" or even "Baal"—remains fundamentally unpronounceable and dangerous. The issue is not decided by the name itself, but by the actual lifestyle and relationships of reciprocity (in social exchange and interaction with the natural environment) envisioned and demanded. In spirit-possession as in material relations, this is a tradition of Sabbath release and regeneration.

Movement Transgression: The Messianic as "Possessed" Samaritan?

But again, the task here is not to expound a lengthy exegesis of gospel narration, but rather to exhibit little tradition moments of artful provocation inside the canonical text. The messianism we are tracking is "emergent," showing hints and traces under the surface of the lion-izing articulation. One such that compels with astonishing brazenness coalesces around the category of "Samaritan" and the way Jesus is rep-resented negotiating such.[31]

In his time, Jewish discourse on Samaritan identity serves to anchor common sense notions of Jewish election and preeminence in the geog-raphy of the "holy" land. Samaritan difference *from* Jewishness had come into being out of the harsh history of Assyrian conquest of the northern ten tribes in 721 BCE, resulting in deportation of some 27,280 Israelites into oblivion elsewhere in the Assyrian empire and their replacement with transplants from five Assyrian cities (Babylon, Cuthah, Avah, Emath, and Sepharvaim), who mingled with the inhabitants remaining in Palestine. Whatever the actual genealogy of the Samaritan people who came to inhabit the terrain around Shechem (they claim descent from Joseph), Jewish discourse increasingly emphasized their hybridity (supposedly born of Jewish fathers and pagan mothers) and contributed to an intensifying conflict between respective practices of Torah, cen-tered in the Jerusalem Temple (on the part of mainstream Jews) and an alternative Torah-observance practiced in a Temple on Mt. Gerzim (on the part of Samaritans). By Jesus' time, Jewish denigration of the Samaritan community had waxed violent and by 6 CE had witnessed a strike of symbolic revenge by a cadre of Samaritans scattering human bones in the Jerusalem Temple sanctuary in the night hours. So trou-bled had relations become that even to say the name, "Samaritan," was anathema for some observant Jews (this refusal is perhaps behind the euphemism used by the lawyer in the "Good Samaritan" parable to sig-nify "the one who" showed mercy, in Lk 10:37). Telling then are the scant references encountered in Luke and John (and the absence of such in Mark and Matthew).

Alone among gospel writers, Luke has Jesus actively lifting up the designation in his teaching. In the so-called Good Samaritan parable, Jesus is indicated as having deftly solicited this pejorative to pique con-science (Lk 10:25–37). The setting is key. Luke had initiated his travel-logue of Jesus' march on Jerusalem in this part of his gospel (chapters 9–18) with a singular account of a conflict about hospitality that frames the occasion of the parabolic send-up (Lk 9:51–56). Jesus has set his face toward the Jerusalem Temple-action while on organizing trek through the mid-section of the country, and seeks over-night accommodation in a nearby Samaritan village. When the villagers discover he only means to remain long enough to sleep, they apparently interpret the brevity as a sign of typical Jewish antipathy toward things Samaritan, take offense, and refuse. Jesus' disciples themselves react according to stereotype, threatening to call down fire, and are upbraided by their teacher for "not knowing what spirit they channel." And in the very first episode of teaching following this incident, Jesus responds with the Samaritan parable. But its bite is now typically lost in having become so familiar.

The Samaritan Parable begins with an attempt at entrapment. A lawyer tests Jesus with a question about eternal life. Sidestepping the stratagem to get him to misspeak—part of the elite plot to destroy his reputation and clear the way for his execution—Luke has Jesus countering the "test" with a question of his own, summed up in the demand, "You know Torah, how do *you* read"? (Lk 10:25–28). The lawyer answers by equating love of God and love of neighbor and is tersely commended by Jesus with the admonition, "that's right, so do it!" Obviously thwarted in his real purpose, the lawyer tries a different tact, asking, "and who is my neighbor?" Jesus counters with the parable about a mugging victim on the road to Jericho, whose bloodied body two typical passersby avoid. Where the priest and Levite shy to the other side of the road out of an unstated fear of contracting "uncleanness," the surprising third traveler—not a Jewish layperson as rabbinic storytelling convention would dictate, but a hated Samaritan—responds with concern. And at the story's conclusion, we find another "in kind" question: "which one was neighbor to the violated man?" The lawyer-spy is forced to affirm what would have been antipathetic to everything his query presumed. An "unclean" Samaritan, "bastard child" of a "bastard" religion, is held aloft as archetype of faithful Jewish response! As a piquant challenge to the cultural imagination of legitimate messianic "help," the vignette's evaluation would have been scandalous to Jesus' enemies and followers alike. But even this pedagogical "monkey-wrenching" of typical Jewish notions of soteriological identity and propriety pales before John's use of the category.

In the idiosyncratic treatment of messianic liberation that John's text offers, Samaritan scandalousness is brought to its zenith. It finds its particular edge of offense in the context of the Temple-grounds that had witnessed the sixth century CE Samaritan profanation mentioned earlier. Unlike in the synoptics, in fourth-gospel narration, Jesus' Temple-clearing is not culminating, but inaugural and programmatic. It occurs already in chapter 2 of John. As paired there with the provision of wine for a wedding in Cana, it serves to telegraph and profile Jesus' movement sensibility as simultaneously prosaic and spectacular. Here celebrated is a messianism mundane enough to secure the honor of a peasant family (too poor to provide for its guests) by supplying festal libation, and at the same time bold enough to take on the priestly elites and their cronies in their own "fastness" (the Temple) by clearing the floor of their money-changing operatives. Recurrently, in John's telling, the Temple-space will host interventions that are renegade and dangerous. We will witness, in Jesus' itinerant visits to that central shrine, a litany of actions challenging the protocols that code the space and police its use. In chapter 5, he will "break" (or more accurately "fulfill") *Shabbat* by commanding a paralytic at the Bethzatha pool to rise and carry away his pallet (Jh 5:1–18). In chapter 7, he initiates a kind of "flash mob" action by interrupting (and "riffing on") the water-pouring ritual at the end of the Feast of Tabernacles (Jh 7:37–39). And by chapter 8, he's once again violating Sabbath injunctions—this time by healing a man born blind using a mud-and-spittle poultice (Jh 9:1–41)—leading immediately to his final verbal showdown with the Temple officials in which he will publicly pillory them as the real "thieves and robbers of the sheepfold" (rather than the shepherd-outlaw bands they so love to hate) (Jh 10:1–21). And the result each time will be a reiterated charge that he is demon possessed (Jh 7:20; 8:48; 10:20).

It is especially in connection with this latter eleventh hour appearance in the hallowed precincts that Samaritan-discourse shows up in a startling fashion. After the Tabernacles action, the Galilean upstart ends up in high-stakes repartee with a Temple cohort bent on securing his arrest (Jh 7:32, 45; 8:20). He provocatively names them as slaves to sin, while they vehemently "beg to differ" by claiming freedom through Abrahamic affiliation (Jh 8:31–49). In what unfolds as a kind of first century Palestinian form of "dozens-playing"[32] (but camped out on the father-line rather than targeting respective mothers), Jesus and the officials go back and forth in the hearing of the pilgrim-crowd of peasants gathered for the feast. The "Nazarene nobody" dares to arraign the leadership party openly as "spawn of Satan" in light of their "will to kill": despite their stipulated genetic connection to the faith-father (Abraham), they preside over a system regularly disenfranchising and criminalizing peasants and their messianic defenders and putting them in early graves. After a series of disclaimers (each stridently rebutted by Jesus), the authorities finally respond in kind, reiterating their long-levied indictment (but with a new prefix): "are we not right in saying you are a Samaritan and have a demon"?[33] And what is suddenly made explicit is their own hidden transcript about this so-called messiah, now figured in terms of the archetypal history of repression and denigration ghosting Galilean geography—the "disappeared" ten tribes of (northern) Israel, replaced by victims of conquest from elsewhere, issuing in centuries of struggle between two related peoples, together suffering imperial predation and translating foreign oppression into internalized repetitions of the same and hatred of each other.

Jesus' answer is cryptic, but jaw-dropping. He asserts that he does not have a demon. Period. What is left unsaid echoes loudly. He *refuses* to refuse being labeled Samaritan. To do so would reinforce the equation, "Samaritan equals demon-possession" (a kind of nascent first century racialization). In the process of breaking such a popular culture association, he is apparently quite willing to be comprehended under the taint. And John's hint here is then even more outrageous than Luke's story. On display is a purposefully agitating Jesus, disrupting Temple protocol, through whom appears a specter of Samaritanness! Will the real "Jesus" please stand up? Read under the influence of Luke's Samaritan pedagogy and against the grain of dominating stigmas, this is a kind of "messianism of the demonic." That which Jewishness considers most abominable—haunting Jewish nightmares and temptations to self-hatred—suddenly shadows the encounter unrepudiated! Defamed in his time as "illegitimate," this charge deepens the murk hovering over Jesus. In the same text framing him as *logos* incarnate and savior of the world, he is also finally "haloed" with archetypal stain. In vernacular key, we might call this a saving appearance of seemingly "unholy ghost." It cautions profoundly: just how do we clarify our respective "possessions"?

Movement Limitation: The Messianic in a Pagan "Prostitute"?

There is one other gospel location that especially begs to be read against the grain in this way.[34] In Mark's narrative structure, geography plays a cryptic theological role. From verse one, as we have noted, it is wilderness, rather than the city or its central shrine (the Jerusalem Temple), that is subtly signified as host space to messianic vision. After his provocative inaugural action in the Capernaum synagogue—breaking through the veneer of official control, galvanizing attention, and hinting the culminating action (the Temple clearing) that will initiate his movement in its vocation—his early activity focuses on organizing in Galilee villages and exorcizing, healing, feeding, and teaching in the outback, away from population centers. Horsley, as mentioned, reads the wilderness sermons (Matthew's on the mount and Luke's on the plain) as indicative of a covenant renewal ceremony, reconstituting "Israel" among the peasantry, enjoining Sabbath-Jubilee practice (debt-release, neighbor-care, enemy-love, and land-respect) as the reestablished norm for relations in the small farming villages of that compromised terrain

("Galilee of the Gentiles") (Horsley 2011, 131–153). But by chapter 7, opposition and surveillance have emerged with such stridency and misunderstanding circulated so widely, that Jesus goes "underground," on the run from the authorities, seeking refuge in self-exile near Tyre, outside Israel proper. Liberation theologian Jon Sobrino—reading out of the context of *la lucha* in Latin America—will even gloss this event as "near-breakdown," the exhausted desperation of a popular upstart, needing R & R from an increasingly high-stakes encounter with local power-brokers bent on his execution (Sobrino, 91–92). In any case, we are told, he is retired, for the moment, from the front lines, and "would not have anyone know it" (Mk 7:24).

But Jesus' reclusive huddle with his male disciples, behind closed doors, does not forestall the spread of rumors—one of which reaches a single, female, head of house in the city, struggling with a demon-possessed daughter, who seeks out his reputed potency as a healer. Pushing through the "quarantine" maintained by his inner circle, she throws herself at his feet in desperation. Unphased by the compromise of her upper-tier status (her daughter's "bed" was a fashionable *klinen*, not a peasant pallet) in coming before him without formal introduction like some hill-country hick, she begs for an exorcism. He immediately rebuffs her importunity with a street adage: "Let the children first be fed, for it is not right to take the children's bread and throw it to the dogs" (Mk 7:27). The tone of this passage may well hint a first century Palestinian equivalent to Native American anger at New Age "appropriation" of native ritual (white "demand" for everything from dream-catchers and sweat lodges to smudging ceremonies and medicine teachings). It unmistakably disdains her eagerness as "presumption" ("it is not *right*"). But it provokes a surprising response.

She takes up the very term by which he has repudiated her—the diminutive for "dog" (literally in the Greek, "little dogs" or "puppies")—and amplifies its form (while seeming to submit to its content). "Yes, sir, but even the little dogs under the table eat the little children's little crumbs." Three times she reiterates the "littleness" implied in his refusal by invoking the diminutive forms for both "children" and "crumbs" alongside "puppies" in her retort. In his ministry, he has again and again championed the little ones (poor people, the sick, prostitutes, small children, "the least," etc.). Here, his own value is subtly thrown back into his face. He refuses her request in the name of a generalized segment of the Jewish population cast as "children in need"; she speaks concretely on behalf of just such a child, albeit not Jewish, whose face she knows and whose need is immediate. He has pilloried her (by implication) as "street whelp," her people as "offspring of a cur." She has flipped the script in an exemplary "dozens-playing" return serve—but more in the fashion of judo than verbal combat. By amplifying the extremity of the insult (the diminutive), she ensnares its barb in a different logic. A "put down" is "sent up" as a keenly retorted "put on." In the conventions of the honor-shame culture of the time, she has implicitly "forced his hand" with a sharp come back that effects a savvy "come on." He cannot longer dissimulate her request without exhibiting bad faith and losing face.

But the rejoinder Mark puts on his lips renders the passage even more provocative—taking the exchange "off the map" in an almost literal sense! He merely affirms her "saying," and bids her "go her way"[35] as the demon has *already* gone off—past tense in the Greek—from the daughter. And she returns home to find it so. The briefly recounted outcome harbors scandalous messianic undertones. The saying for which she is affirmed is, in the Greek, *logos,* a "speaking back to" the messianic subjectivity par excellence (Jesus' own) what everywhere else in the gospels is his prerogative to speak to others. Nowhere else is anyone commended for speaking *logos to* Jesus. It is as if the vaunted "word," the "divine reason" (which he will, in John's gospel, be said to incarnate), has here "leapt track," as it were, and come back at him through a woman who is single, "pagan," and suspect. Her shamelessness[36] in seeking him out in his lodging without a male intermediary would likely have been understood by on-lookers, in the culture of the time, as the action of a prostitute, on prowl for business. At the very least, it signals a female "on her own," with no male relative to intercede for her, no husband to maintain her honor. That she is Syro-Phoenician, a wealthy tenant of the Tyrean metropolitan environs, makes the story even more outrageous, as Tyre, in the gospel corpus, carries a profile roughly equivalent to Sodom. Historically, this Gentile stronghold had recurrently overrun northern Israel, slaughtered its populace, exploited its resources, and disdained its culture. Indeed, the proverb Jesus throws down initially in refusing the woman may have had popular currency among diasporan Jews of the area, suffering under the local regime of extraction, forced to grow crops (i.e., "provide bread") for Tyrean overlords or pay tribute to the metropolitan center. But the implication of his affirmation is that it is *her* word that effects the exorcism—there is no other agency offered in the text to occasion the sudden flight of the demon.

And more subtly, it is even possible to read out from the passage a certain salutary "evacuation," from his own psyche, of any incipient tendency to patriarchal dismissal of her as mere "woman," or ethnocentric refusal of her request as merely "Gentile" and unworthy. It is Jesus' question to the lawyer of the Good Samaritan parable, sneaking outside the text and coming at us from an angle oblique to the tradition at large: "How do you read?" How deeply into hidden transcripts and subaltern silences do we wish to project our imagination? This woman—whoever she may have been historically and however disposed in fact—haunts the text with her possibilities. Certainly she is "spoken for." The gospel of Mark remains a male production, lauding a male messiah. But there are hints and ghostly whispers. So much so that Matthew cannot stand Mark's rendition (Mt 15:21–28). He changes the affirmation from ratification of a "word spoken" to commendation of "belief offered" ("O woman, great is your faith!"). His text almost entirely eclipses the woman's uppity agency and replaces it with more passive acquiescence in receiving a desired benefit ("Be it done for you as you desire"). Yet even he ends up creating intrigue. He has replaced Mark's "Syro-Phoenician" designation for this upstart pagan with the term "Canaanite" and suddenly opened this encounter to a deep past that comes storming into the event without qualification or clarity. Even more spectral and eerie than John's Samaritan apparition settling onto the messiah in the Temple altercation—here we have the violence of the nation's very birth surfacing.

A "Canaanite woman" bests him in argumentation, speaking "his" word back to him with a creative difference, trumping and troping his boundary-drawing with such piquant effect, he is forced to accede. This is a messianism briefly flashing from outside his own intention, coming up inside his word with a kind of subaltern rupture—correcting him, teaching him, perhaps even exorcizing his own temptation to stay captive to a particular cultural orientation. Arguably, her craft mentors his own, a messianic intervention coming from beyond the messianic canon that, somehow, was never quite effaced from the written corpus. How might we read such?

Conclusion

The gospels emerge in history as products of a displaced people. Their very creation already effects a kind of "cover," a necessary dissimulation from the scene of a political horror. They speak from a place of genocidal rupture, from a Palestine that is being ruthlessly suppressed by Roman imperial might, after a brief flicker of revolutionary fervor during the time of Mark's writing. The pain of a kind of holocaust exercises their work. They must bridge from Jewish apocalyptic radicalism to

Greco-Roman subversion, from rural peasant resistance to urban out-law insurgence, without drawing down too much vigilance and polic-ing. They speak in code. They map a social movement in transition. While memorializing outback organizing (in Galilee) and opportunistic seizures of urban space (like the Capernaum synagogue action and the Jerusalem Temple cleansing), they must translate their vision for a radi-cally altered possibility (residential dwelling as contrast communities inside city economies). They move from Aramaic to Greek, from field to street. And they answer to a shifting perception.

Out of a vernacular folk-messianism articulating a movement tra-dition anchored in peasant villages, they begin to convene attention on a personalized figure whose affect and orientation must become intelligible for an urbanized population engaged in trades and imperial "services" (i.e., "slavery"). Certainly the "preacher indeed becomes the preached" (as one theological aphorism would have it), but even more to the point, the sociology becomes a liturgy and the politics a cult. The complex antiurban dynamics mobilizing the marginalized in the out-back of Galilee, schooled in ancient wilderness traditions kept alive in prophetic bombastics, is quickly inverted such that by the second cen-tury the Latin term *paganus*—designating rural-dwelling "noncomba-tants" in the Roman world of urbanized imperial strife—comes to mean the exact opposite of "Christian." Reading the gospel texts across such a divide of evaluation between city and country, urban sophistry and rural savvy, requires an eye attentive to the periphery of both society and vision. If messianism is at heart the use of artifice and artistry to gal-vanize social resistance to imperial domination and memorialize a way of living not answering to its requirements then our reading must itself participate in the artistry. Messianism does not only exist "out there," in the fact of a political movement, but within our own imagination, as the desire to envision such. Daniel's "son of man" apparitions might be said to rest as much with his refusal to capitulate to "Nebuchadnezzar's" (Antiochus IV's) ideological power as with the incursion from without of the sensory data of "revelation." Seeing "triumph," in the very trial and execution of empire's victims (as in Dan 7:1–28 or Mk 14: 53–65; 15:1–20), requires an eye of resolute inspiration (or even naïve "con-fabulation") (Myers 1988, 389–391). Messianism is here the romance of the little, the projection of an alternative reality from the most meager of possibilities, the naming of a mere groan of protest as the birth-sound of a new community.

CHAPTER 4

Metaphysical Speculation: From Messianism to Christology

The Greek oracle at Delphi saw this a long time ago and said, "Woe to humans, the invention of steel." (Prechtel, in Jensen, 2001)

For we are not contending against flesh and blood, but against the principalities, against the powers, against the world rulers of this present darkness, against the spiritual hosts of wickedness in high places. (Eph 6:12)

T hus far, this writing has attempted to take issue with an individualized notion of Jesus as the Christ by focusing on messianic social movements and popular artistry that resist domination systems and structures in part by opening up dangerous memories of other ways of living. I have argued that these memories conjured older social patterns practiced by tribal peoples and indigenous cultures. These (so-called) primitive lifeways and "native" wisdoms are associated historically with what anthropology has designated as hunter-gatherer, subsistence agriculture, and pastoral nomad social forms. In outlining such, I have highlighted biblical messianisms, in particular, as probing and championing more reciprocal social and environmental relationships in which survival was mediated by "otherkind"—by plants and animals in local ecologies, whose adaptive modes of existence and creative alliance with human communities kept "the wild" alive at the heart of the sacred. And in doing so I am positing a kind of fire-break between what the gospels report and what the Pauline epistles represent.

The town and country divide is pivotal. Much of Israel's early formation emerged in desert and highland environments as reactions to—and critiques of—urban concentrations of power and resources. The gospel messianism of Jesus (and of John the Baptist before him) was rooted in wildlands visitations and schooling at the hands of birds and seeds, rivers and mountains, locusts and bees. Most of Jesus' organizing took place in clan-based Galilean villages, chaffing under Herodian royal hegemony, laboring under economic control by urban-based absentee landlords, struggling with scribally interpreted debt and purity codes that deepened indebtedness and disenfranchisement. Towns and cities were scenarios of "exorcistic raids"—Jesus swooping in at the head of a rag-tag cohort to "occupy" official spaces (synagogues and the Temple), "poach" on ritual, stir repressed memory and energy, name the embedded economy outrageously, and just as quickly exit and return to marginal places and crowds.

In this chapter, however, we mark a profound shift. Indeed much of the motive force for writing "gospels" in the first place derived from the revolution of 66 CE that installed a Zealot-scribal coalition in power after a protracted struggle against the occupying forces of Rome. It was clear to any savvy politico of the time that Israel's "liberation" was doomed to be quite short-lived as Rome organized and set in motion an inevitably crushing response. That response came in 70–71 CE and pretty much destroyed Palestine as a viable colony, obliterating infrastructure and wasting fields. Jewish culture—both rabbininc and messianic—was rendered refugee and fugitive in the eventuality. The centuries old and growing diaspora of Jewish communities in regions east (e.g., Babylon) and west (the entire Mediterranean basin) became host sites of survival. And they definitively anchored Jewish institutional life in metropolitan ambiance.

Paul's epistles reflect the shift without really marking out the radicality of the change. No longer will plant-dependent peasantries form the core constituency of the movement. That place will rather be taken by urban-wise traders and the slave and servant constituencies of the imperial metropolis. As messianic Judaism is forcibly expelled from the rabbinic mainstream and gradually becomes known as "Christianity," the communities eventually deciding what will be considered normative and canonical are more and more exercised in interpreting "agricultural gospels" into urbanized theology. As already noted, a Latin term like *paganus*—at once denoting "rural-dweller" and "noncombatant"—will become a major signifier of what is presumptively non-Christian. It is not only the cultural process of Hellenization that is significant here but also the political-economy difference represented by urbanized living. This change alone is worthy of book-length treatment, but again, here, the effort is directed more toward a teasing of imagination than a rigorous proof of a position. As such, we will then open reflection on the Pauline innovation with a brief interrogation of his language of principalities and powers—asking ecosystemic questions of that politicospiritual discourse—and then turn to a similar exposé of John's innovation with the *logos*-concept. This latter move launches a form of conceptual aggrandizement that catapults Galilean messianism toward its eventual role as acolyte to Roman imperial and European colonial projects of expansion and conquest.

Enslaved Things

But first we must detour through a critical difference between indigenous wisdom and urbanized assumption that focuses the concern of this chapter. Osage Indian scholar George "Tink" Tinker describes an experience with a native elder that goes to the heart of the issue. As it offers in anecdote the question that will compel attention, I quote at length. In his *American Indian Liberation: A Theology of Sovereignty*, Tink writes,

> At my invitation this revered medicine person spoke to a large audience at the Graduate Theological Union in Berkeley. In accord with this teacher's request, I had placed a small table holding a fist-sized rock next to the podium. At one point in the lecture, this elder asked the assembled crowd, "I understand that you are all theologians or studying to be theologians. Do you mind if I take this opportunity to ask you something I have always wanted to know? What does God look like?"
>
> Receiving only silence from the audience, the elder finally conceded that it had been a trick question. No one knows what God looks like, of course. But then, this elder picked up the rock and asked, "If you do not know what God looks like, can you tell me absolutely, without a doubt, that this rock is not God?" Again there was silence as this theological audience mulled over the logical possibilities for an absolutely certain answer.
>
> Finally, after tossing the rock gently to me, the elder asked the most telling question, "I, too, do not believe that this rock is God. But tell me, if you cannot describe God to me and cannot tell me with absolute certainty that this rock is not God, how is it that your missionary ancestors told Indian people that they were worshiping a false god when we pray to the sun? The sun is the most powerful physical presence in our lives. Without it we could not live and our world would perish. Yet our reverence for it was considered idolatry." (Tinker 2008, 27)

After explaining that even this was misunderstood, as his people did not really worship the sun, but saw it as a reflection of the sacred, the unschooled elder went on to teach a very complex and sophisticated native understanding of the Sacred Other, says Tinker, to the effect that *wako*^{n}*da,* as it was called by the Muskogee medicine man,

> has no sexual gender identity. Rather, *wako*^{n}*da* is unknown and unknowable until *wako*^{n}*da decides to reveal wako*^{n}*da's* self. Only then does *wako*^{n}*da* take on characteristics that can help us to image *wako*^{n}*da* as a tangible reality. But *wako*^{n}*da* is never limited to a single manifestation but makes itself manifest in a variety of ways to help different people at different times. It is in this context that the elder noticed that the first manifestation and most important manifestation of *wako*^{n}*da* was as a duality of *reciprocal completion* (emphasis JP), as the Sacred Above and the Sacred Below, as male and female, as Sky and Earth (again as representations or mirrors of *wako*^{n}*da* Above and Below).We must not confuse these manifested forms with the euro-western concept of duality as a *binary opposition.* Love and hate, dark and light are dualities, but they are not intrinsically reciprocal. This duality is reciprocal because the two parts of *wako*^{n}*da* are necessary for there to be a sense of wholeness or completion. (Tinker 2008, 28)

Tink goes on to assert that such an image shatters any notion of hierarchy. It offers this mutualistic understanding of "God" not as a commodity to be consumed by New Agers, but as a paradigm for deconstructing colonizing missionary categories in order to replace them "with categories from our own cultural worlds of experience that can speak to our peoples with a new liberating voice" (Tinker 2008, 28). Within an Osage framework, Tinker will go on to claim that rocks have theophanic possibilities equivalent to the sun and to humans and indeed a status as "relatives" possessed of their own "life" (Tinker 2008, 40). They are thus "marked by a particular spirit" (Tinker 2008, 49). And like Vine Deloria before him, his entire argument is not merely that such an indigenous "mythology" demands respect on its own terms, but that *all* of the cultural categories we use to imagine God or describe reality—*including those of the bible and of science itself!*—are culturally specific and patently limited.[1] In particular, it throws down a gauntlet of sorts to the modern Western scientific view that so often joins hands with a corporatized approach to matter as merely "resource"—there to be used and used up—and arrogantly dismisses any other word on physical reality as primitive silliness.

Just here the claim explodes with significance for my own argument. In Tinker's story, a piece of rock is the focus. But it stands in for all of the inorganic material that modern Western cosmology construes as mere "stuff," inert, available for manipulation, reengineering, fusion, melting, cutting, splicing, etc. Thus far in this writing I have tried to assert that indigenous cultures (living some measure of forager, herder, or horticultural lifestyle) stand as collective witness to a radical difference from modern culture in placing *plant and animal life* at the center of ecosystem health and of human identity and well-being. One way or another, such cultures elaborate stories and enact practices that place human life and purpose in intimate reciprocity with otherkind and generally assert that we are younger kin to these mentor-species, who as teachers and nurturers "initiate" our own species in a respectful mutualism carried out by a regular round of ceremony and offerings. What remains unremarked in such an assertion, however, is the status of *inorganic matter* within the highlighted cultural difference. And here is the hardest medicine to swallow for those of us shaped by modernity. (And "medicine" may well be the right designation from an indigenous perspective, as we see in the next chapter.)

Many indigenous cultures will insist that there is no clear line of demarcation between plants and animals, on the one hand, and rocks and minerals (and mountains and rivers and dirt, etc.) on the other. Interestingly, a similar kind of claim is emerging from the far side of modernity's push toward cyborg culture—that the line between organicity and technology is quite hard to specify.[2] In one sense, there is no thing living that is not integrally embedded in an inorganic platform. There has never been life without matter. Trees and birds and humans are, at one level, merely appurtenances of mesas and methane and magma. But for our purposes, this argument will not be engaged with a view to trying to prove something definitively in this regard. Rather the difference in cultural approaches will be explored in terms of their respective discourses and orientations—and the *effects* such have for our vision of religion and being.

Tzutujil Mayan-trained educator Martín Prechtel, for instance, insists that modernity today has emerged in such a way that its primary "slaves" are now *things*—iron ore pried loose from its quartz (or gangue) "home," oil from shale, coal from its vein, and so on. These are then repurposed under tremendous coercive force to serve roles and functions impossible to conceive in the wild, but deemed useful by our species, until "retired" or "released" back into the environment as no longer wanted—and often toxic—"garbage." When we think about it, the claim is patent. Over the course of the last 500 years, machine-culture has increasingly replaced human labor with energy-slaves. (And of course, the city itself is such a gigantic machine, a concrete/steel/

fiber-optic/plastic/vinyl/acrylic surround of materials and formerly breathing organisms rendered so much inert dwelling and moving part.) Marx indeed theorized the human component of this enslavement: factory buildings and manufacturing equipment representing so much human brawn and brain distilled and frozen into hard metal; and capital (as the calculus of such working ancestry) accumulating as a form of dead labor. But in the disenchantment of nature for which the West is (in)famous, what remains naively unexamined in this theory is the prodigious role of nature.

More recent Marxists like Teresa Brennan and Joel Kovel have begun filling in the lacuna in Marx's labor theory of value by including the huge "labor input," performed off the ledger sheets, by natural processes (Brennan 2003, 11–12; Kovel 2007, 10, 40). Brennan, interestingly, argues for retrieval of a sense of natural rhythm—a kind of "Jubilee" calculus—respecting the time necessary for natural cycles of (human and nonhuman) regeneration and recreation to take place rather than seeking continually to leapfrog such by "unnaturally" aggressing on new spaces, after pushing the living vitality of a given locale to the limits of exhaustion (capitalism's typical way of trying to escape reproductive and regenerative requirements) (Brennan 2003, 3, 8, 11–16). And Kovel helpfully specifies that capital is not so much a living organism as a peculiar relationship (albeit like a virus) set up between things, in which exchange value *predominates* over use-value—an invisible hierarchy invested in things by the market that stands in profound counterpoint to the *reciprocity* perceived and honored by native cultures (for instance, as recounted by Tinker in the example earlier) (Kovel 2007, 39–40). But neither uses the language of "enslavement" for capitalism's exploitation of inorganic matter or conceives the possibility that *coercive use* of such might imply a form of *accumulated debt to the natural order*. Clearly, for example, enslaving Africans in North America for the better part of three centuries has resulted in a whole set of social pathologies, including an unpaid labor bill of somewhere between one and five trillion dollars (according to Richard America). The full force of this enslaving violence, its racist legacy of continuing abuse, and its economic consequence of "plunder" now hoarded in white inheritance schemes and physical infrastructure, continue profoundly to warp contemporary social relations and provoke demands for reparation as integral to healing. But what remains unthought in modern theory is the possibility of a kindred kind of debt owed even more broadly to given ecosystems or the biosphere as a whole.

Prechtel is insistent (as, in many varied ways, are most contemporary indigenous leaders still left on the face of the planet). He writes of the "spiritual economy" perspective of the Mayan village whose lifeway he lived for nearly 15 years before the civil war wiped out most of the "old ways" in Guatemala by the mid-1980s. Whatever gives human beings life (whatever humans *take* as necessary to survival) requires for its proper valuation and use a gift in return:

> A knife, for instance, is a very minimal, almost primitive tool to people in a modern industrial society. But for the Mayan people, the spiritual debt that must be paid for the creation of such a tool is great. To start with, the person who is going to make the knife has to build a fire hot enough to produce coals. To pay for that, he's got to give a sacrificial gift to the fuel, to the fire... Once the fire is hot enough, the knife maker must smelt the iron ore out of the rock. The part that's left over, which gets thrown away in Western culture, is the most holy part in shamanic rituals. What's left over represents the debt, the hollowness that's been carved out of the universe by human ingenuity, and so must be refilled with human ingenuity. A ritual gift equal to the amount that was removed from the other world has to be put back to make up for the wound caused to the divine.... There is a deity to be fed for each part of the procedure. When the knife is finished, it is called the "tooth of earth." It will cut wood, meat, and plants. But if the necessary sacrifices have been ignored in the name of rationalism, literalism, and human superiority, it will cut humans instead. (Jensen 2001, quoting Prechtel, 4)

He concludes,

> All of those ritual gifts make the knife enormously "expensive," and make the process quite involved and time-consuming. The need for ritual makes some things too spiritually expensive to bother with. That's why the Mayans didn't invent space shuttles or shopping malls or backhoes [not because they can't]. They live as they do not because it's a romantic way to live — it's not; it's enormously hard — but because it works. (Jensen, quoting Prechtel, 4–5)

And the consequence of not paying off such a debt (which is not actually really paid off in full, but is at least recognized and honored in return gifts of beauty, given back to the natural order in the form of ritual creations and hard-labored offerings like beads or tobacco) is "warfare, grief, or depression" (Jensen, 2001, quoting Prechtel, 4). For Prechtel, the entire scope of technological development—from the earliest tools and the repurposing of plants and animals as "organic machines" that goes by the name of "domestication," on up to the industrial "revolution"—has incurred a continuously growing indebtedness to the sacred in nature. For much of that history this borrowing was at least nominally "redressed," in indigenous communities, by ritual activity. But in modernity in particular—with its post-Cartesian split between mind and body and its rapid disenchantment of the natural order—the tab has been entirely effaced. Any sense of ritual obligation to living nature much less to inert matter has been rendered mute and unthinkable. And the result of this massive project of relentless reengineering is beginning to show—such as we now see in blowback from the environment and climate, increasing levels of mental affliction and addiction, and proliferating technologies and policies of destruction (ubiquitous surveillance coupled with drone and robot capabilities, the threat of nuclear holocaust and the actuality of ceaseless war, chemical pollution of air, land, water and bodies, biological innovations like terminator seeds and nanoinvasives, etc.).

Prechtel reads this result as also effecting a prodigious—indeed monstrous—proliferation of *spiritual* hunger. In indigenous economies, the tearing of the web of life produced by human activity in taking the materials for survival (foodstuffs and minerals for tools) is also a rending of spiritual reality. It leaves the "other side" voraciously hungry and in need of ritual "feeding." A huge portion of the debt owed is due in the form of grief fully tendered—human keening as the spiritual recognition of, and material payment for, the natural beauty necessarily consumed in living. Without human attention given in the form of offerings of beauty (praise language gorgeously elaborated and artistic creations labored over in great attentiveness), the spirit world is left bereft and inflated with appetite and desire. And in the historical employment of such physical extractions for weapons technologies in particular, the effect has been cataclysmic. The desire for advantage has leveraged a five-thousand–year-old project of escalation with ever more devastating arsenals wielded by warrior elites to repress peasant hordes and enforce the hierarchical orders and expansionist designs of settled agriculture and now industrialization. It has resulted spiritually in a growing plethora of *hungry ghosts* and materially in an ever intensifying *flight of desperation* away from such across the face of the planet (with all the violence that continual displacement and conquest entails) (Jenson, 2001, quoting Prechtel, 4–5). Prechtel thus diagnoses our current planetary crises, in indigenous frame, as rooted in what is effectively a multimillennial-old syndrome of terror now elaborated as a colossal (and nearly globalized) cultural pathology called "modern development" (continuously seeking to erect itself out of the decay, death, and composting of all things natural). It is evidence of a newly gargantuan and terrifying "hollowness" at the center of our relationship to otherkind (reflective of both real and ritual debt).[3] And it results in a "haunting" of social life with grief of such depth and duration as to be "un-face-able" (all the "raging" energies of unmourned and repressed loss over millennia of imperial enslavement, native genocide, colonial massacre, pandemic rape, "world" war, ethnic cleansing, genetic mutilation, eco-annihilation, species extinction, etc., that now form the unrelieved and irreducible psychic underbelly of "civilization").[4] Its "discontents" show up as pandemic levels of addiction (to everything from hallucinatory substance to refined sugar, from ceaseless "infotainment" to endless shopping, from binge sex to spectral violence). And its bill for redress is coming due with ever more virulent insistence.

Obviously, this vision of things arising out of a particular indigenous cosmology (Tzutujil Mayan in this case) warrants much more elaboration than I am here giving it. But the general outline that emerges is suggestive. The counter-point to our modern race to the brink of self-destruction is life lived in a radical mutualism with local ecosystems. Indigenous cultures the world over testify to the possibility of a balanced exchange between human communities and otherkind. These visions intimately interrelate material and spiritual planes of existence, organic life and inorganic "platform." Tinker's story highlights the vaunted reciprocity of things in Osage culture and their consequent valuation as having something like "integrity" (if not a modicum of "life" or "consciousness"). The spiritual demand arising from such an approach to reality is for exquisite recognition and continuous care. The sacred haloes all things and does not admit qualitative division between rocks and humans, plants and mountains, animals and stars. Each "thing" is respected as bearing magnificence within its own place and as part of a living whole. Living inevitably demands taking and such cultures clearly participate in the destructive side of nature as well (and do so without sentimentality). But they just as clearly memorialize their (necessary) taking as an "eating of beauty" that immediately incurs debt and will one day require their own flesh as "food." Evidence of such an orientation to the material world is scattered everywhere around the globe, ranging from paleolithic caches of bead (and other) offerings in Africa, Asia, and Europe (as reparations for the "taking" necessary to survival), through neolithic shrines of the same in the Americas, to contemporary practices among those few cultures not yet entirely dismembered by globalization. All of them bear witness to a way of living that creatively (in myth and ritual) routinizes reciprocity with their ecological communities, suggestively maps the cosmos in kinship relations and ancestral affiliation,[5] and effectively inculcates some measure of limitation on human exploitation of the natural world.[6]

Elemental Powers

But the suggestiveness of these indigenous ways for our work comes when we juxtapose such to Paul's language of principalities and powers. The last 40 years of biblical scholarship has witnessed a sophisticated recovery of this particular discourse, initiated by lay theologian William Stringfellow in diagnosing the machinations of empire in the heyday of the Vietnam War, and brought to theoretical precision and activist incisiveness by the likes of Walter Wink, the Berrigan brothers, and Bill Wylie Kellermann. Wink's work especially delves into great exegetical detail and rigorous analytical formulation and will serve as touchstone for the framework I wish to sketch here.

The usefulness of this biblical language of the powers comes clear especially as an antidote to the disabilities of Western individualism and materialism.[7] It enables "depth discernment" of the potency of collective enterprises of every kind. Subtle forces of pressure—institutional, ideological, cultural, pedagogical, etc.—everywhere shape their constituencies in habits of action and modes of perception that are as rigorous as they are inchoate. Wink is ferocious in his insistence that the "spirits" so designated, in the discourse of the powers, form the ineluctable interiority and outer formality of every organized endeavor of human communities, however large or small. They show up as quite particularized "force fields of influence" in everything from the nuclear family to the World Bank, from nation-states to local jails, from media outlets to religious movements (Wink 1986, 4–5).

"Principalities and powers" emerges then as a generic catchall phrase for the entire panoply of gods and mysteries, angels and demons, spirits and *daemons*, thrones, authorities, rulers, and dominions that ancient symbology struggled to bring to expression in its varied mythologies and expressive codes. Its purchase is at once bureaucratic and psychic. It points to both material agency and spiritual efficacy, designating simultaneously the sprawl and reach of a collective institution and the lure and compulsion of its invisible ethos. And its utility for modern thinking is brought into a growing credibility in referencing the confirming insights of what can be glossed as the new physics (quantum mechanics, relativity theory, Heisenbergian uncertainty, neurobiology, etc.). Given the limitations of space here, I am not able to rehearse Wink's comprehensive investigation of the phenomenon, but rather cut straight to what is of most use for our concerns.

Among the seven particular powers (Satan, demons, angels of churches, angels of nations, gods, elements, and angels of nature) dealt with in his second volume (*Unmasking the Powers*), it is Wink's chapters on the last three that especially tease our interest here.[8] Under the Greek term *stoicheia tou kosmou,* for instance, Wink investigates the elementary building blocks of existence as articulated in "the ancient Greek dream of discovering some principle of matter to which all forms of physical existence might be reduced" (Wink 1986, 130). These anchor one end of the spectrum of powers by compelling and conditioning "nature" as its first principles, inaccessible to common sense, but grounding more apparent phenomena. Whether in the form of statistical probabilities, mathematical algorithms, axioms of logic, rules of chance, notes of the scale, regulations of society, basic beliefs, rituals of religion, laws of physics, etc.—the range of these invariant "elementals," as Wink (glossing Paul) calls them, is quite broad.[9] Though working invisibly in and through things as they do, however, they are not merely constructs of thought, but are somehow given within the natural order, functioning in their respective domains much as do electrostatic bonds in molecules.

Mythologies of the past labeled such "sovereign entities and forces" as gods that demanded "obedience," if life was to be successfully lived (Burhoe 1972, 60). But Wink tracks their footprint in the domain of physics—quickly noting the consequence of the ancient Greek quest in modern form, with the splitting of the atom unleashing the most prodigious force yet seen in our time on the planet! Where the ancients accorded the basic elements—earth, air, fire, and water—the status of primacy and embraced them as divinity, we are left with proliferating arsenals of destruction and a demonic parody. Even so miniscule a particle of reality as this very elementary field of atomic force, once interrupted, explodes with god-like terror. Astonishing indeed the corona of raw structure!

And thus we, too, now worship the sun—but in a *danse macabre* of international treaties and second guesses trying to keep its powers of fusion in the heavens and inside atoms—and away from our bodies and societies on earth. But it is not only nuclear reaction that focuses interest. Potency haloes matter from inside out and from macrosphere to microbe. The force of what constrains and moves both planets and life reveals its face on all sides! Gravity, the laws of thermodynamics, sunspot activity, atmospheric ions, floods, volcanism, mutation, DNA, or the .618034 to 1 proportion that "shapes sunflowers and snail shells, the curl of surf and the chambered nautilus, spiral galaxies and pineapple scales, elephants' tusks and lions claws," the inner ear and the relation of rectangles most pleasing to the human eye (Wink 1986, 132). Whether formulated in ancient paean or in modern math, "the elementary powers that be" are indeed powers and ghost reality from top to bottom, conforming all things to their patterns of force! Or if defied—put on ghastly shows of "apocalyptic" numinosity!

But at just this juncture in his discussion, Wink will advert to the apostle Paul's polemic that we are not to become their slaves (Wink 1986, 134; Gal 3:4; 4:8, 9). And herein lays a conundrum. Paul nowhere explicitly teaches about the powers in general—much less the "*stoicheia*" in particular. They were simply "in the air"—taken for granted as part of the cosmology of the time and place. In underscoring his own vocation in Ephesians, for instance, he will assert that it is part of the church's role to make known the wisdom of God "to the principalities and powers in the heavenly places" (Eph 3:10). The mode of doing so is precisely by refusing their demand for obeisance or fear. Looking such "beasts" in the eye without flinching, naming their limitations, and calling for their resubmission to a plan greater than their own aggrandizement—to a "sacrality" centered in wholeness and integrity ("salvation")—entails not mastery on the part of the messianic community, but the kind of bold assertion and forthright acclamation underlined in Daniel's vision of the Human One. It is enough not to capitulate, to refuse to submit to regulation (see Col 2:20), and to stand one's ground, even under threat of death.[10] And it is around this very exemplar of resistance that Paul will orchestrate his admonition to the Colossian community not to become prey once again to the *stoicheia* spirits of the universe (by way of philosophy and empty deceit), but to recognize that the principalities and powers as a whole had been decisively disarmed[11] and made a public example in the cross (Col 2:8, 15).

But it is *to* just such a capitulation that Wink will charge modern science as having succumbed—precisely in its very attempt to comprehend nature as dead matter and not the haunt of gods. By taking the discovery of what is irreducible in nature as its holy grail, the scientific quest invests matter itself with first principles, subtly projecting an "ultimacy" that renders us, its "true believers," simultaneously "exploiters and slaves" (Wink 1986, 141). "For whatever is ascribed ultimacy," says Wink, "functions as a god, whether its devotees would describe it thus or not" (Wink 1986, 137). In divesting matter of spirit or life—in stripping awe from the molecule—we are bound to treat nature as mere mechanism, and ourselves, as part of nature, as an evanescent piece of machinery. No longer participants in a shared mystery, we "are become death" (as Oppenheimer opined, at the first nuclear explosion)—for both nature and ourselves.

But the twist is patent. As dead, matter is merely there as an object of consumption or experimentation—to be used and used up. But as bearing ultimate principles, we also end up elevating its value above ourselves (Wink 1986, 137). The continuing search for the irreducible—from subatomic particles to quarks, from quarks to gluons, and now from these to the Higgs Boson "God Particle"—underscores the primacy of the paradigm of reductionism, attempting to understand the universe by isolating its smallest parts in a mistaken belief that larger ensembles are merely assemblages of constituent "granules." But of course, science itself has of late recognized that what things "are" depends on their relations—that as "the 'elements' (the irreducible constituent parts and their invariant ways of behaving) of a lower level are gathered up into a higher level of complexity, new modes of explanation become necessary" (Wink 1986, 143). Water, for instance, is not something inherent in hydrogen or oxygen as such, but only in their combined relationship to a larger system. Emergent causality, exercising "downward control of the whole over the parts, without interfering with the rules and forces of entities at lower levels," accounts for possibilities not found when the elementary particles themselves are merely added up (Wink 1986, 143). "Scientific objects—atoms, electrons, and so forth—are not basic but derivative; they are intellectual constructs invented to assist us in understanding events" (Wink 1986, 143). In thus insisting that analytical modes of knowing must be held together with synthetic, Wink is pushing toward an embrace of the elements as being ubiquitous in power without slipping into fetishizing their numinosity. The trick, he argues, is rather to "learn to regard them as theophanies" (Wink 1986, 144).

Ghostly Powers

And here there is much that can be fruitfully thought together with the indigenous view rehearsed above. But it is especially where Wink probes the way modernity has simultaneously evacuated meaning from matter only to reinvest it with our own projected shadow that draws attention. He traces a kind of mirroring effect in which violated "elementals"

return the disruption visited upon them (Wink 1986, 141). From popular beliefs in the European middle ages down to contemporary mus-
ings of more sophisticated psychics, there has continued a sense that
something within nature reacts to violence with hostility.[12] Wink reads
such as neither mere fantasy nor evidence of some independent "being"
cohabiting inorganic nature, but as a kind of reciprocity of our own
psychic imagery and our actual relationship with matter. Strip mining,
untreated sewage, chemical dumps, and missile counts are not mere
figments of imagined hostility, but incarnations of our own destructive fury (Wink 1986, 141). The rearranged elements become not only
compliant "servants" of a technological project of ultimate control but
also simultaneously "guerrilla rebels" on the rampage through a newly
fabricated "underground" whose indiscriminate "blowback" is merely
the flip side of our own megalomania. And indeed, in the global ecological crisis we are just beginning to be able to fathom, they may yet
have a "messianic" role. It may fall to these very elements themselves—
"abused, idolized, and rendered demonic" as they are in our modern
employments—to shake us from our sleep-walk into destruction (*if* we
can be awakened in time) (Wink 1986, 152).[13]

What begins to emerge from this way of thinking is something not
entirely different from Prechtel's vision of modernity as a violent mon-
strosity teeming with hungry ghosts and enslaved molecules (indeed,
it is not entirely different from Paul's own vision of creation as having been "subjected to futility, not of its own will" such that it now
awaits with "eager longing" for liberation "from its bondage to decay";
Rom 8:20–21). Wink also has us simultaneously enslaving matter and
becoming its slaves in turn—generating a recoiling of "natural" violence that is both effect and cause, at once a projection of our own
ballooning desire to emerge as universal masters of the planet and a
reflection, in our fevered imagination, of exactly that attempt to leverage mastery. The take-home insight that begins to emerge here is that
"principalities and powers discourse" may well represent an ancient
attempt to figure a growing grotesquery of unstable potency as communities human and "other" are blasted from their home ecologies by
aggressive polities seeking land and resources. Perhaps like a gyroscope
twisting any who would seek to manipulate its balanced spin, the symbiotic wholeness of human-animal-plant-mineral reciprocity (attending hunter-gatherer sustainability) does not simply disappear when
disrupted and forced into the mold of expansionist agriculture. Its
life-force and elemental power rather "submits" to the violent reorder-
ing, but with inevitable consequence. Enslaved matter and constrained

desire knot into a Medussa's head of writhing forces. The energy fields thus warped into forced conjunctures and interpenetrating complexes wax potent with an interventionist logic that cannot but be as destructive as it is creative.

And Wink indeed, hints as much. In his chapter on "The Angels of the Nations," he lifts up the argument of Andrew Schmookler that effectively duplicates the position put forward above (Schmookler 1984, 67; Wink 1986, 100). Hunter-gatherer folk represent the dawn of the species, giving evidence of a time when war was not endemic to humanity, symbiotic relationship with local ecosystems was simply the norm, and harmony and sustainability were typical. But the turn to agriculture initiated a systemic dysfunction—an increase in population, necessitating hierarchy and a militant quest for ever more land and resources—that "selected" for competition, conflict, and conquest. In the mix, neither conscious choice by communities nor ruthless strategy on the part of power-hungry despots drove the logic, but "impersonal forces—what the Bible knows as principalities and powers" (Wink 1986, 101). Caught in a dynamic of warfare unnatural to the species, people were "coerced, cajoled, deceived, bullied, and seduced" into acting against their own self-interest and cooperating with their own oppression, as "civilization" evolved into "the unchosen direction of power-maximization" (Wink 1986, 101).

In his subsequent chapter on "The Gods," Wink touches on this "growth curve" of power at the inception of Christianity in the Roman Empire. The pagan gods of the times, he says, "were too local, too identified with the devotion of certain *cities* [and] too fragmentary... for a world converging on itself": "they were not prepared for a cosmopolis" (Wink 1986, 114). Up until the advent of a Christianizing empire, what polytheism had provided was a map of "those dim regions where the elemental forces of nature mingle[d] without distinction" (Wink 1986, 116). A "god" was a basic structure of reality, a node in the fields of forces articulating inner psyche and outer world, rendered intelligible by myth, coordinated with all the other numinous beings blowing like winds of change or hurricanes of emotion through the crossroads where human "nature" met broader nature in those intrigues and oppositions, allergies and allurements that supersized experience beyond the capacities of mere "individuals." Without the mythology of the gods, he argues, the cosmopolitan world (then and now) is left bereft of sense and direction, subject to being continuously "pummeled and maddened" by the onslaught of forces neither nameable nor tameable (Wink 1986, 116). But the rapid Christian banishment of these pagan stories of power did not eclipse the deities themselves. They simply went underground—hounded out of public life by theological rhetoric and imperial edict—and enacted massive revenge as "demons" (Wink 1986, 116).[14] By the high middle ages the "dark forces" had become pandemic—so overwhelmingly fierce in their perceived vice-grip on psyche, natural ecology, and social collectivity alike, that their terrors nearly eclipsed belief in the one God. And in the reaction to such that emerges as the scientific revolution of modernity, "disenchantment" does not at all translate into disempowerment. Rather these archetypal forces morph once again and become, as Jung offered, "diseases"—Zeus and company ruling from the solar plexus and raining pathology on mind and polity without a discourse adequate to their potency (Wink 1986, 116). Nazism and Hiroshima become their new emblems; rampant addiction and massive childhood dysfunction their new symptoms.[15]

The hint of particular repute here is, of course, the note that these pagan gods—"the very structures by which personality and society are formed"—had been "dumbed down" in the move from Greek city-state to Roman cosmopolis (and lost altogether in modernity). Or more accurately they had been succeeded by forms of power exceeding the comprehension of folk myth as an idiom of restraint through which peasants and workers could pressure rulers with the censure of divine sanctions when their predation became too outrageous (Wink 1986, 215).[16] Even more disastrous has been the modern desire to dabble with "the gods" after banishing them from their material "thrones." "Unprotected by the rituals, myths, and supports of the old city-state *cultus*," the result is catastrophic—an attempt to load up the individual psyche with divine powers that cannot be contained or channeled by such, with all the consequent narcissism or projected fascination with "messianic" *personas* writ large (in hollywood glitz, politico blitz, quasi-myths of sports figures as "stars," etc.) that lands modern humanity in a massively shared condition of delusion[17] (Wink 1986, 118, fn 205). The messianic cannot be borne by the individual, separate from a people's art or a social movement invoking memory of sustainability in a given ecology (or at least so I am arguing). It inevitably becomes drunk on its own grandiosity and demonic in actual social effect (even if it confesses "Jesus").

But Wink's insight here concerns the piling up of power beyond the capacity of representational media to communicate or social institution to adjudicate.[18] The agglomeration of power assembled by empire builds on more local forms of such. Wink references the older city-states as having elaborated cults, capable of rendering "god forces" intelligible and useful—even to oppressed peasantries. But the imperial moment moves power outside local architecture and visibility: Rome exercises its coercions from over the horizon, a nimbus of storm that cannot be predicted or propitiated in local idiom. And of course, once economy goes global after Columbus and crew set foot in the Americas, the game is entirely lost. The emergence of post-modern discourse in our time, as the self-conscious confession of the death of the meta-story, marks not so much the death of the story itself, as of its ability to render a global force-field intelligible (as Jameson, et al., lament; Jameson 1991, xix, 35–39, 53).

Compelling as this argument may be, my interest lies in the other direction. I would surmise that even the older city-state *cultus* already represented a warping of imagination in service of a "tumoring" of power. Power in balance, gods and angels yet in service of human and other beings, the spiritual economy acting in symbiosis with, rather than extirpation of, local ecology, have alone been witnessed in our hunter-gatherer phase. Pastoral nomadism and subsistence agriculture already begin to participate in the growing mischanneling and misaggregation of potency, but at least continue to invoke memory of an originally wild sustenance and the need for regularly reinforced limitation of human aggrandizement. Once the project of domestication launches, and land is reengineered to grow greater numbers of humans, and need for more soil to grow more food leverages expansionist conquest carried out with newly minted weapons technologies, and so on, "power" accumulates in forms anomalous to ecosystemic modes of symbiosis or sustainability. The evolutionary line from settled mono-crop agriculture, through growing urbanization, to modern industrialization and now digitized globalization, represents a development counter to wild processes, to which it would revert, if not regularly coerced by the not-so-invisible hand of humanity.

Up inside the "powers and principalities discourse" of Paul— creatively articulated in his writings but innovated out of Persian theology and Greek philosophy long before its uptake in service of Christian mission—are the trapped powers of nature and the elements.[19] I would suggest, without here being able to argue it out definitively (a book-length project at minimum), that spiritual/elemental power is not outside Einstein's assertion that energy does not leave the universe, but just changes form.[20] It can perhaps be imagined somewhat like a hydrologic phenomenon: pushed out of its natural channels, it floods where it is dammed; inundating those conduits "behind the walls" that have sought to gather its force for other purposes. Prechtel is not far off the mark here: spirit-charged-matter (as all matter thus exists, at least as part of larger force fields of energy and relational ensembles), once enslaved, concentrates spiritual force beyond the capacity of its new organization to control in a healthy manner. It may well be the case, at some level we have yet to fully grasp, that matter coerced, "protests," and ultimately revolts. And organic life, once abused, has its own eventual vengeance.

What a holistic use of the rest of the biosphere would actually look like on a global scale is thus far in our history beyond imagining. It may well be beyond realizing. But holistic relationship within a given ecosystem does have a historic model. Our ancestors practiced such when living otherwise, and remembered such even when coerced by mono-cropping. Some communities on the planet yet know the possibility. None of them live in cities. What a city is, in line with the discussion elaborated earlier, is an amassing of reengineered matter and life forms haunted by ghostly memories of ungrieved violence and "out of shape" matter held in place against itself. The key is that the technologies resulting—whether on the microscale of nanomanipulations and terminator seeds or the macroscale of a megalopolis and a nuclear arsenal—do not happen in the wild, and left "unforced" by human hands, would neither occur nor remain as such.

I am proposing an experimental reading of Wink's take on the powers as signifying just such a gargantuan force field—correlative originally with the emergence of ancient forms of imperial aggrandizement— but now referencing empire's planetary reach in the phenomenon we call neoliberal globalization. This is a titanism of technological power rooted in a billion-billion-fold enslavement of organic life (human, animal, and plant) *and* inorganic matter (extracted minerals, the dead ancestors that we commandeer as "fossil fuels," reengineered earth that is itself teeming with a billionfold of life in each "wild" cubic foot, the rivers and aquifers we seek to siphon and rechannel as life-blood of the mega-machine of industry, and the sunlight we seek to unlock from the atom or capture in a panel). It is telling to me that Wink experienced his breakthrough moment into an "other" way of perceiving power (than merely as human ingenuity exercised on inert matter), through encounter with the writings of Findhorn Community founder, Dorothy Maclean. The latter's *To Hear Angels Sing* opened, for Wink, "the possibility of a second naiveté toward nature," indeed, quoting Sandor Ferenczi, an "animism no longer anthropomorphic" (Wink 1986, 156).

Maclean's exploration of plant communication—discovering a kind of "species-being" speaking to her through written meditation—enabled her community to grow yields of vegetables and flowers otherwise deemed impossible in the sandy environs of northern Scotland. And sent Wink on his own journey out from the typical aridity of modern consciousness into a quest for comprehension of such "angels of nature" as led to his life-work in discerning and rearticulating the language of the powers for our time. Central to that journey was the opening of perception beyond what Wink calls the mental to the imaginal (Wink 1986, 162). Angels do not, he would say, have physical reality (do not fly around up in the sky), but are real as "visionary," as encountered in an altered consciousness. Quoting Maclean, he will recount the report of the Findhorn flowers who said to her, with intensity: "Look, don't think; look directly at us and see God." Likewise the Landscape Angel of Findhorn offered: "All around you, in every bit of matter, is what has come from, is, and leads to the only One: and within you is the consciousness that can know and express this" (Wink,1986, 169).

The investigation thus begun, leads to surprising places. Wink at one point quotes Justice William O. Douglas, contesting a Supreme Court decision on the environment, with an admonition that if a corporation can be a person, so can be "valleys and alpine meadows, rivers, lakes, estuaries, beaches, ridges, groves of trees, swampland, or even the air that feels the destructive pressures of modern technology and modern life" (Mintz and Cohen 1977, 753; Wink 1986, 165;). The river, says Douglas, "as plaintiff speaks for the ecological unit of life that is part of it." But beyond such legal "respect," the summons is back to a basic identity as participants in nature, not mere spectators, a renewed trust in "our own interior depths [as] able to mirror the interiority of phenomena 'out there' because we are set in life as our medium" (Wink 1986, 161). This is a call to repudiate the arrogance that stripped the world of its "within," as James Hillman writes, "stuffing all soul within the subjectivity of human beings, leaving the world a slagheap from which all projections, personifications and psyche had been extracted" (Hillman 1973, 122–123; Wink 1986, 161). It is admonition to assent to living "at the juncture of two ages," wherein "ancient wisdoms take on sudden incandescence" and "recent wisdoms lose all credibility"—in which indeed, "the stone which the builders of the previous worldview rejected may even become the new head of the corner" (Wink 1986, 172).

"The messianic"—the "anointing" of a thing to provoke attention to an alternative possibility for living and acting—may well depend today (as in its very first practice) on learning to listen to a rock which can "speak". Or at least on beginning to intuit the "ghostly place" of power, in urban infrastructure and technology, from which that speaking has been evacuated!

The Power of Resurrection

Wink begins *Unmasking* by linking the principalities and powers discourse with the process of Hellenization as a new phenomenon in Western culture (if not humanity at large). The collapse of the Greek city-states and their rebirth inside a rising cosmopolis is the political reality that the "new language" tries to comprehend—albeit "darkly, as in a mirror." Traditional religions were being broken down and their fragments incorporated "in religious forms and cults capable of universal vision" (Wink 1986, 3). That is to say, powers language is the creature of a new ecology, grounded no longer in savvy relationship with local flora and fauna (as with hunter-gatherer, subsistence agriculture, or pastoral nomad lifeways), nor yet in city-state living, organizing surrounding country sides into suppressed peasantries delivering up rural carrying capacity to the urban core for elite consumption and redeployment. But rather here was the first attempt at articulating an imperial ethos. The groping symbology of angels, demons, principalities and powers, gods and elements of the universe, spirits and Satan did not merely rehash older archetypes, but began to amalgamate them to dimly sensed new arrangements. The "struggle to perceive" that the language reflects (Wink will track its amorphous and imprecise use in the New Testament in his first book of the series) is typical of any such endeavor to discern a novel environment—artists and seers stammering after unfamiliar patterns, marking emergent meaning with extant symbols. In this case, the taxing awareness is of strangely emergent forms of power "operative *among and between people.*" And the alchemic work of translating such is a matter of bending older ideas to grasp "new beings" *intermediate* between God and humanity (Wink 1986, 3).

Wink is clear about the novelty. While angels themselves "belong to all strata of the bible" (but only come into their own under Persian influence in the intertestamental period), angelic "principalities" do not show up until the last of the Hebrew books, Daniel (in the second century BCE) (Wink 1986, fn 4, 174). The rest of the language—powers, authorities, dominions, thrones, names, elements, etc.—does not appear at all outside the New Testament. And though the report of *daimones* has a long lineage in Greek culture, evil spirits as a *class*—provoking prophylactic efforts like the use of "engraved gems, amulets, and spells against demons, phantasms, and night fears"—emerge only in the first or second century CE (Wink 1986, fn 4, 174). (which informs our choice our choice briefly to examine an Ethiopian peasant use of such prophylactics in the next chapter.)

In *Naming,* Wink notes the signal difference that marks the shift in resistance we are proposing here. While the terminology of power is nearly as common in the synoptics as in Paul, its focus there is not at all the same. In the gospels, it references largely "human or structural, rather than spiritual, entities" (Wink 1984, 100). It falls to Paul, however, to innovate the emblematic discourse that will come to characterize the Christian canon, as a *new theology of power.* In a quite unique manner—and probably influenced by the conventions of Greek drama—Paul elaborates the basic "determinants of human existence" in a specialized vocabulary of "quasi-hypostatized words" (Wink 1984, 100). As Latin American liberation theologian Juan Luis Segundo has also emphasized, "Sin," "Grace," "Law," "Works," Righteousness," "Faith," "Flesh," "Life," and "Death" loom large, in the theater of human agency articulated by Paul, as forces or pressures claiming nearly autonomous power and carrying out their own competing agendas (Segundo 1986, 9–10). Impersonal though they are, they function almost as "ghostly militants" or "unappeased ancestors," demanding obeisance, sabotaging intention, deflecting plans and deforming motivation, or opening up vision and new possibility, as the case may be. Rather than the figures typical of Jewish apocalyptic—Satan, Azazel, Beliar, evil spirits, demons, etc.—in Pauline denotation we have these numinous agencies, working anonymously within the psyche and covertly in collective life.

Arguably, for Paul, one of these hypostatized powers is also "Resurrection." And just here, in sketching out his christology, the great innovator's creativity gets quite interesting. Again, my concern is not in trying to delineate an overall picture, but rather to catch certain details in a refractory light that opens the doors of inquiry and imagination. Paul's most mature and developed christological argument is offered from an imperial prison, admonishing an imperial congregation. The first eight chapters of his Roman letter map a striking claim. The life of Jesus of Nazareth—as elsewhere in Paul's work—is tapped for only two images of reflection. Paul lifts the crucifixion and resurrection themes from their embedding in Palestinian politics, and casts them across his theoretical horizon as the organizing tropes of his cosmology. These two moments—of imperial execution and its surprising overcoming—function, for him, not so much as historical-action-to-be-emulated as an interpretive lens to be employed in deciphering existential spiritual struggle. In their light, Paul reads the entirety of Jewish history—reframing "Adam" and "eschaton" (beginning and end) alike within their ambit of meaning. When Paul decides to exhibit the meaning of these now "cosmologized" themes (of crucifixion and resurrection) for everyday existence, however, he does not (like the gospels) make use of details from the life of the prophet from Nazareth, but turns back to the founding ancestor of the tradition. Compellingly, as Segundo makes clear, his choice responds to his audience.

The multi-culturally mixed community making up the Roman *ecclesia* exercises his reading strategy (Segundo 1986, 36, 68). To speak to both Gentile and Jew at once at the heart of his letter to the Romans, Paul carefully *only* solicits precircumcision Abraham—actually "Abram" the Aramean, before his name is changed to "Abraham" (though Paul will simply use "Abraham" for both phases of this forefather's life). The point here is that this is actually a solicitation of "Abram the Gentile"— before Jewishness had been formally introduced into history by way of a clipped foreskin. In this subtle choice of the part of the patriarchal narrative he lifts up, Paul is undoing any privilege the Hebrew line might want to claim for itself as the supposed source of global salvation (salvation "from the Jews"). Rather here, he is waxing cagey, hinting that even the Jews themselves came "from Gentiles" (from not-yet-Jewish "Abram," that is). And attentive readers are thus schooled in the way intra-community politics leverages theological discourse: a doubly constituted polity is addressed through a mixed genealogy (of Jew and Gentile) in a manner that honors a specific ancestry even as it evacuates any claim to superiority. But even more radically innovative is the christological claim put forward in this Abramic reference.

In the most elaborate Pauline letter we have, it is the Genesis texts of centenarian Abram and his nonagenarian wife Sarai that *provides the narrative for christological theorizing, not the gospel stories of the Nazarene.* And it is "resurrection" that supplies the nexus between first century CE messianic witness and second millennium BCE founder. This death-defying power—whose exemplary subject in history, according to canonical confession, is an executed Galilean renegade pulled from an early grave—finds its primal appearance in an old man who can still "get it up" and an old woman who can yet conceive and give birth. According to Paul, Abram and Sarai were already in their day exhibiting "resurrection potency." In Rom 4: 16–25, the imprisoned apostle claims this wandering Aramean herder as "father" for Roman believers (indeed, "for us all") and hails (tongue in cheek?) his hopeful exploits with his laughing wife—neither one of whom was weakened in considering their own declining flesh. In Paul's reading, neither Abram's body "as good as dead" nor Sarai's barren womb were cause for alarm or wavering. Their trust—and willingness to frolic in response to a promise that they will "live again" in their offspring—is read as exemplary "justness" ("righteousness") "in the presence of the God...who gives life to the dead and calls into existence the things that do not exist" (Rom 4:16, 24–25) Thus, Paul admonishes, neither should his Roman hearers waver before the One who also "raised from the dead" the Galilean messiah "who was put to death for our trespasses and raised for our justification."

This conglomeration of ancient memory and contemporary event (in Paul's time) interweaves themes in a surprising conjunction. The sex life of a nomad couple gives testament to the necessary cooperation with larger-than-life forces that conduces to messianic meaning in a novel context nearly two millennia later. Locked away from field and herb in an urban center, laboring under Roman imperial tax and heavy surveillance and militant threat at every turn, a mixed multitude of traders and slaves, maids and servants and the odd wealthy defector, are directed to a highlands couple two thousand years their senior, gone feral from their own city-seat of Ur, in old age under the teaching trees of Canaan, conceiving significance for their late-in-the-day, roll-in-the-hay *as if* it had world-historical import, or even cosmic relevance. "Crucifixion" is swallowed up here in a concern for "Death" *writ large*, lumping together a violently unjust scene of imperial torture and execution with the commonly ubiquitous process of aging and decay. And "Resurrection" is discovered (or really "constructed"), long after the fact, as a force at work even in so sensual an event as unanticipated erection and post-menopausal conception. If scripture itself (in a Christian understanding of the New Testament as such) can give us a use of the life story of Abram and Sarai that reads into its mundane events such a surprising disclosure of the "power of resurrection"— what story, what cultural codes or mythic meanings or historical events or biographies are *not* available for such a recoding? Paul's christology[21] elaborates its primary *experiential* testimony from memory of the lives of non-Christian, not-yet-Jewish ancestors. And it hails the action of "transacting seed" in overcoming the impotence and infertility of old age as the equivalent of exiting the grave. So just how wide open is the door here?

This is indeed a provocative way of "locating" the meaning of a new turning of an old power to a potent use in the hard-to-decipher context of the emerging imperial metropolis. Abram is the exemplar in the tradition of old seed showing up in "waves" of new peoples in both a physical and a spiritual sense. Certainly Isaac is born of the act as are a proliferating succession of Israelites. But under Pauline reinterpretation of resurrection in which he acts like a tree-farmer grafting new stock into an old line (Rom 11:17–24), so likewise are the unanticipated "wild" seed of Abram that come to be called "Roman Christians." And here this paradigm of human fruitfulness shifts toward our most primal experience of resurrection. Now we are talking about shoots and branches of olive cultivars, and life that returns from death by way of plant seedlings. And we hit the root—both metaphor and reality! Whether allied with perennial grasses or annual crops, our species had long witnessed that all things living on land utterly depend for their regeneration on the irrepressible propensity of plant life to die into the ground every year to make way for new growth and every spring return from that seeming "defeat" with astonishing vitality. Primal "resurrection" *is* seed power—in all of its chthonic prodigality! But this most ubiquitous and insurgent of life-powers is now being made "palpable" for a people increasingly cut off from the mysteriousness of that older experience. So Paul only lightly "feints" toward that ancient insurgence. He rather imbeds his "resurrection-from-the-dead" assertions in a "seed-reborn" narrative largely circumscribed within our own species (Abram and Sarai). This is clearly a text for a "christ" of the city, taught by a maker of tents, seeking to renovate, for a new context, a messianism traditionally anchored in a movement of the countryside that had itself kept alive its memory by way of imagery yet rooted in some of the actual alternative "soil practices" it referenced (of foraging, herding, or subsistence growing).[22]

And as Myers so eloquently lays out, Paul indeed brings forward and updates, for a cosmopolitan range of relations, the Sabbath-Jubilee ethos so central to the entire tradition (and *de rigour* for Jesus' own movement) (Myers 2001, 52–59). The intimacy of (150-member) hunter-gatherer band societies is roughly reproduced in local Christian house-church communities, leveling the playing field in labeling all alike as "brothers" and "sisters," enjoying shared access to commonly held resources. But this is a sabbatical practice that is in the process of losing one of its legs.[23] As circumscribed by an urban armature of technology and trade, the movement here has less and less intimate experience with the earth or its creatures.[24] Plants and animals cease to be major "messianic" mediators and "local ecologies" are now increasingly inorganic and architectonic—a piling up of rock and mineral and wood and bronze and copper and the iron (that in modern historical hindsight names an entire epoch) characteristic of city life. "Release of land" and "honoring of the commons" (for hunting, fishing, gathering firewood and roots, etc.) may remain demands of the peasant laborers whose pilfered and horded product makes city life possible in the first place; but in short order "peasants" become precisely those presumed by the new urban "christians" to be "pagan" unbelievers.

The Power of *Logos*

And of course, we would be remiss not to comment, however briefly, on the similar innovation rendered by the "beloved disciple" (glossed as "John") in this context—in many ways the most radical and decisive for subsequent Christianity. The fourth gospel departs markedly from the style and chronology of the synoptics and exhibits a symbology whose artistry and theological gravity reinterpret the political tone of Mark and Q for its own quite altered postrevolt context. It remains trenchantly (and ironically) critical and sharply (and passionately) political within its own social ecology as powerfully clarified in a tome like Wes Howard-Brook's *Becoming the Children of God: John's Gospel and Radical Discipleship* or even a short article like Samuel Rayan's "Jesus and the Poor in the Fourth Gospel." And not too far under the surface of even Johannine reflection lies insurgent memory of an alternative lifestyle rooted in a hallowing of the land (as we shall see). But imperial power (already in the second century, but especially with Constantine and after) will cherry-pick its most stunning theological innovation to recast it (and "Christianity" with it) as a text of apology for Roman aggrandizement and ultimately for Christian supremacy. The "Hymn to the *Logos*" that John appends as preface to his Book of Signs and Book of Words opens an association that has not closed, all the way up to our own time.

Whatever the specific intentions behind John's choice of the *logos*-concept to render his particular vision of messianism, the gospel's shared move to thematize Jesus as "incarnating" something bigger and older than himself (as merely human) reaches its apogee here. Indeed, even the synoptics give evidence of a kind of one-ups-man-ship of reflection, given increasing time and distance from the events narrated, with Mark anchoring his genealogy of the messianic in the prophets, Matthew in Abraham, and Luke in Adam (Howard-Brook 1994, 52). John takes the big leap and trumps them all by going back behind creation itself to invoke *the* beginning (both Genesis and metaphysics), having deciphered within Jesus' movement a Reality, "'tented' (or 'tabernacled'; *eskēnōsen* in Greek) among us," who is the real Subject not just of the gospel story, but the cosmos itself. Compared to the synoptics, his will be an inverted inception. The Johannine narrative does not start with a historical memory of the people (such as the exilic hope of a way in the desert that Mark invokes, the family genealogy of Matthew, or the colonial crisis Luke outlines), but with a metaphysical vision. The centerfold here is not a human named "Jesus" whose "specialness" is then interrogated by way of the Greek word "*christos*" (translating the Jewish title *mashiach*), but rather an eternal, metaphysical *Logos* who somehow enters the world and becomes the human messiah.

The quite concrete characterization in verse 14 of this Word "becoming flesh" and "tenting" in the movement, "full of grace and truth," both references and deflects Moses from his position of primary significance. The subtle herder invocation implied by *eskēnōsen* underscores the trek out of Egypt and into the wilderness as the place of primordial revelation, whence, according to Sir 24:8, "Wisdom tented among Israel." (And indeed, in the subsequent Johannine verse, even the Baptizer will emphasize that something more than mere humanity was present in Jesus: "[though] he comes after me, he was *before* me"). What was at work in Jesus was also at work in the Sinai wandering more than a millennium before. But the Johannine context is no longer the desert or even the highlands terrain of Canaan that carries that memory etched in its hills or flowing along its watersheds.

The new ecology is rather the imperial city (whether Ephesus or some other eastern Mediterranean *polis*). It is the big wisdom of the Hebrew *hokmah*—personified and hypostatized in texts like Sirach and Proverbs 8—that John wants to throw down before his alienated audience to gain traction with their own expectations in a new cultural context. Prov 8:22–31, in particular, offers him the Great Primordial Female of Hebrew imagination, soliloquizing her creation "at the beginning," as the first of God's "acts of old," brought forth before waters and mountains, earth or fields or dust, or even the heavens themselves, "beside" ("with") the Creator like a "master worker" (or in an alternative reading, like a "little child"), delighting the entire (subsequent) creation. But this is a Jewish myth and John must speak to Gentiles. Building perhaps on work like Philo's, he grabs up the masculine term *logos* from the heritage of Greek philosophy to render this feminine *Hokmah* intelligible across the cultural divide he confronts, and goes beyond both Hebrew and Hellenic convention. This is a *logos*, in Johannine conviction, that is not merely the primal artificer, but actually inhabits eternity *with theos* and *is theos*. And this is an innovation whose ramifications we will remark in a moment. But of first import here is the recognition that the concept is culturally "creole"—harboring quite different fields of meaning within the folds of a tradition whose signs, even within its new context, will arc back and forth like wild lightning on a Sinai mountain.

The solicitation of "grace and truth" (in verses 14 and 17) is a specific designation of *chesed v'emet* in Hebrew ("loving-kindness"), the interiority of the Sinai covenant tradition, that at core, again takes us back to the Jewish *axis mundi*, the great storm-mountain, abode of the Wild Sacred that liberated Israel from Egypt and into the desert to be reschooled in the foraging economics of gathering *manna* and the deconstructive poetics associated with YHWH's unnameable name. Of course, by John's time, much of this wildlands association has been tamed and/or lost over the centuries of imperial domination and peasant struggle. But it is telling that John will build his very unique narrative account around creative "I AM" sayings ("I am the light of the world," I am the resurrection," I am the way, the truth, and the life," "I am the Good Shepherd," etc.),[25] whose effect is to pull the theophanic "bush apparition" to Moses right into the center of christic reflection, and hint the movement of Jesus as the new locus of that old disclosure.

And here there is a kind of central thunderclap that the gospel organizes for those willing to be led by its hints into sudden epiphanies. Howard-Brook notes in his commentary on the poetic overture of Jh1:1–18 that the overall gospel is structured around three seven-part chiasms (concentric arrangements of verses that organize insight in a centripetal pattern of parallel sayings, opening into a singular core emphasis) (Howard-Brook 1994, 52). These occur in the prologue hymn, the story of the healing of one born blind in chapter 9, and the trial scene of chapters 18 and 19, culminating in crucifixion. If taken as themselves chiastic, these three would offer the chapter 9 vignette as focal for the entire gospel. Its prime subject, apart from Jesus, is the one healed of his congenital condition who, upon returning from the Siloam pool-washing that had restored his sight, interrupts his neighbors' agitated uncertainty about his identity by saying, "I am the man" (Jh 9:9). And Howard-Brook indeed reads this figure as archetypal for the ideal Johannine disciple, a kind of community parable of the continual struggle "to see clearly" in the post-revolt context of bitter division within Jewish synagogue-based religion (from which the Johannine community of messianic belief had been excommunicated). It is the one time, in John's gospel, when the enigmatic but potent I AM (*egō eimi* in Greek) peeks out from someone other than Jesus. Its possibility stands out as the sharp assertion of Johannine insistence upon reciprocity and equality.[26] Even the apparent primacy of Jesus as the new locus of revelation is not a monopoly: *it is actually a movement possibility*. A blind beggar (and anyone else) can take over the role.

The acute artistry of this assertion gains added depth from the layers of significance curled around its centripetal send up. The healing is by way of "anointing"[27]—in this case, eyes painted over with spit-wetted clay. *And it establishes the blind beggar as also an anointed one!* (Jh 9:11). It takes place on the Sabbath, as an act of civil disobedience that will result in increased plotting against Jesus (Jh 9:12,14, 24; 10:19–21). And it unfolds within the narrative arc of the Feast of Tabernacles celebration during which the Galilean upstart had suddenly come "above ground" in the region of Judea (in spite of the price on his head) and engaged in symbolic action in the Temple (Jh 7:1–10:21; Howard-Brook, 1994, 172). As in synoptic depictions of Jesus sideswiping a Passover parade to stage his Temple exorcism, so here, the Feast of Booths provides the opportunity for prophetic confrontation. And for John's gospel, it is high theater.

The very identification of the feast itself in 7:2 thrusts us right back into the center of the opening hymn (the word "Tabernacles" is *skēnopēgia* in Greek, the noun form of the word for "tent" in 1:14). This is Sukkot as messianic emblem—the Johannine equivalent of Luke's "Jubilee Jesus." It provides a major score for Johannine improvisation. In his prophetic riff on the priestly act of pouring water on the ceremonial altar on the last day of the celebration, Jesus suddenly stands up and cries out publicly like a brazen epiphany of Wisdom incarnate in the public square (Prov 8:1–4). The tension is palpable. Against the controlled choreography of the domesticated version of the feast, rooted in oppressive agricultural practices and presided over by Temple elites, Jesus invokes the original "tabernacle" experience of "tent dwelling" in Sinai (Lev 23:39–43; Dt 16:13). His audacious "Come and drink" baldly summons nomadic remembrance of "free" access to wild resources (like water and grasses) and later prophetic insistence, once Israel is settled, on shared access to "freed" farming products (like wine and bread)[28] (Jh 7:37–38; Is 44:3; 55:1; 58:11).[29] The obvious depth-background here is Moses cracking open the rock in the wilderness, memorialized in Exod 17:1–7 as a struggle between the ex-slaves' continuing unbelief about wild provision (an effect of having long been embedded in an imperial economy) and a herder's grasp of the local ecosystem.[30] The provision of drink in the desert narrated there is not so much a miraculous "turning of stone into water" as a *bedouin* form of local knowledge, savvy about the way desert flood waters, heavy with dissolved minerals, sometimes pool in rock recesses and crust over their cavities before evaporation sets in. Even today, one well-schooled in the ecology knows the signs and can "free the water," shattering the brittle facade with just a gentle tap in the right place. But this Tabernacles teaching on free provision does not really end with the conclusion of the feast.

Its thematic of "living waters" continues on into the episode of heal-ing the beggar. The sequence of "rivers that flow from bellies" of Jh 7:38, followed in short order by the story of "spittle joined to soil" in Jh 9:6, is at once symbolic and polemic. Freely flowing waters, we are told in Johannine commentary, equate to freely flowing spirit (Jh 7:39). Joined as living moisture to the primal element of earth in the poultice of clay in chapter 9, the hint is clairvoyant. The healing is actually an act of recreation, a beginning like Genesis, the very "rebirth" from water and spirit that an elite teacher like Nicodemus (in chapter 3 of John) could neither grasp nor undergo. At the same time, saliva (along with other bodily fluids) comprehended within Torah as "unclean" means the act was also renegade, an assault on the entire scribal apparatus of interpre-tation and denigration. A blind beggar, joined in his jeopardy and impu-rity by a "possessed" Galilean (Jh 7:20; 8:48; 10:20–21), is anointed by this "anointed one" with spittle and mud, and sent to Siloam to wash (a clear reference to the daily Tabernacles procession to that pool to draw up water for use in the fest) (Howard-Brook 1994, 174, 217). The pool name itself means "Sent" (as John tells his readers) and initiates the "blind one" in an extended action of healing that only begins with the washing. Recovery from physical blindness requires for its completion recovery from ideological blindness. The entire chapter rehearses the itinerary of a long climb out of an oppressed condition and colonized mindset to reclaim voice and dignity and wisdom. By its conclusion, the beggar has corrected his neighbors, repudiated the fearful silence of his parents, contested the Judeans brought in to assess his healing, and dared to "teach" the teachers (the Pharisees in John's gospel), resulting finally in his "being put outside" ("excommunicated") like Jesus him-self (Jh 9:9–33). And wittingly or not—like Isaiah before him embrac-ing his own "mission of unmasking" ("*egō eimi*, send me!" in the LXX of Is 6:8)—he has replicated the great I AM assertion that authorizes such a "truth-telling" vocation (Howard-Brook 1994, 286–287).

And just here, we rejoin the concerns of this writing. The oblique references to Isaiah underneath the story of the healing of the beggar are telling. Isaiah's own prophetic task of counseling King Ahaz out of (conspiratorial) reliance on international powers had been cast in the ancient terms of the water politics of that part of the world. In a message delivered "by the upper pool," Isaiah had intoned his word. Failure to quietly trust (Is 7:3–4) the gently flowing springs of Shiloah (Siloam) would result in Israel being engulfed by the "flooding River culture" of Assyrian imperial might (Is 8:5–8). Egyptian flies and Assyrian bees would invade (Is 7:18–19). Where subsistence agriculture previously had purchase, only herding and hunting would survive (Is 7:21–25). And all of this sage advice had burst forth in an overwhelming visionary gestalt of seraphim[31] in the Temple and "glory" in the earth (Is 6:1–13). The bundling of themes here is "thunder" indeed. Highlands watersheds versus lowlands irrigation systems; wild abundance versus hoarded scarcity; pestilential invasives colonizing the Canaanite clefts while agriculture reverts to nomadism; the heavenly host (from above the firmament) "ghosting" the Temple precincts with an angelic ratification of the practices there as "unclean" (the burden of the vision that inaugurates Isaiah's vocation), while the "house" fills with the smoke associated with the desert "tabernacle" (Exod 40:34) and with the sudden stupendous terror of truly natural glory, epitomized in an uncontrollable channeling of the great un-nameable name, "I AM." Beneath the beggar (in John Chapter 9) are both the prophet and the bush. And the entire historical struggle between wild ways and imperial might that Israelite prophecy memorializes.

In a word, this Name that the formerly blind one channels, is a plant-whisper that is messianic. It is a force bridging the human and the wild, the natural and the divine (Ex 3:4, 6; Dt 33:16). But it is also "angelic" (Ex 3:2). Indeed, Wink notes that the "name" itself as an effective entity (*onoma* in Greek) is comprehended as a Power in the ancient world (Wink 1984, 21–22). The I AM comes to be hypostatized as the *shem YHWH,* as time goes on, a "distinguishable though not separate agent of God's will and work," functioning as an intermediary between divinity and world (Wink 1984, 21). As it comes to be associated (not always completely clearly) with the *onoma* of Jesus as "Lord" or "Christ" after the first century, it ascends in scope and potency, often designating a superiority to the names shared with angels (whose names are themselves only derivative forms of *the* name) (Heb 1:4; Phil 2:9–11; Eph 1:21; Act 4:7, 12; Rev 19:16; Wink 1984, 22–23). But it is also the case that *onoma* is used to refer to a power whose effect is satanic (Rev 13:1, 17; 14:11, etc.) or to designate a demonic presence that Jesus will seek to coerce into disclosure (the "Legion" of Mk 5:9) or that the authorities (from their point of view) will seek to have named by Peter and John when they heal a paralytic (in Acts 4:7, 12). (Indeed, Wisdom itself is at times comprehended as a power of evil; 4Q 184; Wink 1984, 20, fn 18). Said succinctly, this is the name of a Power and the power of a Name that refuses the parameters of signifying. It is a Potency that will not submit to univocity. It draws no clear line in the sand. Between God, the Devil and the deep blue sea (or the green flaming bush), it solves nothing (as we see in the next chapter).

And here indeed we close the circle in considering the status of John's focus on *logos*.

The *Logos* as a Power

Certainly it is far beyond what is possible in this space to trace the long career of the *logos*-concept in its many windings over more than two millennia. Suffice it here to note that for the budding aspirations of ancient philosophy, a whole cluster of ideas orbit around or pass through the gravitational field of this Greek arch-idea. My own interest, in light of the argument of this chapter, is to suggest the kind of inflation in perception and conception that the cosmopolitan stockpiling of enslaved "bodies" (discussed above) implied—even (indeed, especially) for this most vaunted of Christian messianic terms.

Of particular interest is the relationship of *Logos* with the notions of power designated as "angelic" such as Wink delineated. Philo, for instance, building on Plato, will speak of numberless Potencies (*dynameis*) grouped around the One, through whom the intelligible and incorporeal world is framed, as an archetypal system of invisible ideal forms shaping the phenomenal world (Wink 1986, 158). Although according to him these were at one time falsely deified by pagans as gods, Philo is nonetheless comfortable with comprehending these idea-forms as angelic powers granted an indestructible existence and generally embraced their reality "as an aspect of the creative *logos*" (Wink 1986, 203, fn 38). But by the late first century this Philoic identification of *logos* and *angelos*—shared in fact by many other thinkers of antiquity—will apparently provoke the "throw down" of the Hebrews Epistle, seeking to combat the equation as heresy (Wink 1986, 216, fn 43). The author of Hebrews will insist that Christ (presumably as *Logos*) alone partakes of godhead. And part of the issue may well be the question of creative agency. Unlike "creaturely" angels, who (we might say) passively function as mere pattern-maintaining "species-beings," early Christian experience held that the Christ-*Logos* exercised a kind of monopoly on both creation and transformation (Wink 1986, 158–159; 213 fn 17; 214 fn 24). And interestingly, just here Wink's own assessment of the debate will equivocate. He edges in the direction of Philo. To the degree everything in nature could be said to have an angel "as its pattern or initial aim," angels are for him simply "the specific initial aim which the Christ or *Logos* provides to every particular being": they are "Logos-made-specific" as that very aim (Wink 1986, 216). And from there, he notes, it is but a slight extension to speak of the *Logos* as "the Angel of the angels." (We might keep in mind here the similarly "supremacist" political appellations of Christ as "King of kings" and "lord of lords".)

In his chapter on "The Angels of the Churches," focusing especially on the role of angelic powers in the book of Revelation, Wink had already clarified that Christ, not the angels, revealed the "reality and vocation of the church" (Wink 1986, 193, fn 18). As the living interiority of the congregation, he there insists, "angels have no message because they themselves are the message" (Wink 1986, 81, 193, quoting Avens, 46). It is rather up to a "Human One" (such as John or Jesus) to deliver the message, call recalcitrant angels back to their own vocation, and precipitate institutional/congregational change. Thus the address of the letters to the angels of the churches by such a one as John (rather than another angel)! John is the "angel's angel," says Wink ("the messenger to the messengers"; Wink 1986, 81). But so would Wink say of Christ (Wink 1986, 194, fn19). And John himself seems to imply as much.

Where John begins his account in 1:1 with the assertion that this "revelation of Jesus Christ" was given by God sending "his angel" to his servant (John), a mere ten verses later (1:10–20) he is describing for the churches the appearance of that messenger as one like a son of man who is clearly Christ himself. Thus for John, *Christ* is the Angel of the Christian Church. And here the terms begin to pile up and cross-propagate. Christ is also equated with the Spirit who speaks to each of the churches (2:7, 11, 17, 29; 3:6, 13, 22). Wink sums up this discussion of the possibilities of transformation by saying "only Christ as the Spirit *of the whole church* can change *a church*" (emphasis JP) and in the relevant footnote to such, quotes the Fifth Book of Ezra (2:42–47) to the effect that as Christians "conquer" (bear testimony even to the point of death), the spirit of Christ *grows larger*. This is signified in Ezra in the form of a "young man, towering above all the rest," who grows ever taller with each crown he distributes, who is identified by an angel as "Christ" (Wink 1986, 81, 193 fn 18). And thus we could say that the messianic term "Christ" itself—at least as a label if not a reality—seems to balloon with "angelic" and "spiritual" inflation in these early efforts to accommodate rural Galilean messianism to urban Roman imperialism.

The hints here converge with our discussion above on a kind of "travail of discourse," struggling to stretch available categories to address dimly perceived new realities in the spiritual and political domains. Not only the language of spirits and demons, thrones and dominions, principalities and powers has been cobbled together creatively to try to open awareness to an emergent dimension of imperial reality (as city-states are engulfed in the Roman apparatus of control). But the categories of "Christ" and "*Logos*" themselves—crosscut with ideas and perceptions signified by words like "angel" and "Spirit"—are morphing dynamically. While "angel" continues its linguistic vocation as a term for the institutional breadth/interior depth of a given local congregation (among other possible references), "Christ" emerges, carrying the aura of *Logos* on its back, as the only term appropriate for a pan-*ecclesial* or trans-congregational dimension of the messianic community, a kind of "whole church" signification—functioning very much like the way "angel" functions, but now in relationship to an imperial dimension of power. To the degree the term begins to reference a spiritual reality that is trans-local—gathering into its meaning a Presence imagined as presiding over and straddling multiple urban centers that are linked in an *imperium*—what is actually being referred *to* is a stockpile of ripped up and repurposed "resources" (animals, plants, minerals, etc.), ghosted with spiritual energies and hungers, now enslaved in city architecture and infrastructure, economy and weaponry. "Christo-logy" itself here begins to edge over into a meaning and a reality as the *prince* of principalities—not simply as "ruler over," but as *participant in,* this imperial rearrangement of local ecosystems and cultures.

And indeed, this Johannine move, opening up *christos* by way of *logos,* proves to be a quantum leap, not usually recognized as such by subsequent Christian theorizing. It marks a shift away from a rural Palestinian ambit of meanings, associated loosely with social banditry and renegade politics, and into an urban imperial set of concerns. It does so by means of a set of rough equivalences and cross-propagation of terms almost impossible to trace or untangle from our vantage point two millennia down the road. The term "Christ" is so deeply structured into our cognitive universe and affective responsiveness (both positively and negatively) as to make it extremely difficult to gain perspective on the articulation and conjoining involved. But the line of succession from the Hebrew "*mashiach*" to the Hellenic "*christos*"—gathering its force by way of "*logos*" and "*angelos*" among a plethora of other terms ("*soter*," "*kyrios*," "*basilea*," etc.)—leads to the theorizing of a quite specific human being named "Jesus" as ultimately hosting within his *physis* a reality coextensive with the universe itself. Principalities and powers will be found operating through and for him; thrones and dominions to have been created by him; the substance of things fashioned and yet to come bearing his stamp of artifice and articulation (Col 1:15–19)—indeed, this super-power *Logos* as the very Word, Reason, Structure,

Salvation, and Goal of the entire cosmos (Pelikan 1997, 57–70) in effect, "mounting" his humanity like a possession cult of galactic proportions, showing through his body as the Hologram of Holograms, and giving rise to the so-far unending battle rightly to parse the metaphysics and buttress the logic that plays out as the Trinitarian and Christological and Iconoclastic controversies like a tragi-comedic "theater of the theological absurd" such as we now see looking back.

This is no longer a mere man, nor even a superhero, but a gloss on the very nexus of reality across the infinity of possibilities that quantum physics and relativity theory, alike, stand equation-less before. Perhaps the claim is true. But certainly its confession is no longer "messianic" in the sense this writing has struggled to establish. Its shift to dimensions literally "unimaginable" likewise opens the door to its use in service of whatever politics one might favor. Its aggrandizement is, however, predictable alongside the historical trajectory of the project of settled agriculture reaching its apogee in cosmopolitan empire (and now neo-liberal globalization). Christological "inflation" (not to mention hubris) is imperial. It is simply fact that no other name has leveraged more conquest, enslavement, and plundering in human history. And quite patently, within the modern theater of genocidal takeover of the planet, and under the spiritual sponsorship of a kind of *Logos*-delirium, "Christ" has been made the Alpha-Male Author and Great Heavenly Apologist of the End Game of the epoch: the maniacal suppression of all of nature's wild sacrality; the gargantuan stripping-mining of its overt potencies and interior secrets; the burning up of its surface, boiling off of its waters, and browning out of its airs; and finally the rendering extinct of its living species—all as the quintessential "divine" Power of the Age of Humans.

What remains for a messianism faithful to its calling is to call for a return to things small and hopeful. Committed to reopen vision on the ground in relationship to local ecologies and their constitutive communities, it must push for a disaggregation of all the spiritual plunder assembled under "the Name." Even as it enters a common struggle—merely as one player among many—to return enslaved matter and reengineered plants and coerced animals and exploited humans to some semblance of sustainable interdependence and embraced symbiosis and reciprocated respect. But for that task, it has merely to turn to its own history and listen to the little traditions not yet entirely silenced under its own heavy foot. Even, and precisely (!), as the way ahead seems impossible.

CHAPTER 5

Talismanic Depiction: Messianic Repair and Folk Arts (Ethiopia)

Some two hundred years ago, an Ethiopian cleric wrote two words, and nothing else, on a talisman he had just made: "powerful medicine." (Mercier 1997, 40)

   Is your eye evil because I am good? (Mt 20: 15)

T hus far we have been tracing a rereading of messianism in terms of our current planetary eco-crisis, moving away from a focus on Jesus as "the Christ," toward a retrieval of the messianic as a Little Tradition memory of local practices auguring our deep past of foraging, hoe agriculture, and herding. This tracery began in an unlikely place of the contemporary—sketching out a brute art installation of inner city Detroit, redeploying postindustrial detritus as "do-it-yourself" ghetto-medicine—and then profiled an alternative figuring of the messianic in terms of rural social movement and rustic folk art. Subsequent chapters coursed through various biblical-tradition samples of such, epitomized in the Sabbath-messianism organized by Jesus in the Galilean hill country, before Paul and John adapted the outlaw movement to the cosmopolitan urbanism of the empire. In the last chapter, I underscored the result of this adaptation: a trans-local—indeed, cosmological—refiguring of the messianic as "Christology," simultaneously narrowing the focus of the movement to the individual man, Jesus, while inflating that *Ur*-Person into an increasingly abstract cipher for the "God-Man" (and in so doing, eclipsing Galilean peasant concern for the coercive extraction of human energy and natural potency and spiritual vitality that urban imperial life necessarily entails). And I glossed the newly coalescing (if not newly coined) language of "principalities and powers" as an index of the emerging political "hypertrophy"—a spirit-ghosted mass of enslaved life forms and reengineered materials ("elementals") organized now into the raging machinery of imperial expansion. I even went so far as to argue that the *Logos* itself partook of the aggrandizing character of these "powers." As such, the last chapter hints the first steps of rendering the movement of Jesus as an imperial force, in which its memories of other (more sustainable) ways of living were adapted to urban hierarchy and expansionist economy. It represents biblical messianism slipping towards the logic (*logos*) that will only become fully clear with Constantine.

A large part of the conviction animating this way of thinking is the idea (mentioned in chapter 2) that we are indeed a species "out of our ecological niche," attempting to live in a now globalized reality with a genetic predisposition still orienting us toward life lived in band societies (of about 150 members and highly localized involvements). Our grandiose cultural adaptations to the larger scale—including a universalizing Christology—so far only perpetuate the fatuous assumption that we can survive as the planet's first "docetic" species, desperately trying to insulate ourselves from a natural world ravaged by our relentless quest to reengineer the biosphere in service of a 5,000 year-old techno-urban project of prediction and control. But increasing numbers of people across the globe are beginning to break out of this agro-imperial delirium to once again listen to the local and to what has actually proven sustainable thus far in our history.[1] Awaking from sleepwalking has meant, among other efforts, a turn to what remains of older indigenous practice and ancient wisdoms, with all the risk entailed in projecting and romanticizing "the primitive."

Modern life itself, however, constitutes a monstrous romance of progress and growth whose interruption and questioning has scarcely begun.[2] In countering such, there is actually need for some measure of counter-romance. Here we offer a magnifying recognition of little traditions and memory fragments encoding an "other" vision of being human that might be capable of reinvigorating the desert of modern imagination like rain on a compost heap full of undigested seeds. But developing this perspective requires probing a domain occulted by a necessary surreption. Front and center here—as with our focus on the Jesus movement in chapter 3—will be vernacular life under imperial duress, in which the myths and practices of peasants, slaves, and indigenous peoples (engulfed by the state) will be lifted up as a kind of halfway house of memory, positioned between the older more sustainable lifeways we have foregrounded (forager, herder, subsistence cultivator) and the state-dominated imperial systems that have become their now globalized (and immensely destructive) successor.

The work of Yale historian James C. Scott has been ground-breaking in this regard, both in tracking the moral economy of the peasant, with its varied "arts of resistance" and arsenals of "weapons of the weak," and in outlining the tactics of state-formation and takeover of conquered populations in regimes of planning and management that seek to render their newly constructed "subjects" legible and accountable by way of imposed standards and policies. Scott's most recent work has detailed the way subsistence economies in difficult geographies—usually forested uplands and hill country—have regularly served as historic "peripheries of ungovernability." For populations struggling against (or fleeing) state-imposed taxation, conscription, and forced labor wherever monolithic systems have come into being, these "edge environments" have hosted experiments of return to the ways of living close to the land in the kinds of vernacularized cultures that have constituted most (some 99 percent) of our experience on the planet. It is this older "outback" orientation to shared risk and mutual aid and conserved resources that will provide the backdrop for the investigation to follow.

In his first major work on peasant morality, Scott offered a breakdown that will shape our focus here. He distinguishes peasant *rebellion*, as an enactment of anger taking place when taxation, rents, and debt have reduced resources below the minimum for subsistence, from what he calls more "tragic options" of *risk-aversion* and *redistribution*, where survival itself has not yet been compromised. This latter situation of quotidian exploitation effectively "creat[es] social dynamite" without detonating it, in which anger is conserved under the surface of compliance in the form of village practices maintaining a basic level of insurance through the abrasive forces of gossip and envy (Scott 1976, 4–5). Examples of little tradition messianisms giving expression to some of these more public energies will be covered in the e-book to come. For this chapter, however, I am proposing a third category that might be called folk *revisioning* or *remediation*—an effort aimed primarily at repair of invasive breaches in the fabric of social and psychic life, where the issue is not so much an expression of anger (whether open or covert), as a subaltern rearticulation of boundaries violated by supervening power.[3]

In one sense, this chapter is counterpoint to the previous one on the powers, even as it mirrors chapter 3's focus on peasant struggle. We seek to listen imaginatively at the margins of expansionist Christianity where largely illiterate populations performed a kind of "vernacular jujitsu"[4] on the imperial invasion of their territories and traditions, translating canonical Christologies into folk resistance and vernacular meaning. Where "principalities and powers" articulated an invasive urban order, we probe a subaltern code of rural exorcism.

But unlike the previous chapters' tracking of the footprints of the messianic inside the biblical tradition, from this point forward the work shifts towards tracing similarly messianic footprints, but now in surreptitious *resistance to* that biblical tradition as vernacular cultures and indigenous populations are forced to adapt to its imperial promulgation. And as before, the effort here can only be a matter of "sampling" (in a hip-hop sense), bringing forward snippets of the past for recirculation in the present under newly imagined possibilities. These will show up less as movement creativity than as resistance arts, articulating older wisdoms in fragmentary practices inside the imperial codes, conserving folk knowledge at the edges of canonical forms. Here the messianic will flicker as a strange intuition at the heart of ecstatic performance, briefly hinting another time and way, offering its sign as intrigue and disguise, but opening a question-mark inside the imperial design.

But part of the difficulty of this kind of investigation is the lack of evidence. Folk culture is largely oral and vernacular resistance by nature hidden. Thus, for instance, the on-going question in the Subaltern Studies Project of the real Subject of a collective action like a peasant rebellion for which there are not written archives detailing the efforts of historical actors but only abbreviated traces in elite annals (usually impugning the revolt and erasing its achievements) and "mythic relics" of such action carried forward in the ritual gestures of folk culture. And thus also, in this effort, our similar question about the real Subject of messianism. But one place we do have access to an enduring artifact of the encounter between Christian empire and folk culture is in the tradition of Ethiopian talismanic scrolls. Though perishable (the oldest extant scrolls only go back as far as the sixteenth century), scroll use and production, as a continuing tradition, reflects ancient practices and orientations. I argue it also encodes a continuing struggle. But deciphering that struggle, and what it means for Christology, will require patient exploration of the material we do have. As such, for this chapter, we hunker down to explore in some depth the tradition of Ethiopic talismanic healing at the southern (African) border of an expanding Byzantine Christianity, in order to elaborate the tactics of folk antagonism inside an otherwise irresistible structure of domination.[5] Ethiopia is described by one scholar as a virtual "museum of cultures," hosting some 70 different languages (and perhaps as many as 2000 dialects), and—in its long political and cultural isolation—preserving many ancient prereligious (prescriptural religion, that is) beliefs and practices that have disappeared from more developed societies (Chernetsov 2004, 41). The effort will serve as emblem of the way folk art can conserve what might be called messianic memory. And, in many ways, this examination will lend new appreciation for the kind of creativity highlighted at Heidelberg Street in Detroit with which we began this work.

Art as Medicine

In light of the previous chapter's focus on the way emergent empire rips up local ecologies (mining, farming, clear-cutting, water-shed interruption and diversion, etc.) and stockpiles the displaced materials as "objects," it is important to look in-depth at the way folk culture itself has used objects to concentrate spiritual force, deflect evil, create zones of freedom underneath a shield of protection, etc. These tactics are not simply responsive to imperial power, but go far back into the untracked footprints of our species' emergence on the planet. Bower birds certainly assemble natural objects, "symbolically," out of place, in order to attract prospective mates. And many species use various objects as tools. But the use of objects as devices of healing or protection may be peculiarly human. Can a stone be "messianic" (as we indicated in the Introduction)? Why anoint a piece of rock, set up as a mnemonic (Gen 28:18)? What is at stake spiritually (and ecologically) when we do art on nature?

This chapter engages a journey that cannot be conclusive. We inquire into a zone of practice and creativity from which we as writers and readers are almost necessarily barred by our already colonized perspective. We who live in modern societies are, after all, captive to texts. Written language looks out from behind eyes and within our minds. The canon dictates the allowable. And modern "common sense" too often closes the door of imagination before we can even fumble with the handle. Nonetheless, here we attempt to listen at length. And dream otherwise.

From the last chapter we can take the idea of things as "powers"—ripped from context like ore from a mountain, pulled apart or melted down, and then redeployed as technology—as fundamentally "imperial" to the degree our species conceives of itself as rightful lords over such matter and matters. Listening closely to indigenous commentary on "tools," we are confronted with a radically unthinkable thought from a modern point of view. Even rocks carry spirit and require recognition. "Taking" or "remaking"—whether soil (in farming), minerals (in mining), water for drinking, or oozing oil for anointing and sealing—demands ritual acknowledgment of beauty disrupted and debt incurred. Among the Navajo, even merely naming a phenomenon—mentioning "rain" when it is falling or "lightning" as it strikes—can be considered disrespectful and damaging. Honoring the powers of nature is a *prima facie* duty of living. Humans exist only within a dense network of exchange and reciprocal "metabolisms." Actively "feeding" what feeds us is *de rigeur* for indigenous cultures the world over (offering tobacco or beads or some other object reshaped by and carrying within itself a kernel of human labor and energy devoted to creating beauty). And that is true whether the taken "object" is animal, plant, or something less obviously "alive."

Even within our modern science we are finally beginning to recognize that Bacon's "torturing" of nature to "make her yield her secrets" has consequences. Disrupting the force field between and among "things" unlocks a charge of power—extremely large in relationship to the nucleus of hydrogen, but undoubtedly there and effective to one degree or another in relationship to any and everything else. Empire in this perspective is haunted by the writhing ghosts of disrupted or dishonored matter as much as by the silenced cries of caged and reengineered animals, dam-impeded salmon, burned-down jungle, or cut-up soil communities. The last chapter provisionally marked out these "living epiphenomena" or "spirited force fields" of our cities and metropoles, our colonized and reorganized country-sides, as the charged up theaters of "the Powers," within which evolving and struggling messianisms wrestled for room to live and breathe and bear "other-worldly" (forager, herder, hoe-agriculture) witness. And almost inevitably, they found themselves colonized and drafted into service against themselves.

In this chapter, we pursue, as best we are able, the counterpoint development among common people undergoing imperial reorganization, as they craft an "effective object" to rearticulate indigenous memory and natural power in service of their own need for healing. Of course, human production of art (symbolic representation of one kind or another) began long before settled agriculture and imperial aggrandizement. Cairn-building for the dead, cave-painting to initiate the living, textile-weaving that patterned mythological subjects into everyday dress, etc., were part and parcel of the indigenous vocation to live "beautifully." And some significant portion of that human-fabricated beauty was continually given back to the (natural) spirit-world from which human living was extracted in the first place. This indeed was art used as medicine to repair breaches in the fabric of the world, torn open simply in the process of surviving. It was fundamentally rooted in an indigenous grasp of a kind of primal social contract—an implicit or explicit covenant "cut" with nature itself—to honor the wild, give beauty back for beauty taken, assent to one's death at the appropriate time, and otherwise remain within certain ritually monitored limits. This was human living that would not pretend to commandeer all of the world's life-force and energy for itself alone, or even seek "to know" except within a respectful boundary. Even under the duress of empire, peasant-folk often enough (wittingly and unwittingly) keep alive memory of this other vision of being through inchoate modes of deploying artifacts as if they have powerful effects for healing or boundary-enforcing within the web of existence. Except that under empire, the ruptures grow exponentially and the powers promulgating them seem to exceed any convention of reciprocal containment. In consequence, what will exercise fascination in this chapter is a concern for a kind of homeopathy of the spirit-world—a treatment of evil by evil, figuring the demon against itself to neutralize its dominating effect, even if its dominating presence cannot be entirely evaded. And the question it will focus is one of folk creativity in the face of an invasive power that cannot easily be defeated with overt resistance.

Spirit-Battle

Empire typically conquers conclusively and rules ruthlessly, even though it clothes its forcefulness in various forms of mystification once a population is pacified. Peasant workers or indigenous cultures forced to undergo its regimen have little prospect of revolting successfully, but do not necessarily simply capitulate. Surviving empire's heavy hand on the inside of its rule often leads to covert modes of protest in occult idioms of communication. Among many other writers, critical theorists like psychiatrist Frantz Fanon (*Wretched of the Earth*), art historian Fritz Kramer (*The Red Fez: Art and Spirit Possession in Africa)* and anthropologist Janice Boddy (*Wombs and Alien Spirits: Women, Men, and the Zar Cult in northern Sudan)* have tracked the way spirit-battles in cultures under duress often enact displaced struggles with political domination. Coupled with Scott's idea of "hidden transcripts" (in *Domination and the Arts of Resistance: Hidden Transcripts*), the insights elaborated by these authors offer critical political perspective on the tradition of talismanic scroll healing that we examine in the following. As the research literature on possession cult performance and trance behavior is an entire library unto itself, here we can only barely hint at the possibilities.

But the hints are rich with irony and cunning. With the advent of colonialism in Africa, possession cults among various peoples (Swahili, Kamba, Sudanese, Zulu, Tonga, etc.) give evidence of the sudden apparition of new figures among their typical repertoire of "spirit-personas" who show up in community gatherings. Historically, many of these peoples "negotiated" difference encountered in contact with strangers (neighboring tribes) by way of possession, psychically internalizing and performatively mimicking certain traits, clothing styles, and modes of communicating of those they identified as "other." Among hunter-gatherer groups, the possession is largely without trance or loss of consciousness; but in more complex agricultural societies, the growing social stratification of the society at large is also reflected in a subordination of will in the moment of possession—a complete "takeover" (i.e., "loss") of agency (if not consciousness itself) for the duration of the episode (Kramer 1993, 90).[6] And interestingly, possession "enacts" relations with foreigners who are despised as well as admired: it is not merely a mode of "identification with an aggressor" (Kramer 1993, 99).

Not entirely surprisingly then, under repressive colonial regimes, the spirit-figures who possess tribal members begin to include a broad array of colonial officials and even Western cultural artifacts. In the Sudanese zar-cult, for instance, possessing spirits began to identify themselves as one or another Turkish conqueror or Pasha (Bashawat spirits), a British military commander ("Lord Cromer"), light-skinned Europeans (Khawajat) and Nazarenes or Christians (nasarin) (Boddy 1989, 291–294). Among the Kamba, Jesus himself was transmuted into the cult as a possessing figure named Kijesu—a strategy for resisting conversion that simply engulfed the invading missionary power in a form of "drag" (Kramer 1993, 100). Tonga Masabe-dancers might even be possessed by the technological accoutrements of the arriving Western powers such as railway trains, bicycles, pumps, motor boats, tractors, or even soap (Kramer 1993, 121–122; 135)! Exactly how to explain the resulting behavior remains a subject of sharp debate and not altogether clear etiology for scientific investigators (for instance, the ability to undergo experiences—like stabbing oneself with a knife or drinking copious amounts of alcohol—without adverse consequences that outside of trance would cause severe damage is notorious in possession cult studies).

But here the interest is political and social, a matter of dissent displaced into symbology and engaged covertly. Especially intriguing is Kramer's material on the Zulu, who experienced the 1920s incursion of industrialization as a particularly terrifying advent of alien forces—the spiritual equivalent of wave after wave of migrant labor that descended on mining areas of South Africa—showing up in the form of attacking spirits (raging hordes of "Sothos, Zulus, Indians, and whites"), unable to be domesticated within the traditional cult of ancestor possession (Kramer 1993, 125). In a very complex negotiation of power relations and spiritual symbolics, the traditional healers (*izangoma*) exorcised the invading troops of amorphous spirits and then "inoculated" their patients with other spirits known as *amabutho* ("soldiers") which they themselves controlled—designed to "prevent other attacks from within" (Kramer 1993, 126). These guardian spirits might speak through their hosts in English or other foreign tongues, or even the language of railway trains, taking up machine oil or the hair of a white man as a magic sign of foreign origin (i.e., as a kind of protective amulet[7] of otherness) (Kramer 1993, 126). This idea of meeting spiritual attack with countervailing spiritual forces that are under the control of the healer parallels what we see in the scroll tradition below.

Fanon's prescience further clarifies the import. Working in an Algeria reeling under French colonial suppression, the Martinique psychiatrist traced out a nuanced reading of the way political struggle was displaced into spirit-battle. Indigenous *djinn* (spirits) that in traditional society might either help or harm people, under colonial violence morphed into full blown demonic forces,[8] appearing as terrifying zombies bent on wholesale destruction (Fanon 1963, 56). The spirit-combat thus engaged opened a realm of ritual enactment capable of discharging pent up anger and revenge fantasies rooted in actual colonial relations, without the risk of direct physical confrontation with French military power (Horsley 2011, 117). At one level prophylactic and creative, spirit-possession also served to "occult" the material situation and siphon off the energies of revolt. But by shifting responsibility for oppression to an array of superhuman powers, Algerians simultaneously relieved themselves of culpability for their own captivity, and ironically preserved a sense of dignity and potency. While arguably capitulating to a degree of debilitating mystification (Fanon 1963, 56), the tactic nonetheless served a survival need. Such a propensity to "code-shift" energy from an intransigent politics to a pliable spirituality offers important perspective for what follows.

Folk Messianism Against Imperial Christology

In the last chapter on the powers, I underscored a remark by Wink to the effect that Greek belief in evil spirits "as a class" does not come into broad currency until the first or second century CE, whence also emerges, for the first time, widespread use of "engraved gems, amulets, and spells against demons, phantasms, and night fears" (Wink 1986, ft. 4, 174). I argued there that the language of "principalities and powers" concomitantly emerges as an innovative discourse seeking to grasp what might be glossed as a new configuration of spirit-charged "relations"— involving human substance and nonhuman matter alike—ripped out of ecological context in imperial conquest and "stacked up" in metropolitan economy and infrastructure all around the Roman-controlled Mediterranean. Not only do reinvigorated "class realities" exhibit new potency in the ramifying structures of imperial polity. But they also intrude inchoately in the symbolic combat enjoined by the resulting spiritual trauma (as we have already seen in the "Prince of Demons" charge leveled at Jesus). Exorcism itself becomes a layered affair, involving devil-kings and subject hordes. How the reality of an enlarging force-field of material and spiritual domination—indexed in the domains of popular demonology (principalities and powers discourse) and orthodox christology (the *logos* doctrine) alike—is negotiated on the ground by subject peoples is no mean question.

What gradually emerges as the Roman imperial economy metabolizes more and more tribal groups and folk cultures on its margins (and "repurposes" more and more natural "resources" and vernacular artifacts) is an intractable question of the spiritual status of material objects and their role in mediating relations between the human and spirit worlds. Once the outlaw messianism of the early church is fully coopted by Constantine and made the official religion of the empire (and rapidly embraced as the new vehicle for Roman aristocratic identity), a problem of genealogy quickly surfaces: how claim continuity with a community of martyrs now that the church has been "converted" to the politics of the executioners? As Robert Markus has argued, the answer was in annexing that outlaw tradition to imperial needs by remapping imperial time and space by way of the very "saints" (including "messiah" Jesus) Roman had itself previously martyred (Markus 1990, 77). The Roman calendar was reconfigured to emphasize dates and seasons anchored by such saints' "birthdays" (execution dates) and dramatic actions (like the confrontations of Holy Week). Likewise, metropolitan architecture and infrastructure was reordered to elevate martyrs' bones and artifacts as the new centers (in basilicas) of urban concourse and celebration. The entire landscape of empire took on a new aspect as "holy land," populated by pilgrimage sites wherein spirituality was negotiated sensually: sacred event remembered on foot; prayer aided by sight (of holy images); comfort mediated by touch (relics of bone fragments, cross slivers, garment tatters), etc. Time itself now disgorged a steady march of ever-recycling spiritual heroes, marking the passage of days with hagiography and vision, investing memory of these "ancestors" with subtle flavors of weather and seasons. And both East and West, the issue of miraculous effects associated with these imperially mobilized images and objects, places and times, brought vernacular concerns and folk customs irrepressibly into the deliberations of imperial officialdom and their Christian apologists.

What their deliberations reveal is the on-going reality of struggle between locally rooted land-based patterns of engaging sacrality and a universalizing and urbanizing Christianity, whose concerns for ortho-doxy are readily and recurrently drafted into imperial policy. Of course, sussing out such struggles is a matter of imaginatively reconstructing traces, seeking to catch glimpses of folk wiles and vernacular wisdom between the lines of official creeds and discipline. To what degree such subaltern creativity under imperial duress can be styled as "messianic" is an open question—largely a matter of how one reads. But that is also true for the reading of the folk movement of Jesus as messianic. As we have seen, Jesus recurrently mobilized peasant arts (parables, proverbs, exorcisms, trance-healing, etc.) and ancestral memory (stories of Abel, Abraham, Moses, Elijah, Daniel, etc.) to combat the devastating effects of Roman occupation in his time and place, and did so in a manner that resisted being read as "messianic" until well after the fact—and even then, in the gospel tracts, only in the context of sharp criticism of that label (Mk 8:27–33; 13:1–37). Here I offer such critical reading of a simi-lar enterprise at the African edge of Roman control, where the Ethiopian tradition of healing with magic scrolls gives fascinating evidence of just such a struggle of indigenous ways with imperial overlays.

As a first moment of characterization of that struggle, the issue might be glossed as one between material objects "christologized" in imperial theology as "iconic" and the mobilization of a quite different economy of the "spiritized" object in folk practices summed up as "talismanic," as we see in the following text.

In the Byzantine east, post-Constantine, difficulty in specifying the exact intersection of the human and the divine in "the Christ" issued in what became known as the iconoclastic controversy. This on-going Eastern Mediterranean elaboration of the Christological controversies that had been engaged by the broader "catholic" church in the councils of Ephesus (431 CE) and Chalcedon (451 CE), resulted in three more major Eastern councils and a seventeen-century-old Christological split

in the Orthodox world between Chalcedonian and Monophysite assertions. A major part of that continuing struggle focused on the status
of images in the divine economy and the imperial polity. The imperially based iconoclasm of the eighth and nineth centuries sought to
retrieve the dispersal of imagistic power back under imperial control.
Instead of common folk having household access to divine interaction
by way of their household icons (especially through the eyes of the icons
understood as "windows" on heaven), the iconoclast position asserted
the emperor as the sole "image of the Image" (of God), whose claim to
a "divine right" of imagistic monopoly demanded that popular icon-use
be abolished. In its outcome, however, the controversy maintained a
kind of "people's right" to unfettered use of icons as long as their actual
production and veneration was governed by theological canon, backed
by state sanction.

And in resolving the dispute, the iconodule ("icon venerating") party
clarified its theology. As Christ was the "image of God" incarnate (*"eikon
tou theou"* in the Greek of 2 Cor 4:4) and the Son was the image of the
Father, participating in the Father's divinity as Nicaea had affirmed, so
the iconic image also then participated in the original—that is, in Christ
and his divinity. The image was part of the inner life of the Trinity
and could thus appropriately be elaborated in the Godhead's "christological" relationship with the world, by way of image-reproduction on
the part of the church. The hypostatic union that supposedly obtained
between Son and Father was also posited between icon and Christ. The
icon harbored an essential or hypostatic presence of Christ—in virtue
of the Word's sanctification of matter in the Incarnation—analogous
to the imprint of a seal or coin stamp (Mercier 1997, 17). Theodore the
Studite would sum up this theology in the nineth century by pushing
icon-painters to inscribe their productions not with the legend "image
of Christ," but simply "Christ" (Mercier 1997, 17).

But underneath that theology we find a complex history of appropriation. Ethiopian art authority Jacques Mercier notes that the cult
of icons was actually modeled on a pagan precursor—the cult of the
portrait of the Byzantine emperor—and that the traffic of influence
went both directions (Mercier 1997, 17). Veneration directed to the
icon had previously been directed to the imperial image. Citing Peter
Brown, he offers further that the iconographic tradition emerged in
connection with the "cult of the saint as intercessor for the *community
of citizens*—as attached to the *city*, that is, rather than the religious
hierarchy" (Mercier 1997, 21, ft 8, emphasis JP). At this sociological
level, icon veneration amounts to an urban transmutation of a more

rural sensibility, adapting messianic roguishness and Galilean rough-
ness to the precincts of "pomp and glory" haloing metropolitan structure with displays of the emperor's visage. And in that appropriation,
peasant-leader Jesus ends up being engulfed in the emperor-cult, recast
as divine patron of the metropolitan *imperium*—at once "king of kings"
and *pantokrator* of the universe—the ultimate guarantee and warrant of
metropolitan imperial authority.

When we turn, however, to the way these Byzantine practices (both
theological and iconographic) are received in one of the more far-flung
theaters of imperial extension, this iconic revisioning gets interestingly
murky. What happens in the production and use of Ethiopian magic
scrolls in some ways partakes of a similar sensibility, focused on spiritual "seeing" in relationship to material representation, but on closer
inspection, reveals a quite radical difference of orientation. It hints of
folk appropriation of an imposed tradition that indeed takes up some of
the canonical subject-matter, but refocuses its symbols in service of an
older and other (more vernacular) practice of exorcism and healing. And
its import as a countertradition in the optics of spirituality is intensi-
fied by the degree to which Christianity privileged visual exchange with
divinity—"contemplation"—as the highest form of human activity.
Catching sight of its difference, however, requires developing a measure
of appreciation for some of the details of the scrolls and their traditional
use. And here a caution is apposite.

For us as moderns stepping back into this ancient world of
Christianizing peasant-cultures, the way is dark-lit and oneiric—even
though especially apropos, in so far as we now inhabit a social order itself
gone hyper in visual media and technologies of surveillance. It is perhaps
like Picasso in his work on *Les Demoiselles*, stumbling into the chimera
of dusty exorcism-masks in the Trocadéro Museum of Ethnography
and having to conceive a new vocation for his art (Perkinson 2007a,
366; 2010, 250–251). We enter a world of angels and demons, spirits
and principalities, seeking traces of the indigenous inside the imperial. In doing so, we must struggle to let a visual and tactile *gnosis* open
us towards a multi-leveled perceptual mode of engaging reality, doing
riddles on the linearity of empire, keeping awareness stretched out in
possibility despite the imperial "will-to-control."

Historical Background of the Scroll Tradition

That the tradition is old is patent. Christianity made its way to the
Solomon-haunted domain[9] of the Axumite dynasty of Ethiopia only

in the fourth century CE. It did so as part of a Byzantine initiative to open an outpost of trade on the Red Sea coast, drafting Axum into a geopolitical alliance against Persia in the interests of securing a pro-Byzantine terminus of the Silk Road. According to Mani (216–276 CE), the Axumite polity had emerged as one of the great world powers of the time, alongside Rome, Persia, and China. It had secured its regional position by enforcing vassalage on subordinate communities of (otherwise) self-sufficient peasants through regular royal "tours," during which the king personally collected tribute and supervised building projects (Kobishchanov 1978, 161). Conversion to Christianity began after a Byzantine merchant ship landed on the Ethiopian coast in 330 CE and one of its subsequently enslaved captives was drafted into the role of educator-counselor for the under-age king, Ezana. Frumentius proved himself a persuasive tutor and ultimately became known as the celebrated founder-saint of Ethiopian Orthodoxy. Axum quickly joined Byzantium as one of the first imperial regimes formally to embrace and promulgate Christianity as a state-religion. In the mix, the Ethiopian Church rapidly became suffused with the Axumite state, lending ecclesial sanction to the *risti* system of land holding, in which a triumvirate of noble, priest, and king enforced the typical peasant duties of land-tithe, taxes on livestock and trade, military conscription, billets and provisions for soldiers, unpaid corvée labor on nobles' land, and compulsory "gifts" for nobles on special occasions (Young 1997, 39–41).

Ethiopian Orthodox Christianity supplied ideological sanction for the state for much of the next seventeen centuries. The church itself was fairly rigidly divided between its wealthy top level officials, who collaborated with the secular nobility in dividing up the surplus product generated by peasant labor, and its local clergy and monks, who usually shared the latter's poverty. While blood-ties across class divisions, as well as the myth of common ancestry and well-defined free-holder rights, damped down impulses toward peasant revolt, the social divide was one typical of early-feudalism, giving rise to persistent friction between differing statuses and locales, social positions and ethnic groupings. Over the course of the next half-millennium, the Axumite kingdom waxed, and then, under pressure from Islam, waned until it was destroyed mid-tenth century by Queen Gudit and replaced by the house of Zagwe. After the thirteenth century overthrow of Agäw rule by the Solomonic family line and a period of religious and literary revival, dynastic succession grew more tumultuous. Taken together with the sixteenth century invasion by Muslims, followed by Oromo incursions, partial European colonization, and later nineteenth century reconquest by Christian rulers, this long history of religio-cultural absorption and political upheaval translated into a complex context of transmission for the tradition to be examined here. The creative art of scroll-production and -use only survived and navigated the process in a continually reiterated process of copying and adaptation.

Today scroll use is widespread and cuts across multiple ethnic and religious divides. Among its practitioners are contemporary populations of Christian semitic speakers (Tigrinya, Amharic) and Coushitic, Agäwinya, and Orominya fringe folk, as well as Jewish "Falasha," and Muslim *jabarti*. But in that practical popularity the scrolls also function as living palimpsests—hieroglyphs of an immensely complicated past. According to Ethiopian art authority Jacques Mercier, the talismanic tradition producing this "magic art" of healing likely traces its roots to pre-Christian indigenous practices (overlaid as they are with ancient Eastern Mediterranean influence and the imprint of centuries of Sabean and Axumite "civilization") (Mercier 1979, 7–8). For our purposes the task is not to trace the historical nuance, but to catch sight of a basic impulse. Mercier's work will supply the witness and commentary. Of particular import is his characterization of what happened to pagan populations and traditions as the Ethiopian state extended its rule in the region.[10] Although Christian missionaries followed in the steps of royal troops and promulgated a Byzantine literary model and ecclesial practice, it is clear that they did not entirely eclipse the preexisting religious traditions (Mercier 1997, 38).

Underneath the Orthodox exterior, indigenous cultural models have continued to influence peasant practice even as they continue to draw down censure as "demonic" from the Church. While certainly morphing into subaltern modes of partial conformance in order to survive, these older orientations remain vibrant under the surface. For instance, local spirits—grouped by species such as *zar, weqabi, awlya*, and *quran-nya*—might "officially" be represented as only "striking or curing" with the permission of whatever Christian, Muslim, or Jewish "high god" is deemed ascendant in a given area. In actual practice, however, folk-sensibility weighs in. They are more typically understood to give ground only when commanded by an indigenized version of the Archangel Michael. Likewise, place-spirits (*qolle*) remain widely extant. But they are attended in ancestor cults that adapt Christian saints to indigenous duty—such as the Gojjam province practice of sheep-sacrifice on Abuna Kiros' day, a local saint whose singular potency is now that of growing the grasses[11] essential to pastoral existence from his very corpse (Mercier 1997, 38). Even today, Mercier notes, these *qolle* are still called "masters of the country" as the topographical powers securing harvests and protecting against epidemics and war for their peasant supplicants. And most amazing for Mercier, in this compendium of practice, is the anti-fundamentalist role of various medicoreligious rites engaged *in situ*. Under sponsorship of one or another *qolle* and channeling various *zar*, these are gatherings that bring together Christians, Jews, and Muslims in a common therapy. At one such recounted by the author, members of these three groups came together on the banks of Lake Tana and sacrificed each in their own god's name. But immediately after, they began inducting one another into trance across group lines, ecstatically dancing a common celebration of a shared "Ethiopian" identity that transcended the boundaries considered absolute among the three monotheisms (Mercier 1997, 39). Here we engage a spiritual/cultural "infrastructure of indigeneity" that remains insurgent and resolute in the face of orthodox stricture and canonical censure—as we see below in the process of reading scrolls that encode such a memory and enact its sensibility.

Ethiopian Magic Scrolls

Abyssinian Christian tradition itself chalks up the advent of talismanic art to ancient "mystery"—either a divine revelation to Hebrew notables such as Abraham and Solomon, or a devilish disclosure to the sons of Seth as they interbred, disobediently, with Cain's issue. The secrets cached among these ancestral savants—in either version of the origin myth—bear the marks of a celestial savvy previously reserved, in Ethiopian biblical belief, to the angelic order. This celestial knowledge included writing with maledictory effect in red and black ink; the creation of "protective gear" for ritual use in summoning and deploying demonic power against itself; and employment of hidden Names of God and talismanic objects for exorcistic purposes (Mercier 1979, 8). These secret arts for doing concrete battle with hidden forces mark the place of fascination for my text—opening perspective on a subaltern zone of struggle between official (imperial) symbology and traditional (vernacular) resistance.

The scrolls themselves are remarkable productions of artistic beauty (Figures 5.1–5.4). Drawn on long strips of hide, they exhibit looming figures in child-like simplicity, or partial faces and disembodied eyes "caught" in a lattice-work of "imprisoning" geometric shapes. The color-scheme is vividly warm: soft amber washes for background allowing the stark forms and bold tones to command immediate attention. Primal colors predominate in the disproportionately large heads, as in the rest of the configurations (Figure 5.2). Fire-engine red faces host huge black eyeballs staring out of white irises, with noses and mouths only barely hinted (Mercier 1979, Plate 14, "A Demon," 66–67). The effect is trance-like, emphasizing sight over speech (Mercier 1979, Plate 11, "Solomon," 60–61). Looming over the top of diminutive bodies, with tiny hands raised in a gesture of surprise, we are drawn into something like a frontal "attack." Clothing patterns framed in simple outline host pulsating contrasts of shape and hue. Indigo-on-cinnabar sleeves or green-and-yellow-striped trunks might be stippled with rows of contrasting zig-zags or little arches bending into each other or multi-layered, checkered borders—creating an oscillation effect that enhances the immobile surveillance of the eyes. In yet other motifs (Figure 5.4), a bare face might be centrally bracketed in a checker-board of squares or a star-pattern (Mercier 1979, Plate 31, Susenyos and Werzelya, 100–101). Surrounding spaces may be filled in with a percussive geometry of crosses and dots and linear "knots," or a border of white ovals hosting black pupils, like a chorus of disembodied eyes. Here the impression is of dismemberment—but one that is still alive! In either case the simplicity of form accenting the power of color within a cadence of repeated curves or angles, has a riveting effect central to the scrolls peculiar use. Like the African "cubism" discovered by Picasso early in the twentieth century, the aesthetic evokes deep response through raw suggestion. The overwhelming impression is one of irresistible intimacy. The piercing gazes commanding imposing faces commanding tiny bodies open a vortex of close encounter at eye-level for the observer.

The striking geometrics and bold palette offer a basic spiritual grammar. The lexicon is vernacular. As indicated, eyes predominate—staring in hypnotic dilation from puffy faces encircled by snake bodies (understood as demons) (Mercier 1979, Plate 14, "A Demon," 66–67). Or they may glance suggestively "offstage" in more pleasantly contoured visages (significant of angels or saints). Or float as little rosette forms at the scrolls' edges (comprehended as either demons or angels). Recurrent graphics include eight-pointed star designs with a face "trapped" in their centers or lattice-like compositions with eyes, faces, and various geometrics "ghosting" the panels (grasped as an imprisoning net) (Mercier 1979, Plate 31, Susenyos and Werzelya, 100–101). Ethiopian-style crosses absent any crucified body (emblematic of triumph) are frequent. Borders might be populated with strands of knot-work (similarly signifying containment) or geometrically rendered wing-shapes (again associated with angels). Occasional elongated or misshapen animal

Figure 5.1 Plate 11, Solomon.

evocations (part of the demonic vocabulary) add a hint of the grotesque. And garment fringes or scroll edges often exhibit ancient Geez letters, terminating in little ringlets (comprehended as magical "characters" or powerful Names, whose circular ends are "leg fetters" for demons) (Mercier 1979, Plate 11, "Solomon," 60–61) (Figures 5.3 and 5.4).

Figure 5.2 Plate 14, A Demon.

Identifiable subject matter mixes a wide spectrum of Mediterranean motifs and biblical themes with more localized concerns. King Solomon looms especially large as an alter-Christ figure, in Ethiopian oral tradition, whose reputed magic words and famous "net of prayers" and demon-portraits subdued the blacksmith kings (arch-demons) who had imprisoned him, and forced them to carry his throne (as we discuss later

Figure 5.3 Plate 27, Solomon, Chief of the Wise.

in this chapter). But curiously, Alexander the Great also frequently puts in an appearance, as having ascended to Paradise on a bird of prey and as having magically closed a protective gate on the northern nations of Gog and Magog, whose *Anthropophagi* ("human-eating") hordes were thus sealed up in their own territories and prevented from invading.[12] Most common among saintly figures are demon-slayer vigilantes like

Figure 5.4   Plate 31, Susenyos and Werzelya.

George and Susenyos. Even more common are similarly "swash-buck-ling" angelic militants like Michael and Gabriel. Alone among prophetic representations is Daniel, holding the imperial lions at bay. And even the occasional Christ-figure may be portrayed with sword unsheathed. Less martial but no less colorful are the depictions of local "celeb" monks like volcano-dwelling Gäbrä Mänfäs Qeddus or Abba Samuel on his lion. And central, as both background chorus and foreground figures, are strikingly alluring protective angels and just as strikingly frightening Gorgon-headed demons, staring dread. The thematic of conflict—of a preoccupation with and summons to "combat"—is not minor.

Talismanic Practice

But what exactly is fighting with what cannot simply be read off the surface of the scrolls. It only becomes decipherable in attending to healing practice. In large measure, it is the use of these symbols—and not only the symbols themselves—that marks the "moment" and import of struggle between indigenous ways and imperial designs. And here it is only possible to imagine the issue on the basis of the present configuration of the struggle. Orthodox Church practice today tolerates the employment of the scrolls in rites of healing, but only to the degree they do not drift towards the kind of divination (*tenqwäla*) associated with idolatry. If made in correlation with astrological coordinates related to the patient's name (based on the numerical values of its letters), or deployed with emphasis on invoking the Names (*asmat*) of God rather than reading the gospels, reliance upon these artifacts becomes suspect. Church use focuses on the scrolls as religious in their effect (hosting written prayers assuring salvation) or representational in design (depicting canonical subject matter like Christ). Though priests may copy prayers and passages onto the scroll parchment, it is book authority and iconic emphasis that anchor the employment.

In traditional Ethiopian medicinal practice, on the other hand, scroll "magic" emerges as part of a two-pronged attack on illness, combining "root remedies" with exorcistic confrontation. Alongside the employment of plant and animal medicines to address the symptomatic side of an ailment, talismanic power is brought to bear on its spiritual "cause" (Mercier 1979, 14). This latter intervention is the specialty of traditional healers known as *dabtaras* whose role it is to prescribe, make, and ritually activate the talismanic scrolls. These un-ordained male or female "clerics" generally function at the edges of official church practice under some measure of priestly censure as (supposedly) impure and "two-faced" maladepts, but historically have been fairly widely embraced by aristocracy and populous alike (and even surreptitiously by church officials) as effective. Typically, the uncertain etiology of an affliction requires consultation with an appropriate specialist to divine its spiritual "root" ("evil eye," "the eye of a witch," "eye of shadow," etc.) and to decide the appropriate animal to offer up as a kind of "body-double" of the sufferer. The divination is usually carried out by the *dabtara* or by a *zar-tänqway* (possession-cult practitioner, consulting a particular *zar*-spirit or interacting with the *zar* of the patient). In *dabtara* and *zar-tänqway* practice, diagnosis and cure involve a double set of rites. Spirits deemed impure and malign are driven out, but *zar* spirits are more likely to be solicited for reconciliation with their client-"horse" (the patient whose body they regularly "mount"). If a scroll is called for in the healing process, it may be used both as a means of exorcism and as a means of protection from repeat-attacks after the expulsion. Once the cause and remedy have been determined, the requisite animal is sacrificed ritually and skinned by the *dabtara,* its blood used to draw off the attacking spirit, its body buried on the patient's land, and the patient washed with a mix of the blood and healing plants. The length of the hide to be used for a scroll is carefully measured out according to the height of the owner-patient ("to protect from head to toe") and then elaborately worked up into a strip of parchment, inscribed with the client's name and the requisite prayers and protective figures and designs, and given to the client as a kind of portable amulet. In this talismanic function, the scrolls might be worn rolled up in a little case or draped over a shoulder, hung from a wall nail over the bed, tucked under one's pillow, or stretched out, in full view, to be gazed upon and "breathed in."

But perhaps the scrolls' most dramatic and telling use is apotropaic. For someone suddenly feeling ill, the parchment may be unrolled and displayed—often evoking a violent fit, in which the patient shrieks, trembles, and struggles until the demon within, confronted with an image it cannot abide (often its own), promises to leave (Mercier 1979, 21–23). And here we begin to move into the zone where canonical church practice is made to harbor counter-practices that eventually I read as "messianic."

Crucial in interpreting this logic of evil "chased away by its own image" is the vernacular-tradition prayer known as the *Net of Solomon.* As the Ethiopian story goes, the king of biblical fame is beset with a dream of demon-blacksmiths who kidnap Solomon and bring him before their own Demon-King (Mercier 1979, 19). The latter is immediately struck with fear, asking what Solomon "has in his belly." Solomon replies that he is full of the "grace of God" protecting him from all spells, and begins chanting Words of Power against the immediately kindled anger of the Demon-King, who, in response, commands his servant-demons to kill the offender. In the battle that ensues, only the Demon-King survives Solomon's words, and, seized by the throat by the latter, is forced to divulge the secrets of all his spell-casting, evil-doing, and shape-shifting (appearing in animal forms like an ass, a horse, a leopard, etc.—thus the need to construct a spiritual "net," to catch the Demon-King on the move!) Of keen interest here is the concern for belly-power—frequently remarked in indigenous discourse as a locus of "shamanic" potency— and the strategy of "seizing and freezing" the source of evil to learn from it and use it against itself. And especially relevant is Mercier's note that "according to Judeo-Christian legend, Solomon controlled spirits by showing them portraits of them that he had drawn" (Mercier 1997, 19).

This belly-speech of powerful words, prayers of magic letters and Divine Names, and the apotropaic use of images that haunts the Ethiopian scroll tradition like a patron-spirit of performance, hint at ancient pedigree. It is unclear whether they arose indigenously on Ethiopian soil or were adopted from elsewhere. But they are attested in Mediterranean talismanic practice dating back to at least the early centuries of the first millennium CE. Among the schools of belief resistive to early Christianity's spread in the Eastern Mediterranean, were those that celebrated the talismanic innovations of Apollonius of Tyan, a neo-Pythagorean of the first century CE. Apollonius is reputed by later writers (in the sixth century CE) to have set up polished-stone storks in Byzantium to drive off real storks, and likewise a bronze scorpion in Antioch, as a barrier against real scorpions (perhaps echoing Moses' desert version). In addition, he is credited with having created a miraculous "mirror," inscribed with Names of God and with magic "characters" (letters ending in tiny circlets as in the scrolls mentioned above), capable of revealing "the invisible," earning him widespread fame East and West, and granting him, among Arab scribes in particular, the name "man of talismans" (Mercier 1997, 18). And in the prospect, the word *telesma* (talisman) takes on a new meaning by the fourth century CE as "effective object," conjoined to its already established significance as "tribute," "tax," and "ceremony of initiation" (Mercier 1997, 21, ft 10).

But even these sixth century attributions to Apollonius, mobilizing the "saving" image on behalf of city centers, only reflect something older, according to Mercier (Mercier 1997, 18–19). Greek magic papyri and rings and medals dating from the second to the sixth century CE, as well as the esoteric traditions of Rome and Islam alike, also invoke powerful Names of God and special "characters." Eighth-century Arab alchemist Jabir Ibn Hayyan—in disputing the magical interpretation of Apollonius' deeds— insists that his power actually derived from a form of nature-wisdom, demonstrating awareness of the properties of earthly phenomenon and the influence of stars on such theurgic works. And indeed, this archaic art of "manipulating the sympathies and antipathies of celestial intelligences and earthly bodies through talismans" already appears as part of Hellenic-era Platonizing Hermetisim, says Mercier. In that tradition, we discover stones engraved with "characters" or "figures" whose graphic elements seem to reproduce celestial configurations, grounding those planetary "gods" and constellations in the very image itself, giving cosmic purchase to the geomantic inscription and its talismanic use (Mercier 1997, 19). This imagistic linking of heaven and earth in a multi-storied ritual process is both ancient and common to indigenous practice across the globe.[13] In so-called "prehistory" it often "figured" observed star positions by way of aligned stone arrangements.

The apotropaic emphasis likewise hints archaic practice. Islamic legend has Alexander the Great similarly displaying images of sea monsters on his buildings at Alexandria when those creatures resisted his construction efforts, and early Christianity encourages apotropaic uses of the cross as a replication of Moses' assertion of his bronze serpent, raised up to heal (and ward off) snake bites. Both of these Mediterranean traditions gained currency in popular culture mythology, as did the story of the Gorgon-head of Greek fame, placed on buildings, fountains, and furniture to repel the evil eye. And indeed, it may be that the Moses-memory is the prototype of the tradition at large.

According to the Numbers text (Num 21:4–9) detailing such, the renegade ex-slaves, on the run from empire in the outback of Sinai, whose terrain for them is a frightening wilderness, are attacked by snakes (or literally, "seraphim," "burning ones"), sent by God because of the Israelites' complaints about having been brought out of Egypt to subsist only on "worthless" manna. When the people repent their lament and their longing to return to empire, Moses is told to fashion a serpent of bronze and put it on a pole for whoever has been bitten to gaze upon and be healed. Exactly how the apotropaic power of the image may have worked is unclear. Certainly it invokes a sensibility in which spiritual attack and actual encounter with wild animals are part and parcel of the same event: the animal is the form the spirit-power takes. The spirit-world and plant- and animal-worlds are not entirely distinct, and both attack and cure are grounded in actual floral and faunal embodiments. What is striking for our purposes is the way this prototype of healing by way of an animistic "shock-therapy" underwrites the primary talismanic potency licensed by the Ethiopian Church in elaborating its own semiotics of the cross. Ethiopian crosses almost never exhibit a crucified body (until later contact with European modernity) (Mercier 1979, Plate 11, "Solomon," 60–61). Rather, they are elaborated in an abstract geometric of interlaced metal-work, some of the strands of which may end up in serpent heads (Mercier 1997, 64, 69, 80). The Moses story itself is reworked into a vernacular legend called "The Thirteen Pains of the Cross" interpreting the iron matter of the image (replacing the bronze of the Hebrew text) as "Christ." But this is a Christ "substance" now annealed into a serpentine "form" of the Devil—an image thus exhibiting the two counter-poised "spiritual forces" (Christ and the Devil) superimposed in a single cipher! As an Ethiopian emblem of triumph, no historical reference is emphasized. Here rather is a talismanic takeover of a canonical subject, remixed as the geometrics of a potent confrontation. The cross is engulfed in indigenous signifying and apotropaic intent.

Folk Resistance

While none of this roll-call of precursors to Ethiopian talismanic practice delineates a clear line between soil-based spirituality and urban-imperial conscription of the same in service of a growing concentration of powers material and sacral, the response of Christian orthodoxy certainly marks a boundary.[14] Something about the talismanic deployment of objects—as opposed to the iconic—remained beyond the pale, too "pagan." It was ostracized as "magic" and despised as idolatry. As noted above, icons could be embraced in orthodox faith in so far as they irradiated heavenly influence in a one way vector of power—from divine potentate to humble believer, by way of images of the Christological mediator par excellence (the Christ) or various other saintly stand-ins.[15] And in turn, believers would venerate the icon in a "hypostatic" dynamic where honor rendered to the image passed back to the original. But a use of charged-up objects and images that concentrated stellar force and earthly (and in the case of stones, chthonic) potency on the point of need, and granted a measure of agency to the human actor, were too self-authorized and assertive for official tastes. Who it is that is being disenfranchised in such theological proscriptions is never really declared, but obvious. There is a primacy of state-dominated literacy (doctrinal and canonical)—rooted in the city, under the control of political elites and their scribal ("Christian") retainers—that renders rural environs and their indigenous practitioners increasingly suspect and outlaw as *pagani* (literally, those who are outside the ambit of both city and army as "nonmartial country-dwellers"). While the argument here is not that the resistances of such local populations (to state dominance and urban exploitation) are automatically to be read as messianic, there is certainly reason to explore their creativity as a kind of "proto-messianism," a set of practical orientations and locally embedded sensibilities that deserve at least empathic attention if not keen appreciation (or even "wonder"). Such is the offering here.

There is then a conjunction of claims. Wink's comment cited at the beginning of this chapter noted a new advent (in the Eastern Mediterranean under Greek influence) of the use of amulets and objects accompanying the *de novo* appearance of a "class reality" in spiritual hierarchies, probed and organized in the emergent discourse of "principalities and powers." Beholden to an indigenous worldview of the entire eco-sphere as charged with spiritual dynamism, I offered a reprise of the imperial metropolis of the early centuries of Christianity as an unstable and necessarily aggressive and violent "overplus" of material and spiritual forces, ripped from their eco-systemic integration in wild nature and stockpiled, out of "niche" and vertiginous with imbalance, for imperial aggrandizement. And our preview of the Ethiopian talismanic tradition—especially in its redeployment of iconic subject-matter for "off-color" apotropaic uses—arranges before our distant eyes a suggestive scenario of "illiterate" rebuttal of demonic invasion by way of scrolls mobilized as folk amulets. How this latter practice might be read as folk resistance will open the matter toward our concern for the messianic.

Of first import is the recognition that this language is one of artifacts—or more literally of a ritual object, charged up with organic "life," that is thrown back at a constraining or crippling spiritual force as a form of material rebuke. The "Word" here is a bit of cut up animal, inscribed with plant juice, painted with mineral, aligned with stars and conjuring their "gravity," anchored (by way of the dead animal's body buried on the client's land) below the soil. Its primary "work" is one of concentrating mythic discernment of an invisible spiritual "war" in a confrontation of gazes, living and represented.[16] It operates in a context of cooptation and suppression of indigenous practice by a Christian missionary orthodoxy that, over centuries and across multiple regime-changes, channeled one or another state takeover of local life. It invokes as its primary spiritual aids, royal figures like Solomon or Alexander the Great, angels like Michael or Gabriel, saints like George, or messiahs like Jesus. The scroll's sudden unveiling—in the presence of the client for whom it is prepared—"outs" the affliction, often enough provoking demonstrative confession of a possession perhaps otherwise hidden (accompanied by shrieks and trembling), demanding from the demonic intruder both a name and a promise of exit. Its mode of effectiveness is thus theurgic and theatrical, rather than contemplative and pacific. And it bears comparison to all manner of modern therapeutic initiatives, rediscovering the role of the body in healing the effects of PTSD-like trauma in past relationships (such as Eye Movement Desensitization and Reprograming [EMDR], Pesso Boyden System Psychomotor [PBSP], or various exposure techniques exploring abreactive forms of shaking, trembling, crying, etc).[17] The "folk genius" in play here, however, only comes clear in *dabtara* commentary on the operation. Mercier offers compelling testimony to a therapeutic savvy that is neither rude nor backward.

Throughout his two books, Mercier emphasizes that *dabtara* remarks on scroll use are patently *not* univocal. There are no "canonical" readings of the talismans (Mercier 1997, 57). Interpretation of the scroll's imagery and indeed of its deployment is multifarious and—from the point of view of a mentality looking for doctrinal coherence—resolutely elusive. Each scroll harbors multiple possibilities of identification and a layered synchrony of associations. A given face, staring out Gorgon-like in trance, may represent, for different healers at different times or for the same healer on different occasions: the demon possessing the client; the demon-king of that first demon (mobilized as an "intimate" of the *dabtara*, terrorizing the lesser spirit into submission and departure); or an angel dressed up as a demon, ambushing the latter by way of its own tactic of "possession" (i.e., a demon that is itself possessed by an angel in the "body" of the scroll) (Mercier 1979, 48, 66, 78, 86, 88). On one scroll (Figure 5.3), Solomon is depicted on the upside of the image as himself, but on the downside as Christ (Mercier 1979, Plate 27, "Solomon, Chief of Wise Men," 92–93). In that same scroll, four serpentine figures in an "X" configuration are spirits tamed into servitude by Solomon's ring, or the brazen serpents of Moses, or symbols of Christ's cross (Mercier 1979, 92).

When we turn from the figurative to the formal and geometric, the proliferation of possibilities is only further amplified. In the recurring graphic of an eight-pointed star, one cleric will see a "face of man;" another, the seal of Solomon or the Cross; yet another, a face in light or the four directions of the compass (Mercier 1997, 57). Gera, a *dabtara* consulted by Mercier in 1973, at one point in the interview indicated that a given face surrounded by four eyes could be "variously interpreted as showing God and the bearers of His throne; a human-faced cherub and his wings; the demon Werzelya with his soldiers; Satan imprisoned by angels; a lord of demons and his servants, bearers of ill fortune; [and]

Christ and His evangelists" (Mercier 1997, 57). Though meaning can (and is) multiplied in profusion, "none represents the truth of the talisman" (Mercier 1979, 31). Beyond all of this possibility, the priority, as Gera emphasized, was the form itself—in the particular talisman discussed, a drawing composed of zigzag lines whose effect was, nonetheless, apotropaic: a matter of the patient seeing and crying out, and the demon fleeing (Mercier 1997, 59). "The multiplicity of possible invocations" of a given talisman is finally in service of the magnification of its practical effect (Mercier 1979, 31).

Complementing this elusiveness of any dominant interpretation or party line in controlling the meanings organized and put in play by the scrolls, is the "shape-shifting" role of *dabtara*-practice itself within the social hierarchy. Notoriously duplicitous from a priestly point of view, these un-ordained "clerics" regularly participate in official church proceedings, singing sophisticated poems for the aristocracy on feast days and joining in banquets in honor of the saints. But on the other side of this public "diurnal" face, "lit by the light of the knowledge of God," is the face of the master of spells, paragon of ingenuousness, ruse, and deceitfulness, mobilizing secret wisdom on behalf of a popular clientele (Mercier 1997, 44). Mercier traces here a clear fault-line, running between canonical sanction and popular appropriation, correlating a difference in sociopolitical positioning with a difference in aesthetic emphasis and use (Mercier 1979, 27).

The more figurative focus in Ethiopian religious art is "connected with the centralization of political and religious authority" characteristic of royal dynasties like those of the Yaqob and Gondar empires of the fifteenth and eighteenth centuries, respectively. It reflects an iconic concern for imperial pomp and ecclesial canon, and works like "photography," telling a story and reflecting what was seen (Mercier 1979, 24, 27). The more esoteric geometric tradition,[18] on the other hand, reflects a deep concern for talismanic practice and is associated with local authority and *dabtara*-work among the people. It seeks to reveal something hidden—like a spirit on a person (i.e., making the invisible visible—"outing" the powers) (Mercier 1979, 25–26). The knotwork and designs of the scroll represent a talismanic "topography" of the everyday landscape of the sick person's life where demonic attack typically occurs (in the field or at the river, in moments of hallucination or dreaming, whether taking shape as bees, or flies, or birds, or stones, or flowers, or arms, or eyes, etc.),[19] investing those places and times and encounters with an opposition, an interdiction, a protection, and a cure (Mercier 1979, Plate 14, "A Demon," 66–67; 1997, 99).

Not surprisingly, this popular talismanic tradition is itself preserved in books (such as the *Net of Solomon* or *Prayers for the Undoing of Spells*) as well as on the scrolls. But whereas these "books of protection," as Mercier will say, "are made for the literate and conceived as reminders and exact copies of ancient models," the scrolls serve a value of extemporaneity. They are "made for the illiterate peasants and must be suited to their sensibility" (Mercier 1979, 31). This latter use exemplifies what Mercier calls an "unusual conjunction": the "wisdom of the learned" brought into service of the "needs of the people," wherein talismanic work takes on the character of a secretive and personalized medicine rather than merely an exhibitionist "art" (Mercier 1979, 33). Both scroll imagery and *dabtara* deployment are committedly improvisatory, adapting codified knowledge to a popular notion of affliction in a "surprising mixture of spontaneity and learning, terror and reassurance" (Mercier 1979, 33).

And it is all centered in the eye that acts. What is at stake is not representation—whether of the good gaze as we find in canonically sanctioned icon use, or of the "evil eye" of folk fame—but of what Mercier calls a modal eye (Mercier 1979, 65). This is the eye as the instrument that takes hold of the image and is caught in a mirror-like reciprocity.[20] It is forced to submit, captured in an exchange, momentarily obliterated—like the *persona* of those possessed for the period of possession. When apotropaic use of the scroll works, latent possession is activated and made to signify itself. The gaze is swirled in a vortex of pictorial shapes triggering perceptive and motor behaviors deepening towards trance, until the possessor spirit, "like a thief knowing it has been seen," halts its operation and flees.

Messianic Reading

How this art of healing intersects with our concern for messianism is a matter of reading. Certainly there is similarity with some of the healing activity of Jesus covered in chapter 3. But where Jesus' artistry was in the form of story (parables) to "capture" and defuse overwhelming power, here the medium is visual. Peasant need sideswipes official sanction for its own purposes. Iconic spirituality is adapted into service of a kind of "body-work" that seems to answer more to African traditional religion than to Byzantine orthodoxy (Mercier 1997, 115, 117; fn 10 above). Obviously scroll use is not immediately connected to an identifiable form of "movement" politics (exorcism here is not connected with public confrontation of the powers as it is in Jesus'

Temple-shakedown). But there is folk craft at work in siphoning off state power and canonical imprimatur into an alternative economy of health. In Scott's terms, talismanic combat certainly qualifies as a "weapon of the weak."

Its particular genius for our purpose lies in mobilizing "the awesome vision of the demon in a liberating way" (Mercier 1979, 30). The scrolls evince a broad-based strategy of confronting overwhelming power with countervailing powers,[21] "roped" into service of folk interest by renegade "clerics" using writing[22] and figuration tangentially to their imperially authorized intent. What shows up in the scroll-form itself are canonical subjects (Christ, angels, saints, etc.) and biblical quotes combined with demonic "Gorgon-heads," oral vignettes (of Solomon, Alexander, Susenyos, etc.) and traditional tropes of mysterious power (magic letters, divine names, geometric invocations, forbidden "scripture")—stirred together and redeployed as talismanic emblems. Known popularly as the tradition of *tebab* (or "Wisdom)," they organize a basic grammar of healing. In context, this is what Asian liberation theologian Aloysius Pieris might call a *folk soteriology*—a grass roots repertoire of symbols offering the messianic its essential vocabulary (Pieris 1987, 63, 90). Here indigenous memory meets imperial efficacy and refuses entirely to surrender—or rather resists precisely *in* surrendering, but on its own terms. The scroll becomes a kind of enacted palimpsest, a screen on which is played out colonial relations, where the rubber of imperial oppression meets the road of peasant life in local affairs. Tellingly, medieval Ethiopian emperor Zara-Yaqob banned from his palace every Name not found in canonical scripture; Ethiopian communists later did the same with the scrolls themselves (Mercier 1997, 41, 60, fn 4). The theme of conflict has already been underscored.

This is spirit-combat gone pictorial, but mediating an economy of gazes that is shamanistic rather than iconic. What is fascinating for our project of reading vernacular arts with a messianic eye is the way so many elements of indigenous practice end up concentrated in a "text." A thin strip of animal hide—divined for its particular mobilization of the appropriate spiritual power, inscribed with inks made from similarly sensed plant powers, anchored in earth through the animal burial and in the sky through astrologically determined timing and etching reflecting stellar influence—comports like a miniature axis mundi, but assembles those powers for a focus on the iris. The text is like a magnifying glass from the past, bringing natural "sacralities" ("powers") to a folk convergence, confronting the imperial eye with its own pretention. The preponderance of concern with faces and gazes opens a "black hole" of questions.[23]

Two uses predominate. As sketched above, swollen faces with vertiginous eyes stare down evil. And disembodied faces, orbited by disembodied eyes, gawk confounded in lattice-works of incarceration.[24]
Apparitions terrifying and "caught" figure large in the talismanic function. Read messianically, this appears as a form of folk judo. Obviously,
imperial power has its way, penetrating vernacular culture, reorganizing
practice under its surveillance of priests and scripture. And spirit-per-
ception matches the political structure. The world of invisible powers
begins to admit hierarchy, with demon-kings ruling lesser hordes. But
"nets" of prayers and letters, Names and figures, older powers of the
earth and sky mobilized in a geometry of memory, are here assembled
to capture the aggressive incursions of the newer "powers" on local culture and at least turn the symbol against itself. Solomon and Alexander
are "drafted" as champions of folk interest,[25] remembered respectively
as having tamed the demon-blacksmith-kings into carrying the throne
(an allusion to the domestication of "mineral power" for imperial technologies?) and as sealing off invasion by the hordes of Gog and Magog
(invasive alien forces from the north—historically for Alexander, the
Scythians, but spiritually for Ethiopian peasants, Mediterranean-
Byzantine or other dominating influences?). Transposed into the spir-
it-imaginary, they now corral principalities and powers for vernacular
concerns. They become, effectively, "people's messiahs"[26] of the spirit-
world.

One commentator remarks that here is an "other" meaning of "religion": the "tying back" signified by the Latin term *re-ligio* not so much
a matter of binding humans once again to the divine, but of tying divine
power back into service of human beings.[27] The imprisoning "nets" are
ingeniously constructed: color variations of the "bars" or "strands" are
irregularly positioned[28]—anticipating, according to *dabtara* comment,
the shape-shifting tactics of demonic savvy (indeed, of imperial hegemony we might add), thus keeping the power contained "in advance" of
its own moves.[29] Of course, for us as moderns, this "magical" use of col-
orfully inscribed matter does not compute as a form of counterpower.
It seems outrageously naïve and "benighted." But so frankly, do many
"Christian" practices seem to indigenous cultures ("You drink wine
and eat bread and think you are consuming a 2000 year old character
whose "body" is suddenly made present by uttering the right formulas
[prayers]?"). Color itself has power, as anthropologist Michael Taussig's
recent work, *What Color Is the Sacred?* makes remarkably clear. He dem-
onstrates rather conclusively that it is one of the disabilities of modern elite sensibility to be frightened by bold chromatics, unconsciously

terrified of being "swept away" into a nether world of ecstasy merely by an eye confronted with a bright palette. Whereas "uncivilized nations and children," "uneducated people" and "southern Europeans and [unrefined] women" just as clearly revel in such "color ecstasies" (Taussign 2009, 3–9). The "power" here is subtle but perceptible even to our urban sensibility. Modern color-phobia is not simply a fear of dark skin. At one level, it would seem "we" (Western educated elites) *do* understand this kind of magic—and seek to keep its powers contained by keeping our cultural semiotics drab. Just who is possessed by what is the deep question of this discussion.

But in any case here, the impulse is to fracture power against itself— not entirely evacuate its force, but reduce its overwhelming aspect back into a mode that is of use to common people. (Thinking Galilean gospels, we might say, "binding a strong man to plunder his goods," or even "casting out demons by the prince of demons"—manipulating Beelzebul against his own hordes.) *Dabtara* cunning requires a quick-step around canonical regulation and a continual ruse-making, keeping from becoming a clear target. What emerges is a resolve to keep univocal signification at bay.[30] The local universe is not simplistically to be divided into good and evil as imperial violence would mandate (seeking to concentrate all positive spiritual influence within a Christological monopoly of determination, consigning everything deemed negative to a domain of Satan, absolutely separate from Christ).[31]

Rather here, both practice and symbol, both natural-world and spirit-world, are maintained in a polymorphous synchrony of interchange, mimicking in culture the eco-diversity necessary to the flourishing of every form of life. And of course, paramount in this perception is the astonishing prolixity of imagistic healing. The apotropaic faces are spirit-flashes now grasped as *dabtara*-tamed demon-kings terrorizing lesser legates into flight, now as angels in demon-disguise, accomplishing the same terroristic goal, now as Christ, or angelic power or saint, peek-a-booing out from behind their others, overwhelming their foes. Shape-shifting is a shared ploy across the spectrum of spiritual struggle. What here is "Christological" and what "demonic," can only be decided after the fact and from the effect. Far too often in history, the imperial Christ has harbored demonic effects. It is simply patent that the opposite has also often been true.

The language itself of the tradition is evocative. Among its other meanings, *"telesma"* ("talisman") signifies "taxation." Within that connotation, exorcism by scroll exhibition emerges as a kind of people's "poaching" on imperial tribute-taking, shunted off into the realm of spirits, refusing entirely to capitulate to psychic aggression even as empire's physical apparatus of extraction has its way. It opens, we might say, a kind of micro-Jubilee in the economy of the "powers"—carrying as it does, a sense of a "finished payment" or "release"—the demon paid its due in the coin of the demonic. ("Render to Caesar..." we might remember Jesus saying during a public confrontation in which he brazenly "throws" the emperor's image back in the face of the empire's collaborators. "Whose likeness or "*eikon*" is this?" he had demanded before commanding that the imperial coin be "paid back." The denarius of Rome was both currency of conquest and cultic emblem—designating Caesar as *Divi Augusti Filius*, "son of the divine Augustus"—and thus also an "idol" or "demonic presence" in that context. While not quite itself an instance of tax resistance, in its sly double entendre for Jesus' followers and his enemies alike, the act signaled a clear repudiation of Caesar's legitimacy by implying that the entire apparatus of imperial tribute-taking should be sent packing to Rome. In effect, Jesus was saying, "Let it all go back where it came from! 'Exorcise' the coinage— and everything it represents—from the land!" And the hovering peasant crowd, very much awake to the double meaning, delighted in the bold-faced gibe; Mk 12:13–17; 37; Herzog 2000, 224–232).[32]

The scrolls "pirate" the imperial canon, redeploying empire's iconic subject-matter in an apotropaic art of shock-therapy, addressing invading "powers" with their own visage, seeking to inoculate peasant vulnerability against further "possession." They accomplish in the micro-politics of everyday struggle a piece of the agenda that messianism as a social movement orchestrates in the broader theater of public life: revealing illegitimate occupation of a body/space *as* illegitimate—and doing so to its very face![33] Through this inverted link with the enemy, the victim becomes, as Mercier says, "the prosecutor," tracking the tracker (Mercier 1997, 102). The shock of recognition breaks the thrall of domination: another part of the psyche, another way of being "human"—heretofore submerged in compliance—is awakened and summoned to the surface. And in negotiating such a delicate economy of visual battle—glances effecting curses or their cures—this folk art can hint much that might be of value for modern struggles against the visual oppressions of racisim[34] or the panoptical technologies of surveillance that increasingly render the entire planetary surface a prison.

It also proves suggestive for our grasp of the messianic. Previous chapters have challenged and reworked the historical imperial fascination with the idea of a God-Man (sic) engulfed within the emperor-cult as a warrant and guarantee of centralized power. If anointing is taken as marking out a special conjunction of powers "Human and Other," I want to push this "artful conjoining" back into its ancient *ecological* incarnation. Way before Anselm's classic feudal society formula, what was actually lived practically and celebrated mythically was a Herd-Human or Plant-Human "hypostatic union"[35] (the indigenous analogues are everywhere—Agave-Human communities in old Mexico, Corn-Human or Rice-Human cultures among the Tzutujil or Anishinaabeg peoples, Inuit-Whale and Sami-Reindeer complexes in the artic regions, Ayahuasca-Shipibo combos in the rainforest, etc.). It is high time we stop buying into imperial "disinformation" about such. Profoundly practical realizations of human-divine "incarnation" constituted the fabric of indigenous life all over the planet. And did so in ways far more true to what a sustainable "holiness" might actually entail than almost anything we have witnessed among "book" religions. This is what messianism gestures towards and what "Christology," if we dare even continue using that term, must now learn to confess. Rather than the abstraction of a "transcendental" God-Human reflective of the way settled agriculture begins to erect human hierarchy over the top of wild vitality, I propose older indigenous codifications of actually experienced and very concrete sacralities, mediating the possibility of human existence within local eco-systems by way of sustainable mutualisms with very particular plants and animals. In this latter comprehension, the spirit-world and the world of "other kind" overlap and interpenetrate organically.

The messianic then emerges here as a particular way of understanding a commensal hybridity, a structure of bridging "natural powers," rooted in the reality of metabolism and food, in which the mediators of the spirit-world are actually living "Others" who school the human community in an entire ensemble of spiritual and material relations constituting a local eco-community.[36] Life is maintained only by consuming an "other." So is healing. The scroll is the hide of a sacrificed life, given as a substitute body for the possessing spirit (Mercier 1997, 115). (The hide becomes a kind of symbolic skin, regenerating the body's outer limits that had been disrupted by an invading power.) And one day, one's own body shall also be food. But in coming close to that moment—in "facing" (giving face to) the terrifying Other occupying and "eating" oneself—time is bought. For the moment, empire is "caught" in an image, "netted' in a lattice-work of self-reference activated by mimesis and forced to confess and concede. (And perhaps for us as moderns, the counterquestion to ask is, "What would it take similarly to awaken *us* to see accurately the spiritual-political force 'possessing' our subjectivity and 'consuming' our substance?" Clearly we live by continuously "sacrificing" untold numbers of others—human and non-human—whose "hides" and "juices" and "faces" disappear without any recognition on our part. And we remain asleep and "occupied." Does the Jesus preached from Christian pulpits really function as a messianic "wake up call" for the average middle class American, beneficiary of the largest extraction-machine of all time, living a lifestyle that is plundering the planet through its market-driven demands for more and more and better and better, destroying its air and water and soil in a culture of wanton disposal of ever-proliferating waste, and giving thanks heaven-ward for the "right" to enjoy such "blessings" while paying for the largest military enterprise in history to make sure those blessings continue to "fall from heaven"? What apotropaic representation *would* be adequate to "activate" our possession and shock us into recognition and a struggle for real freedom?)

And within that understanding, the talismanic tradition offers a quite different spiritual intuition than the iconic: where the icon maintains a linearity of power, an offering of one's being to the all-penetrating gaze of God, anchored in an original "one-way" procession of divine potencies, the talisman appropriates power from power and does so by bringing other power (the "spiritual" power of plant and animal and star and earth "bodies") to bear on the containment of a power that has waxed over-bearing. Of particular relevance here is the Mercier note that the plant medicines used to inscribe the scrolls are only locally effective: each region must substitute its own local flora for the scroll's effectiveness (Mercier 1997, 60). He similarly questions whether the drawings themselves apply cross-culturally. At issue in this way of imagining the messianic are the mainstream Christian notions of transcendence and universality. "Omnipotence" is subtly challenged and put in its "place" (literally). In indigenous practices of a human-divine "incarnation," the divine is only available through a radically *local* form of reciprocity—a mutualism of plant or animal "teachers" or of an ensemble of mountain, riverine, desert, or jungle "communities"—that mediates a living relationship and a larger-than-death existence (everything passing into everything else by way of "feeding") *peculiar to that place*. The scrolls afford a visual grammar particular to the various Ethiopian communities that use them, who fill in the possibilities with their own local plant and animal and spiritual content. The messianic here is ecologically bound—not a "strip mall" version of salvation that everywhere trades in the same set of goods and actors.

And finally we would have to admit, the talismanic is certainly already a creature of the imperial, a necessary reaction to aggrandizing and invading Force. But it refuses entire capitulation. "Yes," it says, "one will be 'eaten' by empire. But not completely!" And that small resistance is crucial as keeping open a memory of something more mutualistic and organically beautiful. The icon is a window, the talisman a blockage of passage; the one is "see-through," the other a rebuff of sight. The latter incarnates an instinct for limitation: it respects the opacity of creatures to any totalizing project of knowing and controlling—even one that is divine. And in so doing, it keeps alive the profoundly wild interiority of *everything* as part of a great *Mysterium*. This is a messianism in which darkness (as apophasis, as unpredictability, as womb-likeness, indeed, as skin color, etc.) has equal claim to salvific power as light does. It asserts cocreatorship and cooperative agency as the fundamental impulse of reality, not the over-lordship and omnipotent agency of a monolithic "one."

In sum in this "magical" vision of darkly beautiful creatures: God *is* ecology! *Christos* is as *manifold* as the varied mix of plant-animal-water-soil-and-mineral communities springing up in their respective niches across the entire planet! *Ruah* is as subtle and multiple and *polymorphic* as the cross-penetration *and* differentiation of winds and breaths and ghostings peculiar to every micro-climate around! And the only possible encounter with any of it is in the only "form" in which it ever "presents": intensely local combinations of *all* of it!

CHAPTER 6

Insurgent Beat: Messianic Decay and Vision Quest

Like a messiah walking amongst us in rags, Detroit quietly delivers her gift of truth to all courageous enough to listen. (Kotting 2013, 3)
  And he was in the wilderness forty days, tested by Satan; and he was with the wild beasts; and the angels ministered to him. (Mk 1:13)

In a recent piece in *The Huffington Post,* Detroit writer Nancy Kotting jousts against the chorus of jibes waxing awful over conditions in Detroit. From the ruins—she teases out an apocalyptic image: Detroit rebirthing in the midst of its own detritus, Sphinx-like in its hard, broken witness, messiah-like in its truth. Her voice contends with—and partially reproduces—an entire discourse, now international in scope, on the need "to save Detroit" (a quick Google search will turn up umpteen articles on the prospect!). Much of the mainstream hoopla lifts up white energy and expertise as the Great Hope for the future—again! Black activists on the ground in the neighborhoods counter with a harsh and necessary reversal: it is rather Motown itself that may be able to "save" white people, if they dare open themselves to the possibility! Certainly, in my own "white boy in the hood" experience, it is the latter insistence that cuts closest to the truth (as explored in depth in earlier writings[1]). Messiah-complexes evoked by surface-appearances are a longstanding temptation to delusion for light-skinned folk, usually requiring some measure of inversion for their undoing.

But obviously given what I have already written here, I do not sit easy with the idea of a city as a deliverer. Detroit is today more conundrum than solution. The City of Cars stands as neither "damnation incarnate" nor "salvation-in-the-making," but as sign to be read. For the eye keen to see beauty in blight, however, the sight *is* messianic in its power. Architecture, says Kotting, is our self-image in stone and steel, at its height celebrating durability beyond our fragile lifespans, but sighing with ennui when crumbling (Kotting 2013, 4). In its architectural grammar, Detroit is a palimpsest of paradox, a ruin occupied with upstart life. Its edge is eloquent with blood, its heart a living rupture. Everywhere Motown's modernist monuments are emblems of the Powers nether-reach of idolatry—fossil fuel pride, now decaying in fecund release of molecules! In a nation still locked up in its own self-absorption as Great American Exception—self-appointed Tutor of those deemed Tardy to Modernity, Righteous Cop of the World Beat, Rainer of Drone Terror on Child Combatants and their Mothers if they resist our demand for oil—the effect is stark.

Most suburban whites think Detroit the poster-child of blight, murder-capital-figure of the perils, since 1973, of letting dark folk rule their own roost. But for young energy of all colors, the 139-square mile sprawl that is 1/3 empty is a matrix of possibility. The creative class flocks to this zone of black humus, eager to sample the brute vigor, giving imagination a jump-start into the figures and flowers of a Do-It-Yourself tomorrow. The vacancy teems with vitality, like a compost bin of germinating life. But the turf is also a zone of war as big money, filtered through the foundation-world of philanthropy, grabs land, imposes its grand designs of privatization by way of public deception, invoking old stereotypes, declaring crisis, naming surrogate managers, taking over educational and governmental structure, evacuating union power, foreclosing an entire strata of populace in service of securing bondholder and banking interest, and putting baton to back and handcuff to wrist of any activist citizenry, begging to differ. It is indeed a sign of the times: Arsenal of Democracy of World War II fame, now site of Disaster Capital plundering, a rumble of thunder for what is coming to a town near you in the near future. It is most proximately this love-hate crucible of struggle called the Car Capital that has most provoked my own query to ask questions on the grandest scale possible, reaching back behind "civilizational" hubris to the root-conundrum of sustainability. And it is this same emblem of urban apocalypse that has seasoned my sight to celebrate "the little"—whether in formal anthropological designation of traditions of indigenous and peasant, or in the creative effervescence of an art emerging from the cracks of concrete like so much shouting chicory, refusing the gray depression of decayed architecture in favor of a wind-dancing mimicry of the blue sky-spirit that is our real medium of being.

In a real sense the city is my "messiah-for-deciphering," a sacked core of Babel, slowly being reclaimed by sapling and root, berry and fox, yielding everywhere guerilla gardens of a people exiting Big Ag and Big Pharma, growing food and learning medicine from the ground itself. A "Messianism of Memory" of doing things otherwise and closer to the loam! Detroit is neither movement nor art, but hosts both with riotous and ribald cheek—a secret love, divined only by those with grit in their teeth and steel in their bones.

But even as I write, there is yet another sign ghosting this troubled horizon. The very day I began this chapter, itself began in the wee hours of the morning with the burning of one of the Heidelberg Project houses, in a fire apparently set by intention— in this case, retaliation for Guyton's interruption of a car theft near the project site (a crime now being dealt with both by police and a community concern for restorative justice). I go this very day of Cinco de Mayo 2013—two days after the blaze—to mourn its passing and sit in its ruins and read its runes (Figure 6.1).

And its water-soaked charcoal shall likewise read me. Indeed, an entire planet hangs in the balance between fire and water, arson and

Figure 6.1   Heidelberg Project burnt OJ house.

rain, globalized "warming" and wild flood of warning. Not merely the city, but the globe itself as now messianic sign, offering weather as its witness, sitting in judgment on a species in the dock, silently pondering whether we will heed.

This book began in Detroit, but quickly leapt to the deep past. Now six full chapters later, we again leap back to my present. A book of caesuras in time, proceeding by ruptures. I have offered as alternative to Christological certainties demanded by imperial polities, a messianism of ruptures, an upwelling of more grounded ways of being human, emerging from the breaks in relationship between our species and the rest of the ecosphere, like a mustard seed in invasive repair of the heavy-handed breaches of settled agriculture. Reading rhizomically into the tradition, seeking roots without unearthing them, guessing at the fecundity of orality beneath the surface of writing, we have scarcely begun.

The Little Tradition is everywhere extant, in nooks and crannies, underneath words, in smirks and gestures—as soundlessly potent as the Ethiopian peasant James Scott remembers bowing before his feudal lord come to collect the rent, and silently farting—the minutiae of opportunistic and alternative liturgies, tendered in subaltern economies under duress, on the run, auguring a messianic hope, rooted in a past not merely nostalgic, but wise (Scott 1990, v). We came forward as far as Ethiopia in the haze of empire, bordering Byzantine might and crafting magic exorcisms underneath its orthodoxy, exemplary of an artistry of the people, waiting a new politics in the outback of history. And now, suddenly, we are right back into the compost heap of the present, where in Detroit, decay is once again birthing green! In between these two emblems of African resilience—an entire unnamed library of creativity, occasionally hinted or traced in the wayward scribblings of whatever militant force happened to reign from the fourth century to the present, relegated here to an e-book footnote, like an after-thought. I succumb to the affliction of our age! I can only offer a writing itself riven by such a huge lacuna, a rupture of genre as well as substance, where the promised trek through an *ad hoc* gathering of Little Tradition samples must now be relegated as subaltern to my own story-line, making use of the very technologies of empire that I largely rue! But such is the demand of publishing. And in a way strange and ironic—and far from anticipated when I began—the displacement is, I suppose, appropriate to the subject. I only pray it can be embraced as syncopation.

This chapter improvises a threefold "Detroit" conversation of concerns for vision, art, and movement, riffing on each other like a jazz jam session. Central to all three will be the conviction that human beings are unhealthy to the degree they try to repress or otherwise domesticate their rootage in wildness. It is the wild that emerges as the true subject of messianic memory—the uncontainable beauty of a planet hosting an experiment in Life, careening across the ages in ever-innovated riffs of everything with everything else. Not a vision of harmony or peace—the wolf actually does *not* lie down with the lamb or the leopard with the kid (except in rare moments of mysterious cross-species care-taking that sometimes *are* part of the wildness of things)! This is a world articulated in metabolism—a fierce vitality, stabilizing its genetic drift and mutational novelty and ultimate entropy in eco-ensembles of diversity that do achieve a kind of "shalom" for periods of astonishing elegance.

Between counter-posed visions of our global future as "cyborgian" or "rewilded," I obviously push for more of the latter. Certainly, there is no going back to some romanticized hunter-gatherer symbiosis with local eco-systems. But there is profound need to listen to what is being plowed under, paved over, or otherwise disappeared on every side. My read of the "messianic witness" of the planet itself is that it is effectively drawing a line in the sand (or more fully a line in the dirt, through the water, and across the atmosphere) and saying: "Stop! You cannot reinvent the entirety of 'creation' in your own image." The diversified inter-dependence that makes up the biosphere exceeds human capacity to control. Imposing limits on our species' "Midas touch" that seeks to recast everything in service of our own aggrandizement is crucial to our own ability to survive long term. Letting the wild remain wild over large stretches of the globe is now the litmus test for whether we indeed honor some version of Divine Mystery as ultimate, or continue our more recent "grandiose idolatry" of our own species' brief epiphany on the planet.

Detroit happens to emerge at this hour as one tiny tinderbox of encounter with this question. Will little people, taking baby-steps to exit industrial pomposity, be allowed to reschool themselves in community experiments of "place-based" cooperation in a mixed "techno-wild" environment like Motown's sprawling expanse? Or will corporate insistence on subjecting everything—including urban decay—to the market, one more time prevail, reengineering the wild zone of innovation in the image of suburb antisepsis and mall culture? The hour is clearly one of having to decipher "apocalypse." Only here, rather than a "natural" warning like Katrina, "disaster" itself has been reinvented by finance capital, unleashed in a slow-motion tsunami of take-over by way of foreclosure, privatization, emergency management imposition, and PR delusion. As I write, the lords of debt are leveraging their bets with impunity. And small cadres of citizenry—a few pastors, various community activists, the odd "exiled" school board and city official, renegade artists, some resolute retirees and animated youngsters finding common cause—are organizing to push back. The battle seems at once futile and epochal. One more little tradition "messianism," up against the Powers! But the truth of growth that is sustainable on this blue marble of wonder is indeed "seed"—sowing and sleeping, and letting earth's wild ways produce its astonishing prolixity![2] As with organic life—so with resistance art and social movement!

The Quest for Vision

Without question, the planetary crises of this hour are dire. A quick listen to an alternative news source like *Democracy Now* confronts one with an almost unfathomable parade of bad news. From planetary eco-cide to rainforest genocide; from a profit-driven perpetual-motion war machine, seeking to blanket the planet in drone surveillance and threat, to a political gridlock entirely captive to a corporatist agenda; seemingly unresolvable slaughter in Syria; seemingly unstoppable plunder of shale and indigenous land in Alberta; melting glaciers the world over, acidifying oceans, coral disappearance, bee colony collapse, and rampant animal torture and mutilation as the condition of industrial eating; a situation of permanent homelessness for 1 billion people before mid-century; planetary heating of between 2–6 degrees, desiccation of land, salinization of water, carbonization of air, release of methane, the rendering of the very "spirit-atmosphere" we inhabit as our "planetary body" increasingly toxic to human lungs (think contemporary urban reality in China)—the litany is psychically lethal and messianically unmistakable—an overwhelmingly blunt "sign of the times." Detroit's agony in the mix is a mere blip on the screen of decimation. But it is the one I must be accountable to and try to read without delusion.

In D-Town today, the emergency character of daily life threatens any clairvoyant possibility of focus, swamping vision with immediacy. But it is especially with the question of vision that I find myself most preoccupied (perhaps because by vocation I have chosen to give my life to the struggle for discernment and have only a little training in things more practically relevant). How develop a "deciphering of the ultimate" that neither eclipses nor capitulates to the demand of the moment? My own involvement in the Motown gardening movement, and most immediately in helping organize resistance to emergency manager take-over, has me regularly engaged in the issue of aims. The chorus of voices weighing in is dissonant: those who pine to return Detroit to its former factory-town glory; those who likewise focus on "jobs," but emphasize finance and service professions; and those resolved to bend current infrastructure and skills toward high-tech conversion and green innovation. And of course, entirely obliterated in the mix are those remaining native peoples whose witness remains present (they were, after all, given "prominence" in greeting the Detroit-hosted 2010 US Social Forum with ritual blessing), but whose disparaged past and numbers mean they are not consulted when dealing with hard economic questions! Overwhelmed in this cacophony of deindustrializing urbanity, I seek orientation from other struggles. One group of urban farmers I work with takes its drive from their leader's 1960's Black Panther experience, seeking to create a "liberated zone" inside the inner city, growing its own food, developing its own educational initiative, ultimately taking on the task of policing its borders and handling its own conflicts through restorative justice techniques in the 'hood. More broadly across the city, the Zapatista Movement of "alter-globalization" fame looms large. Vandana Shiva's eco-feminist farming activism in India inspires attention. Winona LaDuke's celebration of Native American tenacity on Turtle Island hardens resolve. And cooperative economic experimentation like that associated with Mondragon, Spain over the last sixty years, or arising in Cleveland in the last decade, galvanizes practical interest.

But whatever we conceive as a goal requires deep stock-taking of whence have we come. Contemplating ends pushes us back to beginnings. Learning to nurture plants for food and medicine, and reorganize neighborhood communities in various cooperative ventures opens out toward a deeper set of questions about our very reason for being here in the first place—questions that predate and do not merely presume our colonial commitments to conquest and "dominion." What does it now mean to be a human being on this planet? And what is our responsibility to this place? Thinking through such in recent years has pushed me to revise, for discussion in some of my classes, what has sometimes been offered up as a watchword for action in community organizing (what might be called, I suppose, the "Activist's Fish Proverb"). A Detroit version, beholden to recent struggles, would go something like this:

> Give a person a fish, and you feed them for a day;
> Teach that person how to fish, and you feed them until the owner comes;

Organize that person with others to challenge the claim of private ownership in favor of a re-opening of "the commons," and you increase the number of people who can be fed from those waters.

Urban gardeners (some of whom are replicating Will Allen's *Growing Power* initiative in inner city Milwaukee, integrating a system of aquaponics in with their vegetable-growing, circulating the water through a plant-animal nitrogen cycle) might add:

Ask that person, "What feeds the fish?", and you begin to make it possible to feed the next generation.

Mindful of native cultures around the globe, I go one step further:

Initiate that person into the world of fish-spirits, and you open up the ultimate question of our planet: "What is feeding for? Why is life structured such that everything is both eating and being eaten? What in fact is the role of our species in the midst of a bio-diverse symbiosis of everything with everything else?"

The questions on the ground in present day Motown push toward the global issue of the hour: how live sustainably on a finite planet? What actually has worked in our species' evolutionary history? Thus this book's emphasis on messianism as retrospective, opening up inquiry rooted in the indigenous wisdoms of our deep past (hunter gatherer, subsistence agriculture and pastoral nomad) for the sake of our current crises. And in seeking "little tradition" perspective on such, it is then especially the quest for an orienting vision that most summons my attention here at the book's conclusion. Since this work has thus far concentrated its "drive to retrieve" on the formative materials of the Christian tradition, here we continue that focus for one more section. Mark's gloss on movement origins will provide a last gospel reflection.

Jesus' Vision Quest

For a messiah seeking clarity for his first century Palestinian vocation in a situation of imperial Roman occupation, the story-line is provocative. What we encounter at the outset of the career of the Galilean prophet is a time in the desert—"preparing a way in the wilderness," as Jesus' own prophet-teacher also reputedly practiced. Biblical history notes the outback sojourn as a time of testing. African American blues culture might describe the event as wrestling the Great Whisperer at the crossroads at midnight.[3] Native peoples the world over would score the effort as vision quest.

Our reading here is that agriculturally trained Jesus had to be reclaimed by a wildlands sensibility—an entire living, breathing, quivering preserve of untamed habitat: the spirit-world in its own physical body. He had grown up "colonial." Yes, as a carpenter in a peasant village, but one controlled by metropolitan policy with its policing codes and officials. The great need was to gain distance. With the disenfranchised peasant hoards, he takes himself off to the newly emergent messenger, who had appeared Elijah-like as a haunt of the *wadis* beyond the Jordan, wrapped in animal skins and living feral on locust swarms and honey (Mk 1:4–13). This is a social movement in motion and Jesus joins and learns. The central ritual is watershed immersion—a plunge into the most crucial "creature" granting survival in that region. John is the water's baptizer-guru, channeling the voice and lesson he had learned by long sojourn and listening. The wisdom, however, is from the land.

Long before, in another wildlands school of survival, precursor Moses had been taught by a bush about the desert he would navigate as a guide for refugee ex-slaves. His shrub-of-revelation may well have been "aphid bearing" and thus "manna yielding" (the "honeydew" known as *man* that Arab *bedouin* gather even today from desert foliage, as discussed in footnote 5 of chapter 2; Ex 16:31). His vision was the culmination of a forty-year lesson in wildlands living, anchored in an alternative economy of eating tendered by the plant life itself that would become the primal memorial of an antiimperial possibility: the social savvy of gathering manna and living by Sabbath-Jubilee.

Jesus' own spirit-tutor would be a dove—not only hint that Noah's ancient messenger of receding waters and calming weather[4] had returned "reincarnate," but a bird-apparition that many indigenous cultures would immediately embrace as shape-shifting shaman figure, coming to conduct initiation. And such is the scene that unfolds. The waters yield the initiate trance—seeing the heavens opened and hearing the Other World speak. The spirit incarnates (!) as dove (says Luke), mounts the torso, and drives the messiah-to-be into the wild. By lights native and knowledgeable, this is possession. Jesus is plunged into the desert sands of the spirit-world to seek the lost soul of his people. A trek to the wild side that is also a shamanic flight to face the Stealer of Souls, do battle, and return with healing and energy to the community. It is diagnosis as well as training, rupture as well as healing. Afterwards, he will embody both. He is possessed by the Wild.

He also discovers he is possessed by "civilization." A quote by Jim Corbett from his goatwalking days in Arizona's Sonoran desert illuminates the stakes. In discussing his own experience of a kind of reverse of the repression that Freud says is the price of civilization, Corbett emphasizes that going to the wild for an extended period merely to wander without plan or purpose is indeed profoundly revelatory. What is revealed is one's bedevilment. All the discontents of civilizational programming come roaring to the surface. "In the absence of socially supported identities we may discover ourselves possessed by naked demons who have the good manners to appear only in acceptable disguises when we are in polite society" (Corbett 1991, 10). It cannot be different with a fully human messiah.

Jesus goes feral in the outback to uncover his own possession by the "civilized" powers of his time, name their game of deception, wrestle their seduction, and work out a mode of mastery that turns their potency toward something more reciprocal and creative. The more extended description we get in Luke and Matthew hints the equation (Mt 4:1–11; Lk 4:1–13). The thrice–engaged temptations are clearly evocative of Israelite history—moments when the collective experiment faced its inner nemesis: the rebellion against eating desert fare while wandering Sinai (Dt 8:2–3; Ex 16:13–35), the accession by way of Saul and David to monarchical power among other Near Eastern powers (Sam 8:4–21; Howard-Brook 2010, 94–95, 102, 109–111, 124), the triumph of spectacle in Solomonic Temple building (Howard-Brook 2010, 94, 129–131, 142, 280–281). Historically, each crossroads highlighted the possibility of Israel choosing to remain a sign of living alternative to imperial values; each decision enacted a betrayal of the vision and an option for oppressive social structure; each outcome left pain and confusion on deposit in the national psyche. And Jesus must become clear on his own relationship with each of these possibilities—because they are alive inside of his own social formation and psychic memory. He is a creature of his people and of their history and must decipher his way among the ancestral voices that haunt his dreams and desires and fears. Only in risking engagement with the dream-side of life—the Other-World haints that ghost this one with oneiric murk arising from the wounded past of one's people—can vocation be crystalized. Spirit possession is not an option for Jesus—or really for any one of us. The only question is which spirit? Whose trance? What vision?

There is a Native American mask tradition that captures the struggle in an artifact. Among the Heiltsuk people of the Pacific Northwest, violation of community relations was sometimes remedied by putting the

perpetrator "out on the land" for an extended time to face the reality of
having done damage to community. The story emerges in recent times
of an alienated teenage offender, convicted of a violent robbery of other
community members, whose tribe appealed to the white Canadian judge
for an experimental "restorative justice" sentence that would allow them
to implement their own form of wilderness discipline (Brown and
Lucas). Given leave to try the native remedy, the tribe placed the
young man on an island for the better part of a year, ferrying food to
him and keeping tabs on his health, but otherwise insisting that he
remain "feral" until some- thing shifted within. It did and he was returned
to the community for a decade-long period of "testing," after which a large
community potlatch marked his official reembrace by the tribe.

In the course of the gathering to verify his return, his time on the land was
ritually reenacted by him and other tribal members. Among other seminal
moments was one where he felt spooked by a presence behind a tree, and
upon investigation, was suddenly startled by the apparition of a tiny
humanoid figure, peering at him from around the trunk. Terrified, he
suddenly recognized that the creature was his own interior self—hideous and
furtive— ghosting the moment with an uncanny confrontation. In the ritual
reenactment the young man wore a Heiltsuk transformation mask, whale-faced
with a beaked seagull on its head, which was fitfully opened, mid-course
in the ceremony, by means of strings pulled by the performer, revealing
a second human-faced mask within, understood as supernatural.

Here was enacted community valorization and embrace of the young
man's wildlands transformation, gradually worked into his flesh by the
inescapable encounter with his multiple possessions. Only on the inside
of the demonic appearance, could he discover his "real" face, even as
he could only resolve his transgression of community relations by fully
"facing" his own violence.

For the Galilean prophet-to be, the parallel is obviously not exact,
but not all that different either. The only remedy for civilizational delusion
is wildlands immersion, stripping back the façade of order, facing
appetite and need, listening to the inchoate speech of beginnings, gradually
uncovering within, an entire history and cosmology. Corbett notes
that in his own experience of such, the dream-side/waking-life boundary
became less certain, the line between past and present thinned out,
old wounds emerged as fresh injuries (Corbett 1991, 11). This is the
place of primal Presence—God, Devil, Self, Gift, Wound, Life, Death.
The Powers do not merely inhabit institutions, but creep into psyches.
Which voice is which; which desires move toward healing and which
begin one more lap around the familiar track of self-justification and

despair—this sorting is some of the most difficult work human beings ever do—*if* we do it at all. Jesus hunkers down in the lair of beasts and stays put until something happens. Then he wrestles; names; speaks back. His face becomes clear. Once through the crisis, the angels come. The Wild has had its way. He comes back into Galilee preaching...

The inference is unmistakable. The wildlands experience of possession has everything to do with Jesus' inaugural act. His ability to teach in Capernaum in such a way that the spiritual subtext is laid bare, the demons come forth, and the Powers hover close depends upon his desert work. The one is the precondition of the other. Only in clarifying his own inner war can he engage the politics without. Only in immersing himself in water, sand, wind, dew, night breeze, rain, sun, animal scent, plant touch, etc., can he clarify the war within. Wildlands testing has everything to do with demon possession. Only there is it possible to begin to unwind the aggrandizements of the Powers back into their natural theater of operation as part of the spirit-world. Wild-work is a matter of wrestling one's demon into a *daemonic* force, capable of serving an alternative aim than domination. Jesus cannot be equipped to deal with spirit possession in imperial society until he has been reimmersed in wildlands spirituality under the training of a "bird."

And just here, indigenous sense signals an immense difference in how spirit is discerned. Corbett asserts that native folk often "refer to spirit as the air we breathe"—"people living in spirit instead of spirits living in people" (Corbett 1991, 20). Many origin myths "remember" a time when animals once spoke to us. Now we only talk to ourselves. But that self-chatter enclosed within a single psyche has proven elusive. Perhaps, says Corbett, it is because what is speaking is not ourselves, but daemons—that is, angels—"messengers who shape primal presence into specific, personal points of view" (Corbett 1991, 20). The primacy here is shared meaning—the "rhythm of aspiration and inspiration manifest in poetry and prophecy, and other ways of expressing communion" (Corbett 1991, 20). Eco-theorist David Abram goes even further.

During his initial fieldwork as a young anthropologist, Abram remembers sitting outside his hut one morning, watching a woman of the compound go by with a tray of little rice cones set in palm-leaf "boats" (leaves sown together into a cup-shape). Curious, he asked what she was doing. "Making spirit-offerings," was her un-self-conscious reply. Later, Abram began to wonder what actually happened to the rice cones. Following her the next day, he discovered that she was placing them at each corner of the compound. Mid-day, he returned and found that each cone had its own line of ants, in single-file carrying the rice grains, one by one, back to their home mounds. It hit him in a flash. Western interpreters of indigenous communities had probably entirely misconstrued native ideas of the spirit-world according to Western ideas of transcendence. For his Indonesian host, "spirit-offerings" and "pest-control" comprised a single reality. What was given to the spiritual realm was exactly the food useful to animals and plants. They *were* the spirit-world! The latter was an integrated, ecological whole, made-up of human-kind and other-kind in reciprocal concourse and exchange (Abram 1996, 11–13).

Later he would elaborate the insight. In his *Becoming Animal,* Abram traces out an entire deep-ecology phenomenology of human imbeddedness "in" the planet. Working from an exploration of shadow as something virtually "alive," moving around bodies of all kinds until they are engulfed in the great umbra called night, he treats "depth," "mind" and" mood" as also finally realities that humans do not so much experience "within" themselves as move *through* like a field of force. They are far bigger than the individual body and are shared with the rest of living things, indeed with the "life" of rivers, mountains, plains, dirt, rock, and the sky itself. "Spirit," in this compass, is an animate creaturely texture of air that is our very medium of being—not something housed inside our psyches like a kernel of value, but the vast planetary envelope that moves in and out of everybody on the globe: an intimacy that has us in constant exchange with the interior of everything else. For native folks, Abram argues, spirits have all to do with the "myriad gusts, breezes, and winds that influence life in any locale"—from the blasts barreling down a winter river bed, to the gentle zephyrs of evening, or the lisping curlicues enveloping our nostrils in night-dreams (Abram 2010, 149). Earth is not something we live on, but *in.* And what we specifically live "in" is air-wind-spirit-breath! It is an ocean of shared exchange whose every nuance is a product literally of everything else that comprises the planet's surface. Spirit, indeed! Possession indeed!

And the virtuoso of this shared medium—the creature most physically attuned to its every least nuance and shift of character, its vortices of articulation around canyon and cliff, ocean and plain, carrying the scent messages of all material bodies—is the class of animals we call birds. Of course the Spirit came incarnate in an aviary body! It is this body that is exactly the expression of this medium. "Wingeds" are air given physical form. The Hebrew Genesis text had imagined the Spirit hovering mother-eagle-like over the primordial waters in the first moment of creation (Gen 1:2). Wind on Red Sea water (Ex 14:2) had opened a way for the "jail break" of slaves escaping Egypt—a deliverance immediately after spoken of as "being born on eagles' wings" (Ex 19:4). Raven-fed Elijah heard "prophecy" in the barest touch of mountain air on quickened skin. "Spirit" and "breath" and "wind" are distinctions words make out of a medium that is one.

Abram will expand the repertoire even further. Across the planet, day's beginning and day's end is heralded by a moving frontier of bird-song as the light proceeds over the land's surface and then in turn recedes before the march of night (Abram 2010, 183–185). For wood-lands peoples, the various bird species of their locale serve as the origi-nal messengers of the forest. Their five distinctive sounds—territorial song, brief "check-in" chirp while feeding, clamor of nestlings for food, mating call, and warning cry—signal at any given moment what is hap-pening for hundreds of yards around (Abram 2010, 193–194). For for-est wildlife—including acclimated humans—the sounds form a kind of second "body," a sonic texture of moment-by-moment awareness within which life unfolds at a leisurely pace, rests, or starts and takes flight. No surprise then that so many "scriptural" traditions end up imagining divine messengers as winged creatures whose primary responsibility is choral serenade of the divine. Behind our intuition of angelic presence is likely the real physical presence of birds. Inside the notion of spiritual messengers we are probably encountering dim memory of actual mes-sengers of native woodlands cultures.[5]

And it is thus that Jesus was led to the wild and tested and taught, by a bird, by the Spirit *as* bird, with the beasts, ministered to by angels. At least such is one way of reading the text. Not enough for Jesus to prepare by reading *torah* and assimilating the *nabiim* (the prophets). The real school-house of vision required immersion in spirit as wild and multiple—encountered in water, as bird, among other animals, through rock, and sand, and sun, and night, and wind. What is here angelic and what faunal and floral and what demonic is not something that can be entirely differentiated though it must be wrestled and discerned. It is one world—the spirit-world. And it is manifest only through bodies.

The Quest in the City

Again, a leap!—this time, into a wildness closer to home. Taking a cue from the vision quest just explored, how move toward the requisite train-ing when one's surround is city? For me, in Detroit, the demand is dou-ble—responding to the political urgency of the hour while continuing to test my understanding by a deep reading of our species' history. I find I now inhabit a split personality—half of me schooled in an alternative way of being through immersion in the culture and desperation of an urban 'hood over more than two decades (as I have elsewhere written about[6]); the other half summoned by a need to recover more reciprocal relationship with a local ecosystem as a response to our civilizational crises (as outlined earlier and in previous chapters). Both entail a baptism in alternative rhythm that encodes a wild encounter. Certainly my own ventures into the outback by way of camping as a child, or through brief training in survival skills in the Michigan woods a number of years ago, or more recently in an on-going course on indigenous living (taught by Martín Prechtel) in New Mexico, have given me a tiny taste of the kind of recoding of the senses a wildland's pedagogy might entail. The course on indigeneity in particular—taught by a half-white, half-Huron/Cree teacher, investigating indigenous patterns of living that were "native" to Indo-European tradition (albeit, long buried back in the past)—has deepened my appreciation for the depth of the "deprogramming" and reschooling that would be necessary really to begin to exit from empire's ways and pathologies. But it is precisely that rigor that has also pushed me toward learning to value and conserve what remnants of wild memory, or indigenous ferocity, or ancestral beauty, yet remain alive even in modern culture. And indeed, it is that search for what retains a charge of untamed vitality—even inside older imperial traditions—that has anchored my culling of little tradition messianisms in what I have thus far written here. Organizing people in the street to protest on the various battles fronts of neo-liberal imperial conquest—in struggles as different and similar as Occupy and the Arab Spring, Greece yesterday and Turkey now—is necessary and potent in this hour of globalized plundering. But taking care to see and love what continues of an older ferocity, rooted in a clear-sighted embrace of the teaching and example of kindred life forms in this common planetary venture of survival, is a necessary discipline for orienting our action toward sustainability. Ultimately, there is no substitute for schooling in a wildland's pedagogy.

Strangely, however, it was my *inner city* immersion that began such a process for me. One of the quotes of Corbett (mentioned earlier) gets at the connection, when he notes the kind of "communion of spirit" that daemonic encounter, loosed by wildland's work, might engender (Corbett 1991, 20). Alternative rhythms of poetry and prophecy come to the fore. The plunge is into a communicative world of living spirits inhabiting living bodies, giving expression to energies and meanings different from one's own "civilized" programming. But such was precisely my own experience of living for two decades in a decimated east side Detroit neighborhood.

Deindustrializing centers of urban organization are hot zones of breakdown. Things cease to be entirely subject to managerial order and maintenance and are dissembled and redeployed by agents as diverse as rain and wind, grass and weeds, mold and rust, fire and ice, impoverished humans and opportunistic animals. Technocrats and corporate bureaucrats abandon the premises; capital flees "until a more opportune time" (cf. Lk 4:13). What can't leave, adapts for survival. A certain "rewilding" asserts itself. Coerced "coalitions" of natural materials begin to fall apart or are pulled apart for other purposes. Plumbing is pillaged for sale as scrap and recycled use in other projects.[7] Lumber gradually becomes compost and births trees. Abandoned factory sites rapidly disintegrate into more diversified "family" dwellings—housing homeless humans, nomadic seedlings, and teeming multitudes of "four-leggeds," "wingeds," and crawling things. What appears to human eyes as "decay" is actually reincarnation under a wild ethic of ferocious vitality. It is impossible to dwell in such an environment for any length of time and remain entirely "domesticated" and "civilized."

What happened for me in Motown's urban crucible was a furious rearrangement of sensibility, learning a new delight in a wild art of syncopation, giving communicative texture to fierce feeling and valuing the feeling for its own sake, as well as for the energies for change it could unleash. Anger at injustice became a potent weapon for inspiration. My old mode of speaking had to give way to a new velocity, capable of piercing silence with serrated verbiage, freeing up wonder and militancy. Either that—or misspeak! This slow motion "baptism" in urban codes of animation likewise meant opening out my psychic interior to new currents of passion—really, becoming a body adequate to the energies of both entropy and creativity that were being unlocked in the urban ecology all around me. The wild was being "jubilated" from human ordering in forms too manifold to list. Breakdown birthed vision like a cauldron bubbling up fat from meat. It "cooked" me as well.

And in just such a perspective, it is possible also to recognize hip-hop culture writ large as a little tradition memorialization of the urban wild. Its contemporary birth in the South Bronx in the 1970s was certainly a mode of making core city "wilderness" yield beauty in spite of itself.[8] While ceding much of its raw brilliance to corporate poaching and suburban repackaging (as an insipidly capitalist message of "booty, bling and bullets") from the mid-1980s forward, in underground theaters, it has remained insurgent. There is little question that the chosen idiom of young inspiration in Motown in recent decades has been a "word up." Postindustrial blight has required spit lyrics and spinning bodies for its adequate signification. Much of the Motown move to Do-It-Yourself living is fueled by a hip-hop beat. Boombox rhythm has crafted ruin into revisioning, shooting up urgency like a drug of animation, creating entire posses of youth activists remaking Detroit neighborhoods under a tag, full of growing seed, taking over buildings for new purposes. But exploring its own off-timed angle on messianic hope requires writing in its particular vein of knowing. The cadence of this section will thus answer to a beat that cannot be heard except underneath the surface of the writing.

Hip-hop at root is ruins art. Saying such immediately places on the table the question of decay. Civilization in some ways can be construed as an effort to avoid demise, to use technology to fabricate a world of control whose ultimate aim would seem to be sidestepping death. Certainly many of our species' efforts over the entire career of urbanized organization have been to deploy machinery as a bulwark against decimation. In effect, the project has been one of reengineering "nature" as an instrumentality in service of buffering those in power from having to face the task of laboring for food or shelter (or now for the thousands of other technological "armatures" deemed necessary to a "humane" lifestyle). The very creation of elite social classes implies, as well, articulating social structure such that commoners, peasants, workers, migrants, etc. do the work of interacting with the rest of the natural world for the sake of elite leisure and comfort. Hegel, of course, traced in the early 1800s the ironic result—slaves actually "producing," through the practical skills attained in work, their own "independence," while the masters pontificate themselves as "lords" of the domain, but in fact, slide into ever greater dependence upon slave know-how and resourcefulness. As already discussed briefly in chapter 4, modern civilization emerges as an ever-more-precarious projection of our own species' lifeworld cantilevered out over the rest of a biosphere reduced to the role of energy-slaves[9] for that very project. The more civilized we become, the more captive we become to our own techno-constructs, doing the work of "adaptation" for us, reengineering the rest of wild nature into machinery we can manipulate for comfort and entertainment, conforming the biosphere to our image.

But if the energy should ever fail—"woe be!" even to the comfortable denizens of the race (the lower classes and indigenous peoples are already experiencing such "woe" in being "eaten alive" by the corporate juggernaut). Few of us could survive "on the land." At one profound level, the crises today are articulating themselves into a harsh demand that we go back to square one, and relearn the lessons of finitude: life on the planet is one huge, on-going round of recycling. Recycling is not something a few "green-minded" folk practice. It is what we *are*. And integral to the process is decay. Soil itself, from whence all of our food and living, is ultimately a function of composting life—the continuous breakdown of animal and plant bodies, earth and rock, air and sun, rain and gas, combining under tutelage of fungi and bacteria into the matter that mothers everything breathing. In many indigenous cultures, decay is the primal goddess of the cosmos, the one from whose body all things come! The breakdown of bodies by way of compost and metabolism *is* life. It is what our own human bodies are doing moment by moment. Would that our philosophies caught up with the fact!

But in fact, indigenous philosophies are built upon such recognition. And hip-hop, prone as it is to cooptation, can nonetheless be read as an "underground" sign of the same: the hidden power of ruin—given a living shrine in body-rhyme and sample—to offer a new mytheme in the mix. Decay is a womb. Tended with love and respect, it can birth. Like Tyree Guyton's projection of an entire block of blight as a wild statement of insight, organizing garbage into bright puns and prophecy— the culture of up-rock, scratch-riff, and graffo-bomb-on-building-side likewise slaps the eye and mind with a Message! It is the tag on the American Dream, giving currency to the power of a nightmare to midwife life.

Hip-Hop as Vision Quest

In reading the culture this way, I am not so much concerned for its surface appearance as its depth sounding. Incarcerated in corporate glitz, the beat is made a slave of profit and gives game to a few young artists of color. That a 50 Cent would style his ethic as "Get Rich or Die Tryin' or a Jay Z name his empire as Roc-A-Fella, is no surprise, given the ghetto prospects otherwise. But in its origins and underneath its buy-off hip-hop *writ large* is a current drilling deep into the subtext of the country (and now a globe). Lyrics—even in joints that blow up big—often code multi-voiced social commentary. (Think the recent Kanye/Jay Z release "No Church in the Wild," riffing on a religion of desire and a night spent with girls in "all-leopard," but staged in the midst of an anarchic street face-off between riot police and hardcore protestors. Track the blog commentary wrestling with decipherment of the arrangement and the subtlety and riddle-like potency of the piece is apparent. This is clearly critique of both church and high-rollin' lifestyle—Big Piety and Big Capital! But it also is notoriously cryptic, contradictory, self-outing, and finally parabolic, granting no certainty of its thrust. "How do you read?" indeed!) But the power—and the Powers—are in the beat. For many youth, the romance of "the game" is their religion—a mistress fickle and addictive, whose failings cause despair, but whose eruptions of finesse and frankness still save. I know young bloods in both Detroit and Denver who confess without blinking, hip-hop is their salvation. But how that might be so, engages our discussion of "messianism."

What hip-hop opened, in South Bronx in the 70s and globally thereafter, is an aperture to the underworld. Breakdance moves that art critic Robert Farris Thompson describes as "body lightning" might be grasped as a kind of social conduit, tapping forbidden energies in the body politic (Thompson 1996, 211). Adolescence might be recast as a collective trance mounted by a chaos of unnamed spirits. This is hip-hop as *axis mundi!* Climbing its spiritual pole are the repressed "contents" of our age. What is being channeled? Certainly living defiance and vision—against the grain of official silence! But equally, elegy, as hip-hop scholar Michael Eric Dyson has made clear (Dyson 2001, 225–230). Hip-hop is notorious for its RIP libations. In its writhing eloquence—not only the known and lamented losses, like Tupac and Biggie, but all manner of anonymous haints and haunts and saints, wisping up from the streets like so much sewer steam: homeless bodies in back alleys and ungrieved elders in barely marked graves; incarcerated dreams from the streams of ghetto tears; savaged genius shot up with crack; stunted childhoods; beaten heads; "three-strikes" throw-aways, languishing in our prison-industrial dungeons (yielding leverage to ALEC and profits to shareholders); foreclosed mammas; drop-out bangers; deceased fathers, missing diabetic toes and limbs; ex-GIs, nodding in shelters; the whole brood of dispossessed wanna bes, bombarded with visions of Lamborghinis and Gucci, but locked out of the Dream, locked into our varied underworlds of living and dead never heard from in our White Houses or public squares. But not only that! As Gordon's *Ghostly Matters* so eloquently argues, we inhabit an entire landscape now of unfinished business and tightly kept secrets—a globalized underbelly of unprocessed losses, whose split bodies and spilled blood, like Abel's, whisper from the ground. These "unfaced ones" climb the spines of all of us now, unwanted, demanding the grief never yet given—a backlog of mourning and recognition as large the national (or global) deficit. It is no wonder that the country whose power in the last half century has accumulated the largest register of "collateral damage" also now leads the planet in addiction. Were we in the US not to drown our consciousness in beer and blunts, TV triviality and IPod frivolity, we might actually have to stop and look. We might peer in the mirror and discover (like the Haida teenager referenced earlier) someone else leering out through our eyes who has climbed our bones from a zone of deep fright, demanding a living tongue to wail with.

In this compass, hip-hop can function like vision quest. Embraced with discernment, it can make the taken-for-granted possession apparent. It channels more than it knows how to express. But for the first time ever, what is at stake in the spiritual mix is something greater than just our own species' experience. The ghosts of our time also enfold billions upon billions of uprooted "otherkind"[10]—all the dead ibis and elk, otter and mink, walrus and trout and condor, polar bear and tree borer, and elephant and bee and lynx, rain-forests and deciduous growth and habitat-in-general, damned rivers and decapitated mountains and dead mollusk kin from the oceans of our deep past whose unleashed energies now rampage the planet as reorganizing changes of climate, returning in the form of a Katrina or Sandy or melted glacier. Yes, even these otherkind communities may be supposed to have half-lives and zombie-forms! Einstein named the phenomenon in formula. Nothing ever leaves the universe: it just shifts shape. When we ricochet across the planet-scape in ever greater velocities of appetite for "stuff," ripping the earth-body to shreds in the name of the market and remaking the soils into technologies and cities, we should expect comeuppance. At least some indigenously informed churches have begun to frame the reality in ritual. In Zimbabwe since the 1990s, for instance, numerous African Independent Churches (Zion and Apostolic congregations in particular) have begun to comprehend their wanton clear-cutting practices as murder (Daneel 1994, 259–261). Dead trees are now named *ngozi*—alongside other ancestors unhappily dispatched by violence, whose unrequited rage is understood to revisit the living community with affliction. The pillaged trees are given a place in Eucharistic commemoration, as part of the body of the killed, but "undead," messiah. They are also offered regular propitiation in the form of replanted seedlings. Rereading the Christian tradition from within a still functioning memory of ancestral reciprocity with soil and water and plant, these "primitive" AICs are recovering in image and practice an old sense of mutual interdependence. Faced with forms of decimation never before suffered, they have adapted their categories. They give *mythic* expression to contemporary upheaval, by way of collective ritual. But this is also how hip-hop has functioned in relationship to the postmodern city.

What is at work in young bodies splattering bodacious signage across every vertical vacancy, krunking clubs with heavy bass, writhing flesh with impossible contortions of motion, is a kind of mythic comprehension. Yes, the "shout outs" are a party flavor. But the gesture and spin, the tag and braggadocio chop reality into a sign begging to be read. Tricia Rose (quoting Arthur Jaffey) discerns the flux of expression as a set of values convening a community (Rose 1994, 38–39). Up inside the pop and lock flexibility, the oscillating syllables and stuttering vocables, the scratch trebles and interruptions is a body-vocabulary. MC virtuosities of *flow, layering* and *rupture* identify a sonic commons that finds visual and kinesthetic repetition on walls and through muscles (Perkinson, 2013). The community it constitutes shares a basic grammar (Dyson 2001, 233–236, 243–246). In an epistemology of angularity, it makes percussion yield *gnosis* about ultimate matters (Spencer 1991, 10). Life, death, poverty, violence, gender and drug abuse, crime and prison time all receive regular treatment. The rhymes offered may be wise or juvenile. But the default logic is a matter of high amperage: hip-hop gatherings emerge as a "body electric composite" undulated by waves of feeling too dense for language. Amped up flesh and ramped up technologies carry the shared trance toward a climax of aggression. Whether the result goes political or subliminal, cathartic or stupid depends on the group and its consciousness. But the charge is primal.

On boil, I suggest, is the condition of adolescence in the chaos of contemporary globalization. But its struggle goes back to deep ancestry. Charles Long's sample of Rudolf Otto's famous formula opens the analysis toward the kind of wildness I have been underscoring (Long 1986, 116, 123, 178, 197). If indeed there is a "Mysterious Power"[11] at work in the planetary veins of life as Otto argues (his *Mysterium Tremendum et Fascinans*), its evolutionary root is both spiritual and natural. In the state of nature, this Power's deepest "allure" might be said to be the satisfaction of eating, its "terror," being eaten. In the wild, the *Fascinans* is the repose of peaceful grazing—the "power" of a delightful and unperturbed food gathering—when the predator is fully bellied and sleeping. The *Tremendum, on the other hand,* is all out flight before the bared tooth, when the predator is again hungry and on the prowl—for humans and other animals alike. Once humankind begins to "evolve" its social order (from hunting and being hunted to settled agriculture), however, this episodic natural Terror likewise shifts mode (at least for our species): now it looms as the lord come to collect dues, or the enemy lord sweeping forward in conquest. Social organization increasingly walls out the fear of natural predation; "being eaten" becomes a function of war machines and poverty and increases its scale and relentlessness. And once the predatory appetite goes global in modern colonial history, we can witness how native peoples "consumed" by the West around the globe are forced to deal with a "Maw" that is increasingly high-tech and insatiable, steel-toothed and (now) laser-eyed. According to Long, they are compelled to reinvent their lifeways as "religions of the oppressed," capable of leveraging survival in the face of an irresistible and inscrutable Awe-ful-ness, hovering ravenous and Ghost-like over the entire colonial enterprise. They have had to learn to survive *while* being "being eaten," even as those on the "up side" of the operation—today, in suburbs and board rooms, sports arenas and movie theaters, at the drone controls or among the Defense Department planners—"spectate" this *Tremendum* as either statistics or the "Sublime." Ensconced in protection (like Kant watching an avalanche from a distant inn), locked into technology and away from the blood, they ("we") enjoy broken flesh as voyeurism and triumph.

But within the "belly of the beast," in the urban bowels of empire, the veil separating predators and prey is quite thin. On the hard streets, there is little room for fiction about the make-up of social order. The experiences of *Fascinans* and *Tremendum* bleed into each other. Survival dictates a savage calculus. Yes, the urban version of "conquest" is self-destructive and no more worthy of celebration than imperial invasion of one of the planet's "elsewheres" (like Iraq). But the representation is more honest—both in everyday interaction and in artistic exploration. Within this compass, hip-hop in the underground emerges as a secular version of a religion of the oppressed. It grapples with the terror of break-down—of bodies and buildings, neighborhoods and entire cities—in a complex syntax of transfiguration. Like an indigenous religious tradition reinventing itself under colonial duress, hip-hop labors contradiction into beauty and crafts bricolage into virtuosity (Long 1986, 110, 139, 166–170). An urban "Power" (a streetwise "*Tremendum*") is made to yield vitality in spite of itself. The constant work with rupture—syncopated rhyme, scratched "iggities" on top of turntable fluidities, bubble italics cut by lightning strikes of color—is an artistic schoolhouse in social conflict. (Rose will tease its lesson: "*plan* on social rupture"; in fact, wrestle its jagged pressure into a mode of community pleasure as well as a means of protest! Rose, 39, 61.) It is no accident that Occupy and Arab Spring alike were driven by its hip-hop's staccato rhythms. Inside of the stylistic posturing appears something like a living palimpsest that can be discerned theologically. Recurrent encounters with displacement and recovery, violence and its over-coming, can be read as micro-experiences of "crucifixion" and "resurrection," stripped of creed or verse, recast as art. The energies of social break down are "conserved" and layered into muscle memory as a template for action. This is doctrine reduced to a body meme, flow and rupture sequenced like history, stamped into affective structure. Thompson will call its expression "corporeal cubism" (Thompson 1996, 219); I call it a weapon. Absent teaching and aim, of course, hip-hop only siphons off the pain into fantasy or narcissism. But its genius is that it does not prevaricate. It tells both sides of the story. And although mediated through state-of-the-art technology, it too operates as a "little tradition" opening of deep memory. It channels the unfed growl under imperial satiety.

It also channels the deep gene of pedigree.[12] Here is clear witness that the vein of memory opened courses all the way back to our earliest ancestry. Hip-hop has emerged in its brief epiphany on the planet as a kind of body-Esperanto—a global riff whose elements have been taken up by youth as distant from each other as Bolivia and Katmandu, Peru and Belgium, Korea in the East and Bahia in the South, Palestinian Intifada and Israeli occupiers, neo-Nazi supremacists in France and First Nations protestors in the States. The art lends itself readily to movement—of all kinds! That is both its bane and its claim to deeper notice. As a body language unmistakably "African" in its percussive eloquence, hip-hop taps something old in practice. Obviously recombinatory in effect, it spreads without losing its character.[13] Young flesh everywhere splices its body-antics into a cultural tectonics of remix—home traditions put on a flame, cooked up into a creole of beats and rhymes, miming "black" and channeling ghosts and realities of Guinea. This is now a globe going dark under the skin in its taste and vibration.

For the first time ever, there is a common honoring of our mother continent. Yes, supremacies of lightness remain potent across the planet—whitening creams are being marketed hard in Third World countries and Euro-heritage peoples still preside over global finances. Yes, hip-hop culture frequently reproduces multiple stereotypes about race and butt-stupid simplicities about economics. Anywhere in history that politics has grabbed up color to articulate its code, the resulting social hierarchy has featured light at the apex and black in the bottom, and too often the rap game has played right into the ignorance, hyping "getting over" as the ultimate value. But in hip-hop rhythm a recessive gene has also been summoned that is the ironic secret of every racist mania: Eve was African and birthed us all! Like charismatic spirituality suddenly resurfacing in black-led Azuza Street gatherings in turn-of-the-twentieth century LA, the cult of possession by percussion has climbed the spine of the new millennium. A spirit from way back is erupting with a vengeance. Both pentecostal Christianity and hip-hop enculturation could be said to channel a deep pulse of "Africa" in idiom and sensibility. They testify of a rhizome of ancestry. Beneath their surface peculiarities, they insist spirituality is a matter of animated bodies rather than orthodoxy and propriety. Read deeply, they defy the supremacies in which they find themselves embedded. That each in its own way has gone global gives witness to an unrealized fable. We came from the same family and carry a dream of a yet unrealized parable. Our past is the syncopated beat of black blood in heat. And our future could be the shared table of a Beloved Community—*if* we could give up the lie of a gate-able boundary and return to the nurture and pedagogy of local ecology in honor of the root from whence we grew! But if we continue to insist that the imperial trajectory of the last five millennia is proof of a certain kind of "civilizational progress"—resulting (now) in the supposed cultural ascendancy of a thing called "white skin" and the claimed religious superiority of a "Christianity" destined to dominate globally—then the future is dark indeed! I choose rather to augur the memory and seek its possibility. And in Detroit of today, the truth of both the lie and the community is reality. The ruins themselves are revealing the double layer: a pillaged city as the endgame of the practice of empire; and grassroots creativity as the "chicory sprout" of vitality "in spite of."

Detroit Vision

Detroit MC Invincible is a living emblem of what is springing up from the dark loam of Detroit's history of struggle. Transplant from Israel as a youngster, Ilana Weaver earned her chops in the Big Apple, wafted to the Car Capital after sampling the flavor, took in vision from Motown's preeminent activist elder (Grace Lee Boggs), sunk roots, hunkered down into the fruit of an earlier sowing, and now purses her game under the reign of rain and top soil. Recent lyrics have focused on recent conniving: in November, Detroit's City Council voted 5–4 to grant a multi-millionaire real estate mogul privatization rights to 1800 parcels of eastside turf to grow Christmas trees, make land scarce, and reconvene the middle class at the expense of the working poor. And this—against a 500-strong community hearing, heavily weighing-in otherwise with commentary both well-informed and trenchant! The three-year-long closed-door finagling finally trumped alternative plans for a community land trust run by current residents. Never mind that most of the community resistance was black and the entrepreneurial initiative white; the private-public collusion amounted to a land grab worthy of

Global South credentials. This was neo-liberalism in domestic garb. It has galvanized growing community self-organization, despite the losses. And Invincible has begun to warble about "scorched earth" orchards as the new theater of struggle, alongside her other typical subjects like foreclosure and emergency managers, charter take-overs of schools or corporate dollars pooled to elect agents to sell off city assets. Her new riff is the environment, lending clipped consonants and free-style intelligence to all those inner city "residents" who do not speak "human." Hip-hop here is beginning to channel the losses and resilience of an entire local ecology.

Detroit, at this hour on the global clock, is enigma, sign, beloved hope. It breaks hearts and summons heroes and villains (often enough occupying the same body!). On the horizon of our past, it stands as both ruin and rune. Like the Coliseum of Rome, bespeaking days of former might and glory, Detroit blight recalls the last great global fight over world-supremacy, offering its industrial muscle as an Arsenal, championing Democracy. Of course, on the ground, the city hosted something much less singular. In the 1940s, it was indeed the hope of the West against its own historical logic, which had taken shape a decade earlier in what Hegel would once have called the World-Geist on Horseback (now seated in motor car): Hitler, as the epitome of the supremacist delirium of European gene-stock in arrogating to itself an entire planet (in its varied colonial ventures). Detroit supplied the hard-metal jacket of European resistance to its own Demon in World War II. Trucks and tanks, engines and aircraft parts, produced across the nation, but anchored in know-how like Detroit's, eventually helped win the day for the Allies. And in the struggle, black labor, glad to flee Jim Crow terror and exploitation in the south, had settled into northern factory towns to lend sweat and grit to the effort (as well as contributing troops and blood on the fighting fronts). But subduing the Power abroad only sharpened its animus at home. After the victory, racial supremacy rearticulated its social potency by way of policy. Housing, especially, carried out the segregation thrust in northern states—much less visibly, but no less trenchantly than KKK-terror reigning in the south. Detroit quickly became the model of middle class (upwardly mobile) aspiration, hosting more private home ownership by the 1950s than any other metropolitan area in the country.

The city topped out its population in 1951 at around 1.8 million residents, who thereafter increasingly joined in white G.I. desire, returned from the war, to leave the urban core, terrified about formerly "pristine" neighborhoods now under threat of becoming black. White flight had begun especially after the war's end, leveraged by racist G.I. Bill and FHA practices, providing financial support for the nascent suburban movement beginning to sweep the country. Corporate decision-making likewise contributed to the exodus, seeking escape from black radicalism in the neighborhoods, unionization and its demands on the shop floor, and the physical constraints of plants not easily adaptable to the newest automation technologies in its plans for the future. In consequence, over the course of a half century, the Motor City would find itself ringed by 86 independent municipalities, 45 townships, and 89 school districts, sheltering fearful populations behind restrictive covenants and racist real estate policies (Sugrue 1996, 266). Meanwhile from 1948 to 1967 the city proper witnessed more than 200 incidents of white vigilante violence directed against African American families trying to move out of the three overcrowded catchment basins "allowed" blacks histori-cally in the city (Sugrue 1996, 233). White neighborhoods offered the prospect of increasing property values (as well as better funded schools, parks, city services, etc.)—and thus increases in housing equity—in ways that FHA and VA redlining precluded in black areas. But racist white neighborhood associations mobilized entire family constituencies to contain the "menace"—kids and housewives organized to engage in daytime picketing and harassment, teenagers and fathers gathering in angry mobs in evenings, hurling bricks or fire bombs through windows, burning crosses on lawns, splashing paint or salt all over the premises, and hanging black figures in effigy, while white police stood by doing nothing or arresting blacks as threats to the peace.

In 1967, the black community finally exploded in frustrated reac-tion. Young folk in particular registered their anger over white policing practices and policy-making implementing "colonial rule" on the back of "restive natives." Not surprisingly, the rebellion ramped up the flight, as well as opening the way for election of Detroit's first black mayor and a gradual "darkening" of city offices and departments racially. The white exodus bled the city of jobs, assets and tax base. The next four decades witnessed political desiccation of public infrastructure, system-atic gutting of factory employment, and market-cannibalism of commu-nity bonds. Auto company mismanagement and shrinkage (in the face of globalizing competition) amplified the city's economic struggles in the 1970s. The crack epidemic of the 1980s, coupled with a "tsunami" of illegally traded weapons, cemented the shift of Motown's reputation from Icon of the American Dream into Murder Capital Nightmare. Antiunion corporatization precipitated the mid-90s newspaper strike whose union-busting outcome devastated independent reporting and secured a neo-liberal line in both the *Detroit Free Press* and the *Detroit News* from 2000, forward. State takeover of a struggling public school system in 1999 pirated its $1.5 billion bond issue for white suburban contractors and returned the schools to city control four years later, $200 million poorer and even more dysfunctional. The housing meltdown of 2008 registered on the streets as more of the predatory same, with Fannie Mae and Freddie Mac bailouts of banks ensuring that foreclosure would become the latest strategy by which finance capital pillaged public dollars and privatized public assets. By the 2010 census, the population had dwindled to barely 700,000; unemployment engulfed nearly half the working age residents; casinos had become the major entertainment draw; the school system began to be eviscerated and picked clean by a state appointed emergency manager. In the mix, budgetary crises—created by flight and relocation, exacerbated by corporate opportunism and local cronyism, and rendered hyper-dysfunctional by predatory banking and state intervention—crippled city services. But white flight and corporate plundering and state and city mismanagement were not the only agents in this history of deindustrialization.

On the ground in neighborhoods, residents fought back in ways they could. The struggle over this last half century is perhaps most succinctly encapsulated in the activist career of Grace Lee Boggs. Bryn Mawr PhD in hand, the Chinese-American philosopher arrived in Motown in the early 50s, quickly hooked up with African American UAW shop-floor organizer Jimmy Boggs, and together with her new husband began an odyssey of activism that remains in motion even today. Labor Movement and Black Power champions from mid-century, the two continually morphed their vision and practice to confront an ever-changing context. In succession they would open their inner city community-center house to Marxist and Black Panther strategizing, Civil Rights organizing, Women's Movement concerns for gender violence, Asian-America push-back against persecution related to the emergence of Japanese competition in auto-markets, collective struggles of urban mothers to take back streets from crack houses, and ballot initiatives seeking to resist casinos. By the early 1980s, it had become clear that electing a militant and street savvy labor advocate like Coleman Young was not enough to deal with the economic forces at work. Watching this Black Power champion opt to destroy an entire neighborhood (Poletown) in eminent domain capitulation to a General Motors demand for space to erect a state-of-the-art plant had reaffirmed the Boggs' sense that an epochal shift was underway. Not surprisingly, the plant did not deliver on the promised employment. Already in the 70s, Jimmy Boggs had begun to perceive the end of the industrial age, arguing often and vociferously that jobs were not the hope of the future, that technology would eclipse factory work, and that education for citizenship prowess in exercising local community control over local community problems would become the watchword of the future (Boggs and Kurashige 2011, 109). By the 1990s, their revisioning began to take on flesh.

Inspired by the 1960's Mississippi "Freedom Summer," drawing young people to the delta state to assist in organizing voters and creating "Freedom Schools," the Boggs' articulated a Detroit version. They began organizing city youth in 1992 to get involved in concrete neighborhood projects, animated by hip-hop and slam poetry (Boggs and Kurashige 2011, 111–118). Conceived as a multi-cultural, cross-generational initiative pairing urban youngsters and elders, Detroit Summer has pulled together community organizations and active citizens from across the metropolitan region and indeed, the country itself. Clear that a conscious and concerted move from ever-expanding production to sustainable relationship to the land, and from upwardly mobile consumerism to cooperatively self-reliant communalism, is the emergent demand of the hour, the project marks a plethora of grassroots creativity populating the blighted city with new hope and compelling imagination. Head spinning, turntable scratching, rhyme spitting youngsters are making common cause with "Gardening Angels" elders from the deep south, who yet retain the skills to turn vacant lots into community plots of vegetables. Spinning off from, or mutually collaborating with Detroit Summer, a host of gardening and agricultural initiatives since 1992 are converting blight into berries, remediating brownfields with "weeds" and trees, fostering recovery of herbal remedies for illness, reconvening neighborhood solidarity one raised bed, one block, at a time.

Today more than 2000 such gardens—family, community, and school—are slowly altering the city's landscape and its health profile. There are larger-scale east-side efforts like Earthworks Farm, growing from a Capuchin monastery-hosted soup kitchen, teaching skills to kids, linking with the state's Women, Infants, and Children (WIC) program to enable voucher-purchases of organic produce. Or Feedom Freedom Growers, led by a former Panther and his wife, coordinating young energy from around the city in farming an empty lot on a devastated block, using art to educate, while nurturing a Panther-esque vision of the 'hood as a "liberated zone" of self-sufficiency and care. On the west side, Detroit Black Community Food Security Network camps out at Rouge Park, hosting the largest community farm in the city, combining the planting with organizing for food sovereignty throughout the urban core, creating a council to advise municipal and state policy-makers on food security, and contributing input and energy to an Afrocentric grade school. Catherine Ferguson Academy on the near west side has evolved its already unique curriculum for pregnant and nursing teenagers (mostly African American) to now include an entire farming operation surrounding the school (including garden, fruit orchard, bees, horses, ducks, goats, and chickens), such that nursing mothers have begun learning biology and nutrition "hands on," acquiring practical skills as well as academic, eating what they grow, and selling the surplus at the local farmer's market. The school now boasts a roof-mounted wind turbine and solar panels, compliments of a Nobel Peace Center project, and has developed links with the Gandhian-based Barefoot College in Tilonia, India (Boggs and Kurashige 2011, 120). In support of this growing food focus across the city, an evolving infrastructure of organizations now supplies seeds and cuttings, equipment and advice, soil testing and technical consultation.

Meanwhile, at the turn of the new millennium, the Detroit-based International Center for Urban Ecology (ICUE) began focusing global attention among planners and architects on Motown prospects. Founded by architectural historian and theoretician Kyong Park, the Center envisioned development of an "Architecture of Resistance," galvanizing proposals for the city to renovate its vision from factory to ecosystem, machine to community (Boggs and Kurashige 2011, 122–124). By 2001, University of Detroit Mercy students working with ICUE had crafted a vision for "Adamah" (from the Hebrew for "soil creation"), a two-and-one-half square mile section of the east side, unearthing Bloody Run Creek from the current sewer system to once again function as part of the watershed, hosting greenhouses, grazing lands, a dairy, vegetable-, tree- and shrimp farms, sawmill and windmills, and revamping the old Packard auto plant to harbor work and living space, organized in individual and cohousing, and a place-based educational initiative (Boggs and Kurashige 2011, 125). Though the proposals have yet to be realized, they stirred imagination, helped move "urban agriculture from utopian idea to viable strategy" (Howell 2013), and, in particular, fired debate about the difference between "blueprint" and "vision." Local organizers like Boggs resisted any admonition to seek out foundation or corporate sponsorship, insisting that such projects would be "transformative only when grassroots members of the community are moved to act" (Boggs and Kurashige 2011, 125). "Adamah" has not been yet realized "whole cloth" on the east side; it is, however, gaining flesh all over the city in a hundred small projects of like spirit (not unlike tiny peasant villages, in Jesus' time, realizing the vision of messianic hospitality in their little gestures of shared bread and stranger-care; Lk 11: 1–8 as discussed in chapter 4).

The Boggs Center to Nurture Community Leadership (as the house/ community center has been formally named since Jimmy's death in 1993) is merely one way to focus discussion on activism in Detroit over the last half century. The responses of activist citizens have been too creatively diverse and crazily imaginative to detail in a small summary such as this. Sprouting up like wild weeds from Detroit's prairie-land soils has been everything from cooperative bicycle repair shops to mural collaborations between kids and businesses; from restorative justice efforts seeking to head off violence in neighborhoods to 3-D tech shops (combining Fab Lab production, Permaculture design, Solar Energy innovation, and Experiential Learning), making state-of-the-art processes available to ordinary citizens; from restaurants run by homeless and bakeries by returning citizens to neighborhood homes reinvented as museums and community centers; from a safe-space drop-in center for LGBTQ kids with nowhere else to go to the take-over a huge former industrial center hosting art studios and weekend shops.

A vibrant southwest sector of the city thrives as a Mexican-American "village," full of family life and culture as well as the struggles typical of lower income immigrant neighborhoods, laboring under ICE intrusion. Further out on the southwest side, the largest US population of Middle Easterners—many originally from Lebanon coming to work in auto production, but more lately from Yemen and Palestine—likewise struggles and bubbles with life. Ethnic enclaves such as Greektown, Poletown, Chinatown, Corktown (Irish), etc., abound and now find themselves trafficked by agendas and interests cosmopolitan and commercial. More broadly in the city, grassroots efforts, committed to current residents and local control, germinate uneasily alongside foundation–sponsored enterprises, backed by corporate grants and glossy media, energized by a vision of gentrification.

Detroit Summer itself has spun off or helped galvanize an ever expanding ensemble of entrepreneurial youth activity: the Life Arts Media Project, Detroit Future Youth, Detroit Future Schools, and its own version of its Mississippi namesake, the Allied Media Conference, drawing over 2000 youth each summer to the city core for four days of workshops, skill-sharing, celebration, networking, and work-collaboration. Much of the more local organizing has involved the regeneration of marketing and news at local levels, using YouTube, list servs, homegrown video, and digitized production. And now in the face of the latest round of privatizing "takeover" schemes, alternative media is proving crucial to the attempts of local groups to organize resistance and create viable community alternatives.

Detroit Quest

In a word, Detroit has now emerged as the dream-crucible and living laboratory of a thousand competing designs for alternative futures. National publications (like *Time Magazine*) send reps to live-in and report-out on ground-zero of the passing age of industrialization. The zine of the Positive Futures Network, *Yes! Magazine*, has linked Detroit efforts to similar initiatives around the globe, touting sustainable options wherever they are popping up. The city has become the subject of increasing interest and study, nationally and globally, and since 2007, host to a rising tide of in-migration by entrepreneurs and artists, largely white and young. The result is a conundrum. As Boggs offered in her most recent book titled the *Next American Revolution,* the Detroit Summer vision emerged out of the ashes of industrialization, seeking to create a twenty-first-century city, "both rural and urban," understanding the need "of human beings at this stage in our evolution to relate more responsibly to one another and to the Earth" (Boggs and Kurashige 2011, 112). That urban/rural possibility—arising from the large tracts of open space inside the city proper—poses the dilemma in visible form. For whom shall the city be razed and raised?

Certainly, for a site so lately abandoned by capital and people, the influx of young energy and creativity is tantalizing. But much of the reinvention thus far has been at the expense of the vast majority of citizenry of color, decimated by decades of deindustrialization and more recently by foreclosure. But just as creatively survivalist, as the Powers have been insidiously invasive, has been local character. I am reminded of a very recent home-grown video clip of a homeless street genius named Larry, who is known across the inner city for his vivacity and hustler's savvy. The production is part of an on-going parody of the gentrification and corporate plundering of Detroit, regularly updated by a cadre of young "solutionist" activists, spoofing, in their most recent work, "flash retailing." Touting "pop-up" enterprises—little coffee shops or clothing boutiques that "pop up" in an abandoned location for a day or a week or a month at a time—as the tongue-in-cheek solution to Detroit's dearth of retail, at one point the producers zoom their camera in on Larry. He is standing before a heavily tagged Motown ruin with back turned, his ever-present drumsticks poking out of his backpack for ready improvisation on garbage cans or buckets or whatever "echo-chamber" object is at hand. Queried as to what he is doing, Larry finishes his business, turns and says, "Oh, this is just my pop up bathroom!" The send up continues with footage of a "pop up casino" (a crap shoot game) convened in a vacant house and with a stand-in for Detroit's newly appointed emergency manager styled as a "pop-up mayor." If the Powers can't be countered with demonstrations or dollars then picaresque humor at least keeps dignity alive and the pretended aura punctured.

At the moment of this writing, under emergency manager occupation, the future for poor people and local neighborhood initiative does not look promising. Battle after battle with the corporatized players is being lost. The school system is being converted to charters and remedial reorganization putting 50-plus students in classrooms with transient Teach for America recruits, while public libraries are shuttered around the city. The recreation island (Belle Isle) so well-loved and used by inner city folk looking for relief on sweltering summer nights is already given over to Grand Prix and hydroplane races and soon enough may be opened to privatization interests. Some inner city residents have recently been given short notice to clear out for the building of a new entertainment complex close to downtown. Union contracts have been shredded in forced concessions and now are subject to unilateral revocation. Pension and health benefits of retired city employees are slated for cuts as high as 90%; the water, lighting and transportation departments likely to be sold off to private bidders; and perhaps even the world-class works of the Detroit Institute of the Arts put on the auction block for cash to pay off bank loans. Neoliberal empire is winning, by many counts.

But on the ground, grass roots innovation has never been more robust. Community is being forged across racial and ethnic lines, between generations and orientations, led especially by strong women of color, with working and middle classes cooperating. The force of down-pressing power is pushing awake human beings back to the depth questions of the hour: how live? Why be? What are we as a species? There is fervent imagination being kindled to respirit the city as a new urban-rural hybrid, lifting up local decision-making, sustainability, neighbor care, place-based education, cooperative enterprise, bartered services and home-grown entertainment as signs of the times and the only future now possible. The city hosts a recombinant power of messianic visioning, whose portent is legible even if its outcome, like that of all its kindred movements in history, is fragile and in question.

Nothing so provocatively captures the possibilities here hinted than an early June "Food Justice" dinner I attended. It was convened in a central city Unitarian Universalist fellowship hall recently taken over by the Eastern Michigan Environmental Action Coalition and rechristened the Cass Corridor Commons, opening the space to innovation and networking unlimited by religion or creed. Using organic produce entirely locally grown, cooked up in vegan and omnivore options by young inner city residents, the dinner is a once-per-month gathering of neighborhood residents, artists and activists. Predominantly black and Latino, but with a regular cohort of white and middle eastern and Asian-American attenders sprinkled in, the attenders eat healthy, conspire freely, inspire wantonly, imagine vigorously, and recreate memory of a different way of being. Throughout the dinner, a local music producer MC runs an open mike for all comers. A large percentage of the evening's diners stepped up and spit or danced or sang—from the four-year old son of one of the cooks, to sixty-year old Black-Arts-Movement-influenced poets weaving jazz rhythm into a tic toc cadence; from a fifth grader with her partner in rhyme rapping over beats with great panache about the rising of her entire class into political consciousness and "here we come" action, to young bros from the hood showing out their street cred with hard-edged lyrics, throwing down challenge (in this "underground venue") to city officials and corporate "thugs" rather than other bloods from the block. The night was rocked especially by this young black energy, targeting emergency management hubris and championing the turn to care for plants and nitrogen-fixing roots, recycling and muddy boots, compost heaps and hands working soil up into food. Hip-hop is here turning toward its wild-style birthing—but now not merely as fashion like Afrika Bambaataa and his Zulu Nation of the 70s, but in fact, sampling sounds from gardens, giving voice to rootstock (both people and plants) and in general attending to the needs of the ground itself. It spits destiny—with shovel and canning jar squarely in view. Whether the crew can continue to pursue the gestalt to its end-vision of reinventing city life in a sustainable vein with otherkind and with a planet under assault remains to be seen. Deep listening at the well of native wisdom would seem to be one requisite condition. But it already is putting wild voice at the service of wild life, reappearing inside of urban "decay." Perhaps the plants and animals themselves will again be sought as "teachers." But in any case, the messianic has never been primarily a pragmatic solution. It simply insists rather on opening a sign of the deep past for future reconnoitering. What becomes of that glimpse rests with those of "us" who bother to watch and read.

A City Like a Riddle, Like a Seed...

Detroit is not a ghost—though it certainly wrestles its unresolved past. Its youth—like so many elsewhere today—hook their spirits onto an untamed beat rather than a church pew. That beat bears pain like a groan from the ground. Inside that pain is a seed-memory. Inside that memory is ancient beauty. Underneath the beauty is a sustainable possibility. Empires rage; buildings fall; the house burns; the seed is released. May the art inspire movement and the movement art! May the messiah come and do away with the need for all messiahs! May the plants and animals reemerge as kin! Meanwhile, may we rise up robust as ancestors well-remembered and fully-grieved, and fiercely engage the fight!

Erratum to: Messianism Against Christology: Social Movements, Folk Arts and Empire

James W. Perkinson

Corrections/Changes in text

Pg. xvi, line 9 from top: "led by a upright" should be "led by an upright"

The updated original online version for this book can be found at
DOI 10.1057/9781137325198

Pg 10, line 18 from top should have reference added as highlighted: "Likewise, as myth is written down by the early *literati* retainers of these emergent city rulers, it is re-oriented away from memorializing an original "agreement" to remember the wild genesis of things and towards providing underpinning for that new mode of human power (Prechtel, in Jensen, 2001)."

Pg 10-11, line 4 from bottom should have reference added as highlighted: "What is central in primal agriculture is some measure of continued "hallowing" of the wild—a carefully tended relationship with the local ecology mediated by myth and ritual in which plant life, in particular, is regularly "offered" respect (through dances, songs, beads and other human artifacts, etc.; Prechtel, in Jensen, 2001)."

The updated original online version for this chapter can be found at
DOI 10.1057/9781137325198_1

Pg. 45, line 4 from bottom: "I Sam 2:30-31" should be "I Sam 20:30-31"

Pg. 46, line 16 from top: "I Sam 22;1-5;" should be "I Sam 22:1-5;"

The updated original online version for this chapter can be found at
DOI 10.1057/9781137325198_2

J.W. Perkinson, *Messianism Against Chronology*, 10.1057/9781137325198_7
E1

Pg. 76, line 11 from top: should have after "'become' the story": (Prechtel, 2012, 13)"

Pg 84, line 18 from top: "However, we . . ." should be "However we . . ." (remove comma)

The updated original online version for this chapter can be found at
DOI 10.1057/9781137325198_3

Pg. 93, reference after first epigraph: "(Jensen, quoting Prechtel, 5)" should be "(Prechtel, in Jensen, 2001)."

Pg. 103, line 16 from the bottom: "(Burhoe, 1974, 32)" should be "(Burhoe, 1972, 60)"

Pg 109, line 14 from top: "eco nomy" should be "economy"

Pg. 112, line 2 from bottom: "choiceour" should be "choice our"

Pg. 118, line 9 from bottom: "cross" should be "across"

Pg. 124, line 9 from top: "Alves" should be "Avens"

The updated original online version for this chapter can be found at
DOI 10.1057/9781137325198_4

Pg. 174, line 2 from bottom: "Haida" should be "Heiltsuk"

Pg. 175, line 20 from top: "Haida" should be "Heiltsuk"

Pg 179, line 12 from top: "half-white, half Anishinaabe" should read "half-white, half-Huron/Cree"

Pg 186, line 15 from the bottom: get rid of "it" before "hip-hop"

Pg 187, line 5 from top and line 20 from top: get rid of "it" before "hip-hop"

The updated original online version for this chapter can be found at
DOI 10.1057/9781137325198_6

Corrections/Changes in Footnotes

Pg. 204n20: "Bola" should be "Boal"

Pg. 206n3: clean up *'abod* (I don't have the necessary symbols on my computer, but it should be as you have it in the hardcopy version, except for the first letter which is just " ' "--a kind of reverse apostrophe for the transliteration of the Hebrew letter *ayin*).

Pg. 218n23: add at end of note: "(Prechtel, in Jensen, 2001)."

Pg 222n13: "An inscription on one scroll, for instance, reads, 'Wisdom of Alexander, Greek king, who made requests on the stone of the horizon' (the mountain on the horizon that supports the sky) (Mercier, 1997, 57). This is a mode of invocation strongly reminiscent of pastoral nomad practice on the Asian steppes of setting up standing stones with demarcations of deer antlers, that are also maps of the riverine valleys whose funneling of snow melt from area mountains (e.g., the Altai) determines the fertility of the grasses on which their animals (and they) depend (Prechtel, 2012 lecture).

Corrections/Changes in Bibliography

Pg. 229, "Aves" should be "Avens"

Pg. 229, insert the following after last entry for Brennan: "Brown, Frank, and Lucas, Phil. 1990. *Voyage of Rediscovery.* Vancouver : Moving Images Distribution (video)."

Pg. 229, replace the Burhoe entry with "Burhoe, Ralph Wendell, 1972. 'Natural Selection and God,' *Zygon* 7 (1972): 60."

Corrections/Changes in Index

Pg. 239, right-hand column, Eisenberg: should include "202n6, 202n8, 203n9, 203n11, 203n12, 206n5

Pg. 240, left-hand column: "Haida" should be "Heiltsuk" (before "transformation mask")

Pg. 240, right-hand column, hip-hop/ciphers: "221, 224" should be "221n6, 224n22"

Pg. 241, right-hand column, Loewen, James W.: "200" should be "200n5"

Pg. 241, right-hand column, *logos*: "214" should be "214n34"

Pg. 241, right-hand column, Long, Charles: "199" should be "199n3"

Pg. 243, left-hand column, possession/ Jesus' own: "23n30" should be "213n30"

Pg. 243, right-hand column, Prechtel, Martín: "93, 97, 179" should be "10, 11, 93, 97-101, 179, 201n1, 203n10, 218n23, 222n13"

Pg 244, left-hand column, salvation: "203, 213" should be "203n15, 213n29"

Pg. 244, right-hand column, Solomon/*Net of Solomon*: "212n223" should be "212n24"

Pg. 244, right-hand column, spirit-world/spirit-battle/combat: "213" should be "213n26"

Pg. 245, right-hand column, wild, etc: "204n" should be "204n21"; "204n5" should be "204 n22"; "219n" should be "219n29"

The updated original online version for this book can be found at
DOI 10.1057/9781137325198

Notes

Introduction

1. Tim Burke salvages his found objects especially from abandoned buildings and churches.

2. An interesting postmodern equivalent might be found in hip-hopper Tupac Shakur's body tattoo of "50 N . . . Z" (the N-word ending with an "A" and a "Z") adorning his sternum, signifying, according to him, that when "you come up against me, it's like coming up against fifty n . . . s, because I've got the souls of all my brothers in me" (Dyson 2011, 243).

3. And here is opened a deep question of the character of revelatory experience in a given ecology as wildly numinous and "terrible"—an aspect of indigenous experience of land as "haunted" in certain places, and not to be lightly trafficked by humans except at times of crisis. Native American scholar Vine Deloria gives thematic expression to such in his essay, "Reflection and Revelation," in *For This Land* (Deloria 1999, 250–260) and African-American historian of religions Charles Long characterizes something like this level of experience—by way of Rudolf Otto's *mysterium tremendum*—as the differentiating element in "religions of the oppressed" organized out of the agony and ruins of colonial conquest (Long 1986, 123, 137–139, 142, 162–16, 196–197). In connection with such an awesomeness (or "awfulness" or "dread") that becomes his own most primal revelatory moment outside the city of Luz in Gen 28: 17, Jacob names that potency as primary in his ancestral litany of protection—in this case, the great "Fear of Isaac" whose numinosity warrants his rights to his own flock and to a just wage (Gen 31:42, 53). Later this stone will also attract to itself an invocation that associates it with "shepherding" in the deathbed blessing of Jacob over Joseph, who apparently inherits the protecting name, if not the anointed stone itself, in the prophecy that "his bow would remain unmoved (despite provocation) and his arms would be made agile by the Mighty One of Jacob, by the name of the Shepherd, the Rock of Israel" (Gen 49: 24). And all of this gives biblical coloring to a broader thematics of the way boundary stones in primordial times were associated with protective spirits and marked the "herm" (that eventually becomes

"Hermes," the messenger between worlds, for the Greeks) delineating the living from the dead (Shepard 1982, 25, 133; Harrison 1963, 11–12). Anarcho-primitivist scholar Paul Shepard notes that early agricultural villages marked out their watershed boundaries with sacred pillars, creating a horizon line of security for the communities huddled in their lowland dwellings (Shepard 1982, 25). Veneration and consultation of such standing stones was a matter of seeking ancestral help—protection for crops in agricultural societies, or for flocks if pastoralist. Anthropologist Jane Ellen Harrison further elaborates that once the stone "gets a head and gradually becomes humanized," it becomes a primal signifier. Among a pastoral people, this "Herm-figure" is depicted carrying on his shoulders a ram, "and from the Ram Carrier, the Criophorus, Christianity has taken her Good Shepherd" (Harrison 1963, 11–12). The genealogy of these ancient "standing images" is evocative when compared with the amulet-like presence of Heidelberg hulks, marking out Guyton's particular block as a refuge space and safe zone for inner city residents (in this case, particularly *for* children and homeless and *against* crime and drug trafficking).

4. To situate my own terminology in broader contemporary reference—if I were to camp out on Derrida's distinction between "the messianic structure of existence" shared by all and "messianisms" formulated and promulgated by historical religions, I would say I am using the latter term somewhere in-between Derrida's two formulations (Derrida 1989, 60). I am interested in underscoring historically emergent movements that answer to the (messianic) "waiting," characteristic of his structural "hypostasis," with provisional concretions that are not simply controlled by historical religions, but remain in some sense "subaltern" even to their own hegemonic orthodoxies. These would be collective gestures momentarily realizing a qualitative social approximation to "messianic justice" that are given emblematic expression by means of artistic figuration generating insurgent energy (such as what happened on Tahrir Square during the 18-day Egyptian Revolution of 2011, as conveyed in various Internet documentations).

5. See the intriguing historical correction offered by James W. Loewen in *Lies My Teacher Told Me* to the effect that black slaves can lay claim to the dubious honor of having been North America's first non-Native settlers to have continuously occupied the continent in the modern era. The year 1526 witnessed a group of 500 Spaniards founding a town in South Carolina from which 100 slaves revolted by that November, escaping to join the Indians, while the Spaniards fled to Haiti.

6. See Taylor's elaboration of the term borrowed from Avery F. Gordon's *Ghostly Matters: Haunting and the Sociological Imagination* (Taylor 2011, xi, 14, 34, 70, 139, 206; Gordon, 17, 21, 195).

7. In the sense of Hardt and Negri's careful deployment of the term as a counter-globalization alternative to neoliberal visions of corporate globalization. The "multitude" points toward grass roots "events" of spectacular

resistance and zones of solidarity that no longer organize around homo-geneities like "class" or "race," but embrace a plethora of positionings and identities that nonetheless make common cause in struggles for the commons, privileging the experiences of marginalized groups (Hardt and Negri 2009, 61).

8. Using FHA and VA policies up until the mid-1960s and default patterns of white racist behavior after that.

9. Not to mention that drug traffic and crime have been sharply reduced in the neighborhood and young people and homeless finding a place of hos-pitality and refuge.

10. For similar work with "shamanism" as a trope of analysis, see the section entitled "Black Creativity, Shamanic Remedy, and Afro-Polyphony," in my book *Shamanism, Racism, and Hip-Hop Culture: Essays on White Supremacy and Black Subversion.* New York: Palgrave Macmillan Press (2005), or my article "Tupac Shakur as Ogou Achade: Hip-Hop Anger and Postcolonial Rancor Read from the Other Side," *Culture & Religion: An Interdisciplinary Journal* (special Issue on Hip-Hop and Religion) Vol. 10, No. 1 (March, 2009), eds A. Pinn and M. Miller, 63–79.

11. The emphasis here is not on "interfaith dialog" between so-called world religions, but rather attention paid to more "indigenous" traditions, engaged with their land base, articulating their wisdom and memory in vernacular symbols.

1   *Wildlands Memorialization*: Messianism Mapped

1. I am indebted for this image to Martín Prechtel who has powerfully devel-oped this idea into a kind of mandate for the work of transforming impe-rial pathologies of all kinds into emergent possibilities of creativity.

2. There is even some reason to suspect that the 150-person limit on mean-ingful social networks is nearly "hard-wired" thus far in our species' evolutionary experience according to evolutionary psychologist Robin Dunbar, reflecting a brain-size to social-interaction ratio that reflects all kinds of natural human groupings, including the average size of regular Facebook contacts (Dunbar 1993, 681ff). Beyond that number, social contacts become increasingly depersonalized and instrumental, ever more dependent on hierarchical systems of "representation," both political and symbolic.

3. See *Rabbit Proof Fence*—the Hollywood work up of the true twentieth century story of an 11-year old Aboriginal girl who leads her 8- and 5-year-old siblings across 1,200 miles of inhospitable Australian outback, walking home from the residential school to which they had been sent after being kidnapped, with the whole colonial administration chasing her. She was able to do so because she had internalized the major form of "capital" of her society—the knowledge of how to live off of the land—that allowed

her even as a prepuberty female the kind of autonomy that translates into social empowerment.

4. Thomas Hobbes, sitting in his Malmsbury house, never having met a hunter-gatherer in person or laid eyes on their domain, is nonetheless certain their "state of nature" lives are to be abhorred as "solitary, poor, nasty, brutish, and short" (Hobbes 2010, ch xiii, 9).

5. Even as recently as the 2004 tsunami ravaging Indian Ocean countries, evidence surfaced through a BBC investigation of an island-hopping fishing tribe called the Mokan, off the coast of Thailand, for whom concepts like "need," "want," "worry," or "take"—much less "murder" or "war"—are simply nonexistent in their language and thus largely unthinkable. The Mokan survived the tsunami—despite never having experienced such in any living member's lifetime—because their myths "remembered" a "man-eating wave" whose tell-tale signs they instantly recognized as the sea receded and because their instincts had them paying close attention to the resident animal life that all fled to higher ground. They simply followed suit.

6. Eisenberg notes the shared evaluation of agriculture's advent as "fall" (Eisenberg 1999, 467). For the Bobo of Burkina Faso, "primal world harmony" was destroyed by farming. The Khasi of Assam lament the loss of human contact with heaven, ended when the great-tree was cut down to clear garden space. And Dogon myth remembers the noise of women grinding millet as the cause of God separating sky and earth and introducing mortality among humanity.

7. Via cyborg amalgamation, drug intervention, genetic splicing, reproductive cloning, and so on, much less the more gradual reprogramming accomplished through advertising, media saturation, education, and therapy. See, for instance, the claim of postmodern theorist Fredric Jameson that multinational capital has so effloresced as to have colonized and recapitulated even the few remaining niches of precapitalist order (Nature and the Unconscious) that had previously served as "extraterritorial and Archimedean footholds for critical effectivity" (49).

8. This is especially the case given our quite recent alliance with a third partner—this time our dead Mesozoic ancestry of ginkos, ferns, mollusks, plankton, etc.—called up by the new social "creature" called a corporation and reengineered as "fossil fuels." This new mode of being on the planet, in effect, recreates our species as a new kind of "saprophagic" scavenger, continuously perforating the bowels of our "mother" and unleashing, in the form of spills and pollution, a literal "night of the living dead" (Eisenberg 1999, 52–54). The oil/human alliance is abolishing practices of "Jubilee rest" underground communities need in order to rejuvenate, and over time, "deskills" soils and ecosystems alike, decanting genetic information into the waste bin of extinction, as grainfields replace biodiverse ecosystems.

9. Between the end of World War II and 1990, for instance, 38 percent of all the land under cultivation in the world had been damaged by what

Eisenberg calls "agricultural malfeasance"—the result of the human/ annual alliance whose destruction of soil nutrients and biota has the effect of inverting the food chain. Instead of "eating the recycled remains of our ancestors...we are eating our children" (Eisenberg 1999, 33). The alliance itself is not really ecosystemic, but the continual disturbance of such relations.

10. See respectively here the works of Martín Prechtel (2012, 294–297), Howard Gentry (1982, 4–5), and Winona LaDuke (2005, 167–190).

11. Though the Genesis texts do not explicitly identify Eden with a mountain abode, its characterization as the source of four great rivers would imply as much (Eisenberg 1999, 90–91). Ezekiel in the 6th century BCE, as indeed scholars from Philo's time on down, have placed the great garden of God, with its full compliment of celebrated trees, in the peaked heights (Ez 28:12–16; 31:4–9, 15–16).

12. Eisenberg offers a crude index of such in his examples. Compared to industrial agriculture's expenditure of 10 calories of energy for every 1 calorie we consume as food, for instance, "Tsembaga farmers in highland New Guinea, using Neolithic slash-and-burn methods, invest less than 1/10th of a calorie for each calorie they eat" (Eisenberg 1999, 53).

13. Diamond notes the tragedy when in 1835, New Zealand Maori land on the Chathams and quickly enslave and then slaughter their Moriori kin, whose centuries-old hunter-gatherer traditions of peaceful dispute resolution had them responding to the new arrivals with an offer of "peace, friendship, and a division of resources" (Diamond 1999, 53–57).

14. This is actually an anachronistic use of the term—indigenous cultures generally do not compartmentalize spirituality as something separate from simply living. Spirituality rather suffuses everyday life, is part of everything that is done.

15. And theologically, herein lays a potential scandal. In one sense, these alternative social formations represent peoples who still know how to read the "book of creation" and thus have less immediate need for the "book of the bible" as an antidote for the loss of focus (and increase in violence) evident in settled agricultural settings (see, for instance, Rasmussen's discussion of Luther's *larvae dei* in this regard; Rasmussen 1997, 273–274). Former Trappist monk Daniel Quinn explores this possibility in his *The Story of B*, asserting, in a chapter entitled "The Great Forgetting," that the notion that everyone universally "needs to be saved" would have been virtually unintelligible for most indigenous cultures before Western colonial contact (Quinn 1996, 240–243). Where existential experience gives little sense of being lost or alienated from the "world" (rather than meaningfully involved in a sustainable set of relations) salvation appears beside the point.

16. I am opting for a use of the messianic more in keeping with that of Clastres in her discussion of the Tupi-Guarani migrations of the sixteenth century, distinguishing such movements focused on shoring up traditional values (in the face of foreign incursion or social disruption) from prophetic visions

questioning the older values and venturing onto new terrain (though even these latter often project from the past, as the myth of the "Land-Without-Evil" indicates) (Clastres 1995, 43–45, 48–49, 57). See also the discussion of "messianic shamanism" by Giesler (*Shamanism: An Encyclopedia of World Beliefs, Practices, and Culture*).

17. *Reducido* was the term coined by Spanish conquistadors for their systematic effort to tame and domesticate Native Americans, pulling them out of hunting and gathering lifestyles and into supposedly "productive employment" farming and mining (Corbett 1991, 4). Even the utopian Jesuit communities of the eighteenth century in South America, reorganizing the Guarani in cooperative ventures where much of the product was shared equally were entitled "the Jesuit reductions" (Dussel 1995, 68–69).

18. Mk 4:30–32, where the "kingdom" is compared to a grain of mustard seed.

19. In hasidic Jewish terms, a *tikkun or mending whose "reach" goes as far as the divine itself*—in a creative reading of the trauma of exile as having not only "cut off" Jews from a homeland (whether Israel itself in 70 CE or late middle ages Spain in 1492), but indeed "cut into" the interiority of the sacred itself.

20. For instance, some of the first century Palestinian Jesus movement activity (e.g., his reenactments of covenant renewal in Matthew's "Sermon on the Mount" and Luke's counterpart, "Sermon on the Plain," or some of the parables, or, indeed, the Temple takeover), could certainly be productively analyzed through the lens of Augusto Boal's *Theatre of the Oppressed*, especially where Boal talks about peasants coming to new levels of bodily expression and active agency through theatrical experimentation (Boal 1976, 126–142).

21. Using the Jesus Movement by way of example, these would include respectively, the Sabbath-Jubilee tradition of economic "release" exemplified in food- and resource-sharing (Mk 2:15–17; 10:17–31; Lk 11:4–8); episodes of gathering (Mk 1:6), gleaning (Mk 2:23–28), subsistence sowing (Mk 4:26–29), and wilderness "pot-latch" cooperation (Mk 6;30–44; 8:1–10); use of the symbols of Elijah or the Son of Man (Mk 9:9–13; 2:28); parables as a response to defamatory ideology (Mk 3:22–30; 4:1–34); and recourse to lake-side and wilderness to recruit, strategize, teach, and rest (Mk 1:16, 45; 2:13; 3:7–8, 13–19; 4:1, 10–12, 34).

22. See James Scott's benchmark work on the way political resistance is often coded in "hidden transcripts," seeming to confirm the official public transcript of society, while occulting and maintaining a quite different evaluation for an insider community (Scott 1990, xii–xiii, 14, 40–41, etc.). Again, looking to the Jesus Movement we could note, respectively, Jesus' move away from cities and towns to lakeside and wilderness for so much of his teaching (Mk 4;1–34), going into self-exile near Tyre (Mk 7:24), and retreating to his Bethany "safe-house" during the Jerusalem campaign (Mk 11:11, 19); speaking "frankly" only to his inner circle (Mk 8:32), or

privately in explanation of parables (Mk 4: 10, 34) or in challenging fatuous thinking (Mk 9:33–41).

23. See the way the synoptics structure both the Galilee and Jerusalem campaigns as an ongoing struggle between various leadership elites and Jesus, who works continuously to peel the people away from loyalty to the authorities and dismantle their "colonized" mentality (Mk 3:23; 7:14; 11:18, 32; 12:12, 34, 37; 14:1).

24. The epigraph with which this chapter is prefaced continues (after Abel's shed blood cries out from the ground): "And now you are cursed from the ground, which has opened its mouth to receive your brother's blood from your hand. When you till the ground, it shall no longer yield to you its strength; you shall be a fugitive and a wanderer on the earth... Then Cain went away from the presence of the Lord, and dwelt in the land of Wandering, east of Eden... and he built a city" (Gen 4:10–12, 16–17).

25. For a graphic description of such in late medieval Europe, at the time of Columbus "discovery," see Stannard (1992, 57–62).

26. Although it is important to note that, in reality, it is the North that is dependent on the South. One estimate "clocks" that transfer of wealth at a rate of $25,000 per minute being paid northwards by Southern economies, some $200 billion per year that the North pulls from its victims south of the border (Susan George, Chair of the Transnatinoal Institute of France, as quoted in Cobb and Diaz 2009, 50).

27. Cited in Brain Willson's *Blood on the Tracks* (Willson 2011, 338, 464).

28. And more loosely in my deployment, messianism will encompass all three uses: a marking out of political meaning in an artistic figure that proves culturally and spiritually effective for a social movement seeking to articulate and embody that meaning in a context adverse to its implied critique.

29. As I frequently reiterate to my students—*no one* lives out the whole bible. Every one of us picks and chooses the particular texts *we* will let "speak to us with all "divine" authority and which ones we will dismiss as only relevant to the culture of the time, but no longer binding. But it is actually culture all the way up and down the line of interpretation, and it is always "we" who do the choosing and the dismissing.

2   *Ancestral Invocation*: Messianic Traces from Abel to Isaiah

1. And just by way of anticipation, the "city of God," the heavenly Jerusalem—invoked in both the Hebrews and Revelation visions of things to come (He 12:22; Rev 21:2–22:5)—is a "city" unlike anything else we mean by that term: by the measurements in Revelation, it is about 1500 *miles* long, wide, and *high*! Its most important features are its mineral-jewel-encrusted walls and foundations, its river of the waters of life, its trees of life whose leaves are for the healing of "the nations," and whose luminescence effectively abolishes night, or the need for sun or moon.

2. In the Hebrew, the emphasis seems to be on simultaneous beginnings: the *birth* of a son to Seth that he calls Enosh as also *inaugurating* the practice of calling on the name of YHWH. In this reading, the condition as "mortal" itself gives rise to the memorializing of YHWH's name in a set of ritual practices that craft a certain artifice of performance as the protective covering or even "spiritual armature" of Enosh's condition as vulnerable. The other way of reading this etiology of the use of YHWH's name is in terms of the beginning of idolatry, marking the moment when human mortality seeks to cover or hide its weakness through manipulation of the name in relationship to its own artifices and technologies—literally setting up tools as gods.

3. Hiebert will note that the Hebrew term for cultivate, ʿābōd, is "the customary verb in biblical Hebrew to express servitude," elsewhere used to connote the servitude of a servant to a master (Gen 12:16), or one people to another (Gen 27:40; Exod 5:9), or Israel's service to God in worship (Exod 4:23, 7:16, 26) (Hiebert 1996 64, 33). To what degree this "servitude relationship" to land reflects the oppressive conditions of peasant subservience to city-centers (in monarchical Israel of the Yahwist's own time of writing), or conversely, a remembered relationship of apprenticeship to land, depending on riparian watersheds replenished by rainfall and seed fertility nurtured by arable soil, as the primary structure of relationship to YHWH lifted up by the Genesis texts (in contrast to the "hi-tech" irrigation systems of superpowers like Mesopotamia or Egypt), remains a question of "how one reads."

4. Midrashic commentator Avivah Gottlieb Zornberg will note the condition as a "loss of a particular standing ground," that is synonymous with having no place of rest (Sabbath) and no capacity to "stand tall" in the presence of God (Zornberg, 21). In the Hebrew, Cain will speak of being driven from "the face of the soil and from your face" (Gen 4:14).

5. Eisenberg notes that what likely was foraged here was "treachy syrup that aphids and their cousins exude, known to us as honeydew [and] to the Israelites in the desert as *man*, or mana." It is actually a highly nutritious excretion still gathered by the Arabs today, "who [also] call it *man*, and by Australian Aborigines who call it 'sugar-lerp'" (Eisenberg 1999, 15–16).

6. Corbett will bring Buber into the picture here, exegeting the text by reference to Cossacks' self-naming as *kazaks*, "feral strays" who are "free wanderers" (also *khirgis* as in Khirgis Kazak), "undomesticated adventurers," "masterless guerillas," or "freebooters" (Corbett, 2005, 221).

7. It is interesting here to note that Abel's blood cries "from" the ground (wherein it is actually received and swallowed) and it is likewise "from" such that the curse arises that thwarts Cain's tillage and renders him nomadic. The laboring of the text to express a kind of intertwining of human blood and arable soil itself hints a kind of symbiosis that has been violated, a destructiveness that strikes at the very nexus between human and soil, such that the resulting cry emanates irresolvably from both. It is

the soil that speaks through the dead nomad and the nomad who speaks from the violated soil.

8. Indeed Corbett will offer that pastoral nomads "may claim their separate identity so stridently because they usually have peasant serf ancestry that they want to leave behind them, yet they often continue to maintain familial as well as societal connections with peasantry, which keeps a way open for peasants to go feral but also for nomads to settle back into domestication" (Corbett 2005, 218).

9. Indeed in the synoptics, Jesus will hold a teach-in on the Temple mall after taking it over for a day and throwing out the street-level representatives (money changers and pigeon sellers) of the predatory exchange system controlled by the priests. The core of that teaching will be clear exposition of the temple itself as the primary place of piracy, the quintessential "den of robbers" of the time, in direct opposition to its intended function as, in general, "a house of prayer for all peoples," but even more particularly—as noted in the Isaiah passage Jesus is quoting—a Sabbath-sanctuary for "foreigners, eunuchs, and outcasts" (Mk 11:15–19; Is 56:1–8).

10. In this vein it is worth noting Eisenberg's reprise of ancient Near Eastern myths of the World-Axis, the place from which circulates everything necessary to life (genes, nutrients, waters, diverse life forms, etc.). The deepest reservoir of such thinking, at the advent of agriculture's invention, looks back toward the higher Northern mountains, which act as "spigots for the circulation of wildness through the places made hard and almost impermeable by long human use" (Eisenberg 1999, 75). This "World Mountain" site of the earliest Canaanite (and thus Israelite) gods, was, in effect, "mythic shorthand for ecological fact"—the carefully preserved recognition that wilderness is the source and necessary condition for anything to exist, including the human agricultural enterprise (Eisenberg 1999, 75, 78). Sinai (as indeed, the stories of Eden itself) find its root-significance here.

11. Although the psalm (Psalm 110) being quoted here was likely written during the Maccabean period, in relationship to the high priest, Simon Maccabaeus, antiquity believed it to be a creation of David.

12. And this is a sequence that will include the regimes of both David and Solomon, as Howard-Brook points out, whose oppressiveness—in spite of all the royal propaganda otherwise that appears in the Deuteronomic History—shows up in stark glimpses, when Northern-dwelling "Israelites" seek redress from the harsh policies of labor and taxation suffered under these two (supposedly) "paragon" kings (Howard-Brock 2010, 110–133).

13. Although an alternative interpretation (based on a different vocalization of the same Hebrew consonants) yields the idea of Elijah being fed by "the Arabs" of the area. In this case, Elijah would have been embraced and given hospitality by local *bedouin*, who themselves live "on the land" as savvy nomads. It does not really alter the notion of Elijah as becoming "indigenous" to the desert *wadis*, chthonically rooting his vocation in the local ecology.

14. Cf Hillel for the reading of *qol dmamah daqah* as "sound of thin silence" (Hillel 2006, 138, fn. 298).

15. In subsequent figuring throughout Europe and the Caucasus (e.g., Slavic, Estonian, and Georgian folklore), Elijah is embraced as successor to, or embodiment of, various mountain-top lightning gods. For more on weather magic see the discussion in chapter 3 on Jesus' own "weather powers."

16. Presumably attempting to "lean into" and "face up to" the political conspiracy tightening its noose around the movement by talking about it explicitly with his closest followers, much like Martin Luther King would attempt to defuse tension and face down fear after a hard day on the streets by breaking out into a spontaneous funeral elegy for one of his inner circle once back in their motel room. King's preaching was not only wickedly funny but also seriously pedagogical and therapeutic, trying to prepare spiritually and psychically for what was almost sure to come—by getting it explicitly up into language and consciousness.

17. And here we are not just dealing with metaphor: Isaiah labored in continuous lambast to keep Israel *out of* alliances with Sennacharib, whose imperial violence included clear-cutting the cedars of Lebanon in the ceaseless appetite of royal might for lumber (Is 37:22–24). Isaiah will even lend prophetic voice to the arboreal relief envisioned when Assyria itself falls: cypresses and cedars exulting, "Since you were laid low, no one comes to cut us down!" (Is 14:3–8; cf. Myers 2005, 5–6).

18. Myers notes the fact that the only time this word (*ta skeuē* in the Greek of Mk 3:27) reappears in Mark's narrative is in 11:16, when Jesus locks down the Temple Mount in a sit-down strike, forbidding any transport of "goods" across the Temple mall.

3 *Parabolic Incantation*: Movement Messianism and the Jubilee Jesus

1. Hosea, for instance—after certifying destruction of all of Israel's agricultural supports and celebrations—will announce YHWH's promise "to allure her and bring her into the wilderness, and speak tenderly to her" . . . to which she shall respond as "in the days of her youth, as at the time when she came out of the land of Egypt" (Hos 2:14–15). The focus of that "reschooling" will be the making of a covenant "with the beasts of the field, the birds of the air, and the creeping things of the ground," abolishing "the bow, the sword, and war," making it possible for Israel to "lie down in safety" (Hos 2:18).

2. Such resistance was often covert and calculated—as in any situation of occupation and exploitation, much of what pushed back on the domination system was coded and tactical rather than overt and direct. For readings of the Jesus movement that discover such modes of resistance, see Wink on Mt 5:38–41 (counseling sabotage of power dynamics when forced to carry a Roman soldier's pack), see Herzog on Mt 20:1–15 (exposing the rapacity of landowner "attacks" on day laborer vulnerability and hinting at the

possibility of organizing against such), and Herzog again on Lk 18:9–14 (parodically "sending up" Pharisaic pretense to justice as a tithe-giver and -collector) and Mk 12:13–17 (brazenly using inference publicly to repudiate the imperial tribute system) (Wink 1992, 179–184; Herzog 1994, 79–97, 173–193; 2000, 224–232).

3. A different way of making the same point would have been to focus on Jesus' way of suggestively invoking the ideology of a return of a king like David to the throne, in his procession into Jerusalem at the head of a chanting throng of peasants, only to subvert its militant overtures with his choice of a nonviolent "prop" like a donkey to ride upon. Indeed, his choice of an inner circle designated by the subtly significant number 12 can be read as indicating an option for organization of his movement much more like a "feral" retribalization of the "nation," away from imperial dreams and urban concentration, seeking to recapitulate earlier Israel as a "counter-kingdom" movement, anchored in more egalitarian and sustainable land values and social practices, rather than casting himself as a "true" king, worthy of the Davidic throne and court bureaucracy.

4. See the discussion of Jesus' way of rooting a vision of "greater Israel" (reaching beyond Roman political jurisdictions) in the specific lifeways and traditions of Galilean village culture (Freyne 2011, 31–34).

5. There is even talk today of a third "search for the historical Jesus," this time focused not on his persona, but on his context—the actual political economy of first century Galilee, as its small-holding farming operations were increasingly restructured in service of aristocratic interests centered in the two Northern cities of the region, Tiberius and Sepphoris.

6. A rural Galilean north/metropolitan Jerusalem south "divide" that continues to show up even in John's much later gospel writing, where the primary axis of contention is between "the Galileans" and "the party of the Jews." The latter references not all Jewish people in first century Palestine (Galileans were Jews as well), but the controlling Jewish interests rooted in the Temple-State-dominated economy of Jerusalem.

7. Horsley and Hanson, citing Josephus, will characterize the situation as a virtual police-state (Horsley and Hanson 1985, 33).

8. This may well represent a crafty bit of innuendo, on the part of the scribes sent from Jerusalem to disrupt the growing movement, hinting that Jesus' time spent in the south with John the Baptist is to be understood like the ancient Northern ("Israelite") scandal of king Ahaziah, dwelling in his capital city of Samaria, turning for healing to Baalzebub, god of the southern border town of Ekron, after falling through a window (2K 1:1–18). In the older story, the "treasonous turn" away from Northern traditions of divination and healing results in confrontation by Elijah and ultimately in Ahaziah's death. There are vague subtextual shadows here that can be neither illuminated nor dismissed: the ancient rebellion of Moab (2K 1;1) in a region that is later the setting of the Baptist's ministry and hideout (whose head is also supposedly buried in the city of Samaria); a mythological

genealogy linking the fiery Cuthim (Hebrew for "Samaritan") underworld war-god, Nergal, with the Phoenician "Lord of the Flies," Beelzebub, both of whom are associated with plague and its cure; and the persistent rumors of Jesus' own genealogy as illegitimate and "Samaritan" (the charge in John 8:48, "are we not right in saying you are a Samaritan and have a demon?"). How much the strategy of the Jerusalem-based scribes in charging this particular "possession" is a disingenuous disinformation campaign, seeking to impugn the Northern Galilean-centric orientation of Jesus as false because of supposed connections with a Samaritan spirituality informed both by southwestern Philistine/Phoenician sympathies with an older Canaanite god ("Beelzebub") and eastern Assyrio-Cuthim powers (the Samaritan demon), remains open to conjecture.

9. As already indicated, in the archetypal confrontation at Capernaum he had begun to clarify and confront the linkage between possession by an unclean spirit and scribal promulgation of the discourse of uncleanness (the purity code), rooted in Temple practice, that imprisoned the poor in stigma and shame. By his second major encounter in Mk 1:40–45—declaring "clean" a leper on the road and sending him to the priests in Jerusalem as a witness "against" them (*martyrion* in Greek)—he had definitively tipped his hand (Myers 1998, 152–153).

10. To what degree this immediate response inveigles the charge in one of the oldest memories of anguish in Israel's history is an open question. Wes Howard-Brook articulates his wide-angle overview of Israel's history through the struggle for hegemony between the Northern kingdom, Israel, and the southern house of David, whose breakup after Solomon is memorialized in the archetypal cry of Jeroboam and the people, "What share do we have in David?...To your *tents* O Israel," even as Solomon's son, Rehoboam, continues to rule "over the Israelites who were living in the *towns* of Judah" (I Kg 12:16b-17; I Sam 20:1; Howard-Brook 2010, 123–124; 131, emphasis JP). Tent-dwelling is here opposed to town-living—one more time evocative of the way herder skills leverage the possibility of resistance to monarchical rule that constitutes a "heavy yoke" of "hard service" (the "true" character of both Davidic and Solomonic rule that subtly flashes through the coded textual writing; I Kg 12:1–17). Howard-Brook will even underscore this North-South polemic of one son/shrine/geography/lifeway struggling against another son/shrine/geography/lifeway as the basis of the Genesis story of Cain and Abel, retrojected back behind the royal history "after the fact" (Howard-Brook 2010, 126, fn 61, 131, 137). How much the Galilee-Jerusalem axis of conflict haunting the gospel texts reflects this primordial "break" is an open question. In any case, Jesus *will* clearly emerge as a force for breakup of the house/kingdom of David/ Herod and redistribution of such a "satanic" monopoly of goods/powers back into a more dispersed and localized disposition.

11. The exorcism he ultimately intends is the whole of the imperial apparatus: the regime of "powers" that are channeled through primary institutions

like the Temple and its satellite synagogues by way of elite-controlled interpretation of *torah*, colonizing the entire landscape and locking peasants and the poor into exploitative relations with the rich (and often enough, into early graves).

12. It is worth noting Matthew's rendition in which it is the spontaneous line up (for healing) of blind and lame and the suddenly boisterous clamor of kids in that freed-up Temple-space that provokes attack by the chief priests and scribes (Mt 21:14–16).

13. The actual "unclean spirit" in the Capernaum synagogue had *not* done that, but did call him "holy."

14. Elites would likely have gained their own economic power through careful calculation of returns and tightfisted control of "social claims" on their resources, and would typically have mobilized social disapproval toward peasant villagers who "squandered" their already meager fare in more fluid practices of reciprocity and hospitality (putting their elite patrons in the position of having to make up village shortfalls, if any occurred).

15. See respectively, Mt 17:24–27 as discussed in footnote 26 below; Mk 7:1–14; Lk 11:46.

16. Yamm represents the underground "sea" whose saline concentrations can percolate to the surface and leach into the soil over time; Mot is the lord of death.

17. And indeed, Baal and consorts—as also YHWH-Elohim in the Israelite choice for monarchy—eventually become guarantors for city-life—prey to the typical elite cooptation of indigenous stories in service of dominating polities that everywhere becomes part of the tactics of takeover.

18. It is worth noting, in this regard, that the irrigation lords of Babylon and their city-dwelling populations knew of a "different" Sabbath—or rather knew the Sabbath differently. They feared the seventh day's "release" of untamed powers whose wild force, threatening their fields and urban order, "cowed" them indoors, where they huddled and dreamed of the taming of all things "uncivilized" (Corbett 1991, 81, 84).

19. There is an Edenic hint in the parable, a sudden looking from wild mustard in the field to towering cedar in the heights—in prophetic verse and popular imagination, the place of origin among the mountain trees in the "garden of God," source of the four great rivers (Ez 28:12–16; 31:4–9, 15–16,

20. Biblical scholar Dominic Crossan notes that while cultivation of mustard was dangerous in household gardens, it was utterly ruthless rampaging through a field (Crossan 1991, 278). The Mishnah, accordingly, forbade its use in Jewish gardens, mandating that it be kept segregated out at the edges of larger field-plots where its intrusive drive to intermix could be controlled (Scott 1989, 374, 380).

21. In the long view, invasives like wild mustard do function to "mend" ruptures in woodlands ecologies that are destined to become climax forest when restored to their own wild trajectories (Hemenway 2009, 13–14). In that sense, mustard does eventually issue in "branches."

22. It is worth noting Newcomb's critique of "Christen*dom*" in this regard—in tracking down the metaphorical purchase of the suffix "dom" in its root meaning of "domination," he points out that "king*dom*" and "free*dom*" likewise become suspect terms to work with. "Freedom" itself derives from a German word, *freithom*. which literally references a "barons' estate" within the feudal hierarchy of land control, over which that ruler had a right of dominion (Newcomb 2008, 59). Here we might then extrapolate that the opposite of slavery and oppression is not "freedom" but...what? Indigenous folk would likely say, "wildness."

23. As well as the response of his extended family, who seek to "arrest" ("seize") him before the authorities do so (cf. 6:17; 12:12; 14:1, 44, 46, 49, 51 for the political valence of the term), having heard of how beleaguered he was in his exorcism activities (Mk 3:20–21). They perceive him to be "standing outside himself" ("*ekeste*" or "ecstatic" in Greek)—a perception Jesus will immediately "flip" in his characterization of a kingdom and a house that cannot "stand" in being divided against themselves. As we see, this amounts to a kind of "battle of possessions," in which he challenges the "possession" of the kingdom/house by way of his own actions while possessed by countervailing "Powers" (Mk 6:14 and discussion of Davies below).

24. I have taken up this particular way of describing Jesus' parabolic tactic of folk resistance from Ethiopian (and broader Mediterranean) practices centered on vernacular traditions such as *The Net of Solomon* (discussed in chapter 5). This latter tradition will show up as a "visual graphics of the spirit" (literally) "writ large" in Ethiopian use of talismanic scrolls to "entrap" invasive spirits. What Jesus seeks to accomplish in an artistry of words, Ethiopian healers will elaborate in a geometrics of color.

25. The debate about the exact meaning of the charge is undecidable. What it does make clear is that Jesus is popularly perceived as not aligned with the "Power" of the Jerusalem Temple-State, but with a country-side spirit of pagan folk of earlier time that he brings to bear against the Temple regime. Whether Beelzebul references something like "lord of the heights," "prince of the lofty house," or "lord of the flies," the invocation of "Baal" pulls into the equation the deep history of this god as a storm-figure. As a "fly-king," Beelzebul was understood to be an apotropaic power, bringing healing from fly-born infection by appeasing the flies or using their own power against them; while in later Christian tradition he is depicted as a prince-demon, leading a revolt *against* Satan himself. Whether or not Jesus can be understood as "reworking" this old power as a subdued and now captivated "familiar spirit"—reoriented into apotropaic service of a more sustainable "messianic" vision (the "leading captivity captive" of Eph 4:8)—the entire episode gives strong hint of a use of spiritual power against itself, not a simple division of "good versus evil" or merely exorcistic banishment of the "principality."

26. As noted in chapter 3 in connection with Elijah, I am not here interested in debating the difference between "magic" and "mysticism" (or "grace" or

"charisma" or "miracle-working," etc.). Biblical accounts of "exorcisms," "healings," "calming storms," "walking on water," and so on, all involve representations of a certain level of agency on the part of Jesus (as indeed of Elijah before him and, later on, Peter and Paul after him; Acts 5:14; 19:11–12). The issue of legitimacy around spirit-combat is not simply a matter of having the name right, but of an entire posture of living engagement toward the powers in both their personal and structural aspects. The concern here is to read with an appreciation for "indigenous" and "vernacular" wisdoms.

27. The account gains added traction when we remember that the half-shekel Temple tax—mandated by custom, not by Mosaic law—implied a form of reciprocity: a payment tendered to guarantee the rains necessary to an abundant harvest. But this was a tax, as Herzog indicates, that Jesus, in effect, taught was not legitimate (Herzog's take on Mt 17: 24–26, pointing out that Jesus' question to Peter implies that this Temple-tax is no different than what "kings" like Caesar or Herod coercively extract, but that *kinship* relations to the real "divine" owner of the land void the claims of any would-be "ruler," whether Gentile royalty or Temple priests; 2000, 220–221). What we then have in this reading of Jesus' "weather action" is the Temple marked as "Tower," as illegitimate World-Pole, usurper of the role of guaranteeing rain and fecundity, trying to replace the "Power" of mountain wildness and storm vitality.

28. Also of interest here is the immediate juxtaposition, to this Beelzebul passage, of the story about a cast-out spirit returning to his house with seven more" (Lk 24–26; cf. also Mt 12:43–45). What the connection might be between a "Rain-God Principality" (Baal) and "spirits unable to find rest in waterless places" remains unclear but intriguing.

29. Leading immediately to Moses' threat to Pharaoh that if he still will not let the people go, swarms of flies (what later becomes a "Beelzebul Power") will be sent to establish a "saving division" ("to set redemption" in Hebrew), articulating a boundary by way of natural powers (insects) between the geography of Goshen and the rest of Egypt, and between Pharaoh's people and those of YHWH/Moses (Ex 8:16–24). For a contemporary example of a similar "salvation by way of the swarm," ecofeminist scholar Gloria Orenstein writes of reindeer-herder Sami folk above the Arctic Circle who have identified summer-time mosquito swarms as "shamanic protectors" of their lands, keeping out European interests that otherwise would have long ago colonized that area (Orenstein 1993, 177–181).

30. Again, the background of the word in a Jewish context ranges from wind as a natural force, through breath as the life of living beings, to the hovering of an ancestral "haunt" or power. And indeed, here there arises the question to what degree "anointing" itself pointed toward a propensity for possession, as in the Is 61:1–4 text that Luke adopts as inaugural for Jesus' ministry: "the Spirit of the Lord is 'upon me' because he has anointed me to preach good news to the poor..." (Lk 4:18–19).

31. For a more in-depth treatment of this category in the gospels, see my chapter, "Upstart Messiahs, Renegade Samaritans, and Temple Exorcisms: What Can Jesus' Peasant Resistance Movement in 1st Century Palestine Teach Us about Confronting 'Color-Blind' Whiteness Today?"

32. Referring to African-American skills at "signifying'" (ironic and parodic modes of using language to combat seriously, or relativize playfully, dominating forms of power)—most especially in the tradition of "playing the dozens," involving two antagonists trading insults in a rhythmic cadence based on sexual innuendo (and frequently referencing mother-lines) until one of the two could no longer wittily invert the chain of insult and thereby either lost face or got physical. In addition to generating entertainment, the practice was actually a form of street pedagogy, training young blacks how to use language to sidestep abuse and put down, in a society where facing such was a certainty.

33. Whence the association here remains unclear. But it is just possible that the earlier charge of channeling Beelzebul (Mk 3:22, Mt 9:34, 10:25, 12:22–32; Lk 11:15, 2 Kgs 2:1–18) itself hides a deep anti-Samaritan abhorrence referencing Samaritan ethnic genealogy going back to the Assyrian city of Cuthah (the Talmud calls Samaritans the "Kuthim"). Cuthah's central cult honored Nergal, at times said to be the chief of Hell's "secret police" and honorary spy in service of Beelzebul (2 Kgs 17:1–41; de Plancy; Weyer).

34. For a more complete treatment of the Syro-Phoenician encounter covered here see my piece, "A Canaanitic Word in the Logos of Christ: or the Difference the Syro-Phoenician Woman Makes to Jesus.".

35. In Mark, as Myers makes clear, language about "the way" is heavily coded as a cipher for discipleship, for living the regime of Sabbath-Jubilee practice alternative to empire and its predatory demands (Myers 1988, 124, 174–175). In context then, release to "go her own way," after affirmation of her particular saying, carries interesting overtones of a way beyond "the way."

36. A gospel virtue, as Herzog makes clear in his unpacking of the parable about the "Friend at Midnight," where peasant enactment of hospitality for a stranger, refusing (shamelessly) to be bound by the self-interest calculations of the elites in allowing village resources to address a need that could not be repaid, are subtly signified as "messianic" (Herzog 1994, 212–214).

4 *Metaphysical Speculation*: From Messianism to Christology

1. Corbett will note, for instance, that all of our naming of "God" is edging toward idolatry—and inevitably so.

2. Eisenberg offers, for instance, that though describing machines "as if they were alive" is a conceit, it is "a useful one" (Eisenberg 1999, 57). "It reminds us to keep an eye on them." "Like our living allies, machines coevolve with us." "We think we control them; in truth, they have a life and a logic of their own."

3. Brian Willson, who had his legs severed when a munitions train ran over him during a 1987 protest action against US support of Nicaraguan counter-insurgency efforts, notes, for instance, that the problem is technology in general, not merely the uses to which it is put (such as weapons innovation). He cites the "cost" of manufacturing a two-gram microchip, running our computers and cell phones, as entailing 3.7 lbs. of fossil fuel inputs, 8.5 gallons of water, and baking temperatures necessary to fix information on the chip that render such a commodity hundreds of times more expensive, in energy terms, than manufacture of an automobile (Willson 2011, 361). The extractive "hollowing" of the planet ramps *up* with the shift to information technologies, despite the vaunted energy savings involved in "paperless" communication.

4. And obviously, there is a richly suggestive intersection here with indigenous understandings (of ancestral domains, underworlds, spirits of the violently killed and the "ungrieved deceased" returning to haunt the living community) and the scholarly work of Avery Gordon, already mentioned, tracking the effects of "ghostly matters" in a sociological vein. We are simply expanding the register here to include ghostly "matter."

5. Lakota Sioux vocalization of *mitakuye oyasin* ("all my relations") to conclude various ritual actions is merely one of the better known.

6. Which is not to say that indigenous cultures did not ever ravage their own ecologies. Obviously many did (though with much less destructive effect than our modern forms of predation). The point is that many did not. Even one such is evidence that human beings *can* live differently and deserves deep pondering and careful attention.

7. Even a Marxist like Brennan finds the history of demonology requisite to begin to articulate the extra-individual dimensions of life, resorting not just to a reprise of older languages to describe the "visitation" of things like passions and anxieties, but theorizing such, in depth, and juxtaposing to it recent work, for instance, on the relationship of smell to consciousness. It now appears that extra-corporeal "agencies" like pheromones are so integral to human awareness that it is likely that "the problems of consciousness and intentionality will not be solved" until olfaction and influence from outside the subject are understood (Brennan 2004, 68–69, 75, 97, 164).

8. Wink summarizes this range as follows: "What I propose is viewing the spiritual Powers not as separate heavenly or ethereal entities but as *the inner aspect of material or tangible manifestations of power*. I suggest that the 'angels of nature' are the patterning of physical things—rocks, trees, plants, the whole god-glorifying, dancing, visible universe; that the 'principalities and powers' are the inner or spiritual essence, or gestalt, of an institution or state or system; that the 'demons' are the psychic or spiritual power emanated by organizations or individuals or subaspects of individuals whose energies are bent on overpowering others; that 'gods' are the very real archetypal or ideological structures that determine or govern reality and its mirror, the human brain; that the mysterious 'elements of the

universe' (*stoicheia tou kosmou*) are the invariances (formerly called 'laws') which, though often idolized by humans, conserve the self-consistency of each level of reality in its harmonious interrelationship with every other level and the Whole; and that 'Satan' is the actual power that congeals around collective idolatry, injustice, or inhumanity, a power that increases or decreases according to the degree of collective refusal to choose higher values" (Wink 1984, 104–105).

9. And of course, Greek philosophy traces its rise out of Greek mythology as a nascent attempt to identify these base-line principles and irreducible elements of things, beginning with the focus of Thales on water, Anaximenes on air, Parmenides and Heroclitus on earth and fire, Aristotle on "hot and cold, dryness and moisture," and even Empedocles on "love" and "strife" (Wink 1984, 74–75).

10. In *Naming the Powers*, Wink emphasizes that it is precisely those persons and communities that publicly refuse the "ultimacy" of the imperial institutions—symbolically calling out and contesting the fetish form or "spirit" of such, like early Christians kneeling to God and praying *for* the emperor, rather than bowing *to* him—that will draw down the most ferocious wrath and furious punishment of imperial might. Whereas robbers and thieves—who actually embody the spirit of imperial operations—will incur much less severe repercussions, as their antisocial acts really confirm, rather than contest, imperial power (Wink 1984, 108–111).

11. Public symbolic actions like Jesus clearing the Temple (and consequently suffering the theatrics of ritual degradation on the cross as punishment) do not so much seek redress for particular grievances as expose the spirit of a system of domination in its entirety (Wink 1986, 67). I comprehend such as a kind of inverse dramaturgy of indigenous practices of ritual offering (that sought not so much exactly to make up for the "hole" created in reality by human taking as to "mark" and honor the entirety of the sacred in nature by way of a small gesture of "beauty returned").

12. Where Jews and Christians posited angels as presiding over the elements, northern European folk belief grasped gnomes, fairies, elves, and dwarves as "nature's little blue collar laborers," working angelic patterns "into the stuff of rocks, trees, and so forth" (Wink 1986, 140). Hildegard of Bingen (1098–1179) will pen that she hears "a mighty voice crying from the elements of the world" to the effect that because of human corruption, they are "being spun like the sails of a windmill," and left "stinking from pestilence and from hunger for injustice" (Fox 1984, 101).

13. The biblical tradition concurs. Where the element of water offered early judgment (in the days of Noah) on the aggrandizements of settlement and city-building hubris, Peter warns that it will be fire's role in the time to come (2 Pet 3:10, 12; cf. Wink, ftn. 32, 209). This could be read, on the one hand, as water itself rebelling against its enslavement in irrigation systems serving nascent imperial formations in Mesopotamia and, on the other, as fire in revolt against its industrial servitude (in smelters,

internal combustion engines, lasers, nuclear reactors, etc.), threatening either explosive (nuclear war) or slow motion (planetary warming) come-uppance. Unlike our modern romance of the flame, blacksmithing, in cultures across the globe, was recognized as a violative and dangerous human intervention, needing careful quarantine from everyday life in terms of both ritual activity and (often) physical sequestration at the margins of the village.

14. Wink clarifies that "the demonic" is not a quality inhering in particular "gods" as such, but rather "in the way we relate to them" (Wink 1986, 125). Powers become demonic when we abdicate the creative tension in which we should be "wrestling" blessing from them (integrating their force in psyche and lifestyle alike), in what amounts to "worshipful deference" to their appearance as inflated and overwhelming.

15. See Canadian physician Gabor Maté's devastating critique of the destructiveness of modern culture for children, resulting in societies constructed on pandemic forms of addictive relationship (Maté 2010, 263–280, 417, 438–442).

16. Although there does remain a remnant of such in European feudalism's fascination with relics, as we examine in subsequent chapters. See, for instance, the way "sacral potency" associated with either a living holy person in the neighborhood, or the dead remains or artifacts of such (toe bones, skulls, pieces of clothing, even slivers of wood from the "true cross"), could be mobilized on behalf of oppressed peasants to restrain elite aggression (Markus 1990, 116–119).

17. Communication scholar Robert Jensen touts the third major revolution of our species' history on the planet (after the so-called agricultural and industrial "revolutions") as the "delusional revolution" of the early twentieth century, by which he means the emergence of the public relations and marketing industries, now tipped off by Sigmund Freud's nephew, Edward Bernays, to the possibility of linking imagery and language with subliminal desires and fears, and the massive mental "colonization" that results (Jensen, Robert, 2).

18. In his chapter on Satan, for instance, Wink will insist that our modern rationalist "killing" of the devil (or reinvention of the image as merely a personalized bogeyman) hardly eliminated the reality to which the term referred. It is rather the case that "the evil of our time had become so gigantic that it had virtually outstripped the symbol and become autonomous, unrepresentable, beyond comprehension" (Wink 1986, 10).

19. In one sense, "principalities and powers" could perhaps be imagined as the numinosity of materials and life forms plundered from various ecosystems. In this view, natural biodiversity—now stripped from its local context, unnaturally amalgamated with other plundered "elements" and piled up in the infrastructure of imperial bureaucracy (slave bodies, food economies, urban architecture, military technology, aqueducts, ships, etc.)—is rendered unstable and overbearing: a newly minted imperial "eco-sphere" of

formerly wild forces, simultaneously reduced and hypertrophied in these novel employments.

20. One intriguing example of this might be found in the etymology of our understanding of "angels." David Abram wonders if these "winged messenger" figures are not simply flattened out memories of indigenous woodlands cultures for whom bird-life—once carefully observed in context and the various song-sounds correlated with subsequent behaviors and events (like the sudden arrival of predators)—was embraced as the primordial messenger-species, a kind of "second-skin" of the community, granting it early apprehension of what was coming toward it through the woods from a great distance away (Abram 2010, 192–199; 1996, 12–13). Are "angels" an imperial refiguring of this indigenous "bird-sensibility," at once appropriating and hiding its primal import?

21. We could almost say Paul's "gospel"—the emblematic narrative by which Paul "fleshes out" his meaning of "messiah."

22. The role of "pastor," for instance, inherited as a Christian leadership term from the older appropriation of the idea of a "shepherd" for kingship, grows increasing remote, in its actual informed experience, from the lifeway from which it takes its meaning.

23. These practices did not only codify the demand for regular reestablishment of a basic structure of social solidarity and rough economic equality. But they also gave critical practical effect to the memory of the postslavery experience of being reschooled in the wild and given a covenant, issued from a storm-clad mountain, that established "going feral" from Egypt as primary for this people's identity. Central to such practices was revisiting the experience of *manna* foraging as the touchstone for—and mythic limitation on—the subsistence agriculture rhythms the people would settle into in Canaan (given ritual form for seven days in every year's Sukkot festival and given social expression every seven years in the required Sabbath year release). This can be read as a form of regular practical recall of an original "agreement with the wild," similar to indigenous examples of such the world over that license human captivity of natural forces—domesticated herds, reengineered fields, extracted minerals, etc.—in exchange for regular ritual return to, and recognition of, the sacrality of the *wild* ("uncaptured") source of life itself (Prechtel, in Jensen, 2001).

24. It may even be that Paul's vision of the entire creation "groaning in travail together for the epiphany of God's children" is his own lament for the growing devastation—even in his time—of imperial predation on local environments. But however constrained his "reading" may be by urban assumptions and imperial limitations, even Paul argues that creation will obtain the freedom "of the children of God" (Rom 8:18–27). It takes only a slight heart skip to read in this a perhaps unthought intimation that "children of God" includes within its compass "creation" itself as equally hosting both "liberty" and "glory"—that is to say, as equally being itself a sacred "child of God." In any case here, "the Groan" shared by creation,

"ourselves," and the Spirit would appear itself to be a "power of the commons," a kind of elemental force-field rooted in nature that throbs with spiritual longing in mineral, plant, animal and human alike, that shall not finally be thwarted. Paul's conclusion that "no creature"—whether the humanly instituted powers of "tribulation, oppression, political persecution, impoverished hunger, etc." or the more eco-cosmically reengineered forces like "death or life or angels or principalities or height or depth, etc."—will be able to separate us from the love of *theos* in *christos* Jesus, is a conclusion anchored in a vision of freedom that unrolls all the way back to undoing the enslavement of the created order itself.

25. Which Howard-Brook will characterize as Johannine stand-ins for synoptic parables (Howard-Brook1994, 32).

26. A defining value for the Johannine community that stands in sharp contrast to other discipleship communities that John's gospel engages polemically. John's refusal ever to use the noun form "apostle" for leadership is only one index of the entire programmatic posture of this community's oppositional stance regarding hierarchy and authority (Howard-Brook 1994, 32–33).

27. Which represents the only occurrence in the gospels of Jesus anointing someone else—although in the Johannine address to the angel of the church of Laodicea, the angelic power that "is" that church is counseled to buy from the messiah salve with which to anoint "its" eyes in order to see (Rev. 3: 14–22).

28. Products whose possibility depends on agriculture and tillage. Both water and wine are central in Sukkot ritual.

29. Sukkot densely compacted layers of meaning and experience: the years of wilderness wandering and living off the land in Sinai (as we covered in chapter 2, especially in the discussion of Corbett's Arizona desert practice); agricultural rites borrowed from neighboring peoples; and the struggles of exploited "day laborers," living in temporary "ramadas" (or "booths") for the few weeks of harvest. For aware practitioners, Sukkot should have been a 7-day "schooling of the senses" in all of that historical memory. It also offered prayers for rain to terminate the long hot summer and provide water for the fall harvest, and indeed looked to an eschatological "retooling" of Jerusalem as a "city" full of light, from which living waters would flow (Zech 14:7, 8).

30. The subtext of Sinai here is reinforced by the "murmuring" theme (Jh 7:12; Exod 17:3).

31. Themselves a hypostatized power of the element of fire or burning (Wink 1984, 30).

5 *Talismanic Depiction*: Messianic Repair and Folk Arts (Ethiopia)

1. Growing advocacy for a return to a "paleo-diet" (typical of hunter-gatherer communities before the advent of agriculture and large-scale consumption

of grains) and the research of physicians like Gabor Maté on ADD and addiction, arguing that we have much to learn from hunter-gatherer child-rearing practices, are just two quick examples (Maté 2012).

2. And tellingly here, for many, the questioning is arising not from any theoretical analysis, but from the interruptions and interrogations of nature itself. Hurricane Katrina, for North America, served as a kind of wake-up call (largely ignored). Hurricane Sandy has punctuated the growing reports (not least from the World Bank) of catastrophic climate changes afoot. Melting glaciers, acidification of oceans, record temperatures across the planet, typhoons (like Bhopha in the Philippines) in new places, etc., beg to be read in line with our analysis here as "ghosts" of dishonored natural powers (animals and plants rendered extinct, mountain tops removed, oil-corpses dug up, etc.) whose after-lives are coalescing into the kind of gargantuan "blowback" alone capable of "standing up to" human technoimperial pretension and once again confirming that our race is not master of the planet, but only one among a billionfold of living organisms and other forces whose gestalt answers to no single name and whose "power" remains, at core, wild. From this perspective, it is interesting to trace the career of indigenous "weather magic" as one of the spiritual practices most coveted by early empires in their projects of subduing restive peoples. Weather, and on a larger scale, climate change (and of course tectonic, volcanic and meteoric activity) comport as a kind of "natural rebuke" to our pretension to single-species mastery—an ecosystemic reaction whose material power effectively defies domestication.

3. Subaltern modes of microresistance, still alive in the half-lights and hidden transcripts and coded longings of peasant existence, become perhaps even more important today in light of the closing out of "ungovernable spaces" through state-controlled technologies like highways and railroads, satellite surveillance, drone penetration, helicopter over-flights, and so on.

4. Cf. Scott's notion of "symbolic jujitsu" (Scott 1990, 98).

5. And part of the choice here is informed by recognition that already in ancient Greco-Roman texts, as indeed in early Christian literatures, "Ethiopia/Ethiopians," "Egypt/Egyptians," and "Blacks/blackness," were adopted as tropes to anchor the bottom levels of moral and theological hierarchies (and by the fourth century, Ethiopia/Ethiopians had emerged even in Egyptian writing as the defining yardstick of inferiority) (Byron 2002, 12–13, 78). Indeed, black African subjects were used by Romans—alongside images of other startling novelties and supposed deformities (like pygmies or hunchbacks or large phalluses)—as an apotropaic defense against the "evil eye" of envy. As we see in the following text, this tactic will be inverted in Ethiopian scroll use, redeploying imperial images apotropaically against imperial incursion. Remarkable, in this context, is an ancient folk tradition extant all over the Mid-East and Asia that associates the evil eye especially with blue and green eyes (and with the peoples of Pontus and Scythia in particular), often creating blue-eyed charms (such

as the *nazar* of Turkey) to ward off the "curse effects" initiated by the gaze of envy. What historical experiences underlie this association can only be guessed. (It is curious that blue-eyes emerge in evolution at the same time and not too far removed spatially from our first efforts at domestication of other species. It is likewise curious that recent European research indicates that brown-eyed people (to the degree such also correlated with bigger mouths and noses, broader chins, and more prominent eyebrows), are generally perceived as more trustworthy than blue-eyed folk.) But the folk struggle to deflect the "invasive gaze"—as the advance "force" of a more material incursion—is a striking precursor to the modern struggle of people of color against the curse of racialization invented by white ("blue-eyed") people (to legitimize colonial extraction).

6. A host of questions arises for our argument here. In the *Ecology of Eden*, Eisenberg offers the theological concept of *tsimtsum,* popularized by Isaac of Luria in the sixteenth century, as a possible model for modern humans to adopt in relationship to the necessity to maintain the wild, if our species is to survive long term (Eisenberg 1999, 361–364, 390–392). Luria theorized creation as an act of god's "self-limiting," opening space for creatures by reducing the divine "footprint." Possession practitioners have at times remarked on the experience in terms of a kind of inner shrinking of self-awareness and intentionality—not always entire eclipse, but a moving of the self "off-stage," to make room for, and observe, other powers emerging in the psyche and body that then have their say and have their way (Hall 2009, 87). Esaki details something roughly similar in hip-hop ciphers or battles, when MCs must maintain a realm of inner silence, keeping themselves perched peacefully at the edge of an intuitive upwelling of words that they then "spit" against their opponents (Esaki 2007, 370–374). Once human society has aggrandized or "ballooned out" in an agricultural mode of settlement that is relentlessly destructive of habitat, some kind of practice of self-limitation is utterly necessary for survival. This set of concerns represents perhaps *the* moral question of our time for our species. "Possession" may well represent a trope for rethinking ecological health in the key of inner life and psychic ecology—a kind of indigenous model for what anarcho-primitivist author Daniel Quinn calls learning to "stand aside and make room for all the rest" of the world's various creatures (Quinn 1992, 242).

7. Interesting in this regard is bell hooks' discussion of the way some black people would try to adopt "white ways" as a kind of "amulet" to deflect the terrors of white power invading their communities or their persons (hooks 1992, 166).

8. This accords with my argument above that the demonic—especially in its imperialized form as "principalities and powers"—may represent a kind of inordinate "piling up" of the elementary spiritual potency attending everything natural (animals, plants, minerals, etc.), which in its wild state is neither "divine" nor "demonic" in any simplistic sense, but is rather its own

thing, part of a spirit-world that does not easily parse out into reductionist equations of good versus evil. Many origin myths "remember" a time when humans and spirits readily comingled and communicated more easily, until the unfolding of historical alienation resulted in a situation where illness is now a primary language between spirit and human (Mercier 1997, 46). I would merely add that we may be speaking historically here of the shift from hunting and gathering to settled agriculture and urban hierarchy.

9. The fourteenth century Amhara *Kebra Negast* legend of a son (Menelik) produced by sexual contact between Solomon and the visiting Queen of Sheba—as indeed the genealogy of Ethiopian Jews (commonly known as *Beta Israel*) in the country—remains the subject of scholarly debate. Certainly the legend was used to buttress the Solomonic dynasty that solidified its rule in the thirteenth century, while the genealogy may represent a "rebellious archaism" of converts out of Ethiopian Monophysite Christianity at some point, or some more ancient derivation (a breakaway part of the group Moses led out of Egypt, Southern refugees from the split of Israel under Solomon's son Rehoboam, remnants of the tribe of Dan, ending up in Cush following Babylonian conquest of 586, or Yemeni Jews crossing the Red Sea, etc.). The DNA evidence, in any case, suggests African ancestry rather than middle-Eastern.

10. Throughout the history covered, but especially after the thirteenth century.

11. Grasses, in much herder ritual around the globe, honored as a primal spiritual power (god or goddess) necessary to life.

12. The career of Gog and Magog in the legends and discourses from ancient times to the present is prolific, referencing whomever various cultures deemed "barbaric" or "threatening" (cf. Gen 10; Ezek 38–39; Rev20:17). For Josephus the term clearly references the Scythians, whom Alexander is reputed to have locked up behind a gate of iron in the Caucasus Mountains, keeping them from invading the south. One subgroup of this people was the Sarmatians—a blond-haired, blue-eyed people whose name ("Sauromatai") according to folk legend, meant "lizard people—an apparent reference to their scale-like armor and dragon-standards. In the scroll tradition, a number of talismans associated with Alexander take a serpentine form, replicating, in their spiritual function, the gate of iron or bronze closed against "the snake people" (Mercier 1997, 50, 90, 92).

13. An inscription on one scroll, for instance, reads, "Wisdom of Alexander, Greek king, who made requests on the stone of the horizon" (the mountain on the horizon that supports the sky) (Mercier 1997, 57). This is a mode of invocation strongly reminiscent of pastoral nomad practice on the Asian steppes of setting up standing stones with demarcations of deer antlers, that are also maps of the riverine valleys whose funneling of snow melt from area mountains (e.g., the Altai) determines the fertility of the grasses on which their animals (and they) depend (Prechtel, 2012 lecture).

14. Clearly the scrolls emerge historically in Ethiopian medicinal practice as a concrete "site" where older ways and newer Christian belief meet and wrestle. Here is historical change rendered emblematic. Mercier underscores the evident creativity and polyculturalism. Lack of certain archaeological evidence or written testimony does not preclude him from positing (what he calls) a Sahelian zone of "African therapies and art forms" wherein mix motifs of the Mediterranean north with West African stylistic emphases. While Greek, Mesopotamian, Byzantine, Iranian, Jewish, and Muslim influences are clearly evident, the scrolls' focus on geometricism, frontality, face, and eyes share an ethos more characteristic of *kifwebe* masks of the Sonye and Luba, or steles of the Cross River region than the Mediterranean. Frequent thematic references to cosmological and cosmogonic symbolism, as indeed the attribution of physical malady to spirit possession and the crafting of medical/religious objects of therapy or protection correlated with users' bodies, likewise favor an African rather than a more northern influence. Though not necessarily indicative of direct linkage with societies south and west, the evident motifs push Mercier to hypothesize an Ethiopic role mediating encounter between black African and Christian Mediterranean cultures that he likens to the way Ireland similarly remixed Mediterranean culture and the Celtic world (Mercier 1997, 115). Form and function clearly appoint the scrolls as medicinal rather than iconic, linking body and trance in a mode of remedy quite similar to Fon *bocio*, Minyanka *boli*, Kongo *nkisi*, and other African "objects of power" deployed in cultic practices as a physical double of the patient. Much more than mere representation is at stake in their production and use.

15. And it is interesting to note in this regard that religious paintings, if not made in concert with orthodox conventions of prayer and fasting, are rendered "pure" for church use by being "anointed" (Mercier 1997, 73–74).

16. It emerges almost as a form of "folk bible," whose interpretation demands the requisite cultural competence, mobilizing the menagerie of scroll-personas resulting from such work as a vernacular ensemble of "texts," negotiated by the eye, quoted with power by a "people's" evangelist (the *dabtara*).

17. Convulsion would seem to be a key index here of the psychospiritual depth "activated." In its political dimensions, as we discuss below, exorcism tampers with ideological "programming." Uprooting the latter, I would venture, is never merely a matter of new information, but of breaking up an emotional-cognitive structure that necessarily sends tremors through the body and upsets kinesthetic habituation.

18. Geometric representation, in many indigenous cultures, signifies (or contributes to causing) trance experience—the whirling vortex of passage out of "normal" consciousness and into its alternative that often seems to give rise to a visual impression of everyday objects suddenly condensing into flowing or writhing patterns of geometrically shaped fields of energy (Clottes and Lewis-Williams 1996, 16–17; Perkinson 2005, 147–151).

19. Again, the sensibility in evidence here is one in which animal and plant and mineral encounters are not separate from the spirit-world, but are rather the "incarnations" that spirits operate through.

20. Physician and scholar of ADD Gabor Maté notes at one point that, "Everyone has the experience of suddenly feeling intense physiological and psychological shifts internally at trading glances with another person; such shifts can be exquisitely pleasurable or unpleasant. How one person gazes at another can alter the other's electrical brain patterns, as registered by EEGs, and may also cause physiological changes in the body" (Maté 1999, 71). The "represented" gaze can be received with similar effect.

21. In folk idiom—using "a thorn to remove a thorn" (Mercier 1978, 88).

22. The entire tradition can be read as preeminently one of magic "literature," in which writing is commandeered into a role of power not as a set of signs to be deciphered through reading practices, but rather as mysterious ciphers to be worn on the body or displayed on the wall as an amulet (Chernetsov 2004, 42). Writing, historically, is a state technology, designed to control populations through census-taking and keeping track of debts, taxes, and rents. Here it is "thawed out" and put in motion as a numinous advocacy for people's defense against invasive powers.

23. A reference to French philosopher Gilles Deleuze's construction of the "machine of faciality," mixing "the white wall of meaning with the black hole of subjectivity" (Mercier 1997, 95). Deleuze's phenomenology of this "machinery of the face" offers an entire treatment that in many ways underscores the argument here. In a philosophical poetics dense with suggestion, he tracks what he calls the "semiotics of significance and subjectification" that coalesces in the "year zero" (of the Western calendar) into the face of Christ, subsuming all other semiotic systems into its ever growing, but nonuniversal facialization of bodies and landscapes. Overcome and destroyed—in this "emergence of Christ" as what Deleuze calls the quintessential "White Man"—were (and are) the preexisting "primitive" semiotic systems rooted not in the production of faces but in "shamanic, warrior and hunter organizations of power" operating through "corporeality, animality, and vegitality," capable of receiving "souls" (of jaguars, of orchids, of rocks, etc.) as friends while repulsing enemy souls (Deleuze and Guattari, 1980, 175–176, 190). The resulting regime of racialization anchored in the face of Christ totalizes its signifying and subject-making into a social and geographic topography admitting no exterior and no other. Not surprisingly, for Deleuze, "popular Ethiopian scrolls representing demons" appear as the purest case of this despotic countenance of signifying that everywhere looms, multiplying eyes, snapping up the gazing subject in its black holes (Deleuze and Guattari 1980, 182–183).

24. Perhaps akin to a scribal "face" caught in a parabolic "net" in Mk 3:22–27?

25. How far different is this from a "Finger of God" Beelzebul figure rounded up into a thunder-chorus for certain of Jesus' works as discussed earlier?

26. Scott traces the wide-ranging historical evidence for peasant use of what might be called "naïve monarchism," projecting the Myth of the Return of the Just King (in Russia, for instance, the Myth of the "Czar-Deliverer") onto the royal incumbent in a savvy brokering of supposed peasant backwardness into the public expression (and possible redress) of grievances (Scott 1990, 97–101).

27. Chernetsov notes, among other analogs, a Moroccan practice of tying rags to trees or objects near the shrine of a saint (usually Sufi), that accomplishes a "transference of a conditional curse"—a material form of petition in which the petitioner announces that the saint is "tied up" and will not be released until the request is granted (Chernetsov 2005, 195).

28. Only black (maledictory), red (flames), and white (light) are deemed effective against demons; blues, greens, and yellows are merely background "support" (Mercier 1979, 58). The contrast between the abstract white and black of the eyes and the raw materiality of the reds and blacks and other colors of the rest of the composition creates a percussive effect, doing with sight what polyrhythm does with sound in service of trance.

29. One dabtara reads the geometrics as a "throne," which once perceived by the Devil, is recognized as his proper place and occupied, leaving the possessed person empty (Chernetsov 2004, 41). The power of red lines to entrap (a kind of ancient and inverse "redlining") ensures that the person will not be "resettled" by the demonic power.

30. What Deleuze would call the either/or "bi-univocalization" of the racialized face system, followed by its yes/no "binarization," adjudicating sameness and tolerated (or not) deviance (Deleuze and Guattari 1980, 176–178).

31. As one dabtara interviewed by Mercier remarked, after dreaming, horrified, of eating impure hyena until he heard God admonish him to resume the "calling of the spirits" (or "divining") that he had previously given up as being against God's law: "My god and I understand each other" (Mercier 1997, 42).

32. Using Scott's insights, Herzog reads Jesus' response as an instance of "peasant dissembling," appearing to conform to the pubic transcript of deference and submission required by the authorities, while loading into that public posture, various "coded" gestures and tonalities that simultaneously communicated the "hidden transcript"—the "real" evaluation of the situation—to the on-looking peasant crowd (Herzog 2000, 225). That the authorities were "astonished" is textual evidence that he had slipped the noose of their trap, and "poached on" their very challenge, managing to affirm defiance of the entire apparatus of occupation even while conforming to what it utterly demanded. The tribute was paid (under the implicit threat of arrest and execution), but honor and spirit were not!

33. We might think of the way the Occupy Wall Street movement "revealed" the face of capitalism as savagely "demonic" in the grimacing faces of white collar police officers pepper-spraying demonstrators. Capitalism was not

thereby "dethroned"; but its spell was certainly broken in the public square and its character clearly unmasked.

34. Cf., for instance, Du Bois' accounting of the way a little girl's glance in grade school shattered his world and locked him inside the veil of race (Du Bois 1961, 16–17).

35. In classic Christological terms, the underlying "substance" permitting different entities (e.g., "God" and "human") to share an existence together.

36. It is interesting in this regard that even Orthodox Christianity, both Ethiopian and Byzantine (and for that matter for the Roman Catholic West as well), emphasizes that while devotion to an image is a form of veneration, adoration or actual worship of God is reserved for Communion—that is, "eating God"—alone (Mercier 1997, 74, 85, fn 21).

6 *Insurgent Beat*: Messianic Decay and Vision Quest

1. See especially, *White Theology: Outing Supremacy in Modernity and Shamanism, Racism,* and *Hip-Hop Culture: Essays on White Supremacy and Black Subversion.*

2. Cf. Mk 4:26–29, as indeed, a mid-west ecoactivist like Wes Jackson, involved in a grassroots (!) initiative attempting to repopulate the US prairie with its native species of perennials. Counter to the scientific hubris of the likes of a Richard Dawkins, Jackson argues that an "epistemology of ignorance" has become necessary to contain our species toxic overreach in presuming that we can "know," plan, and manage the entire ecosphere of the planet (Jensen 2005, 1; Jackson 2005, 14–15).

3. Such as we find in the legends about blues genius Robert Johnson, supposedly trading, in interaction with the "devil," his innocence for gifting, ever after able to plumb depths and embody conundrums in his playing that evoked the underworld of human experience and drove people "crazy." And of course this legend is itself camped out on West African traditions relating to the trickster figure, Eshu Elegba (or Eleggua, or Papa Labas in Voudou, etc.), Great Presider over the crossroads of decision, Opener of the Way, and Provoker of Desire.

4. It is worth remembering that for the Deuteronomic Moses, standing on Mt Nebo and delivering the covenant-song to be read at the time of every Sabbath-year-release during the feast of Sukkot, the ultimate witness called into play to secure the words spoken "against" Israel was "heaven and earth" (Dt 31:10, 28). The "Power" of last resort, brought to bear against the excesses of empire with its seductions and might, is the ecosystem itself, organized as "weather." In apocalyptic vision, the ultimate agency of antiimperial rebuke typically takes the form of some kind of geocosmic revolt.

5. It is worth recalling that most of the religious traditions whose scriptures invoke angel-like messengers trace part of their origins to forested

environments (e.g., Judaism, which arguably learns its language of angels from Persian-Zoroasterian influence; Christianity and Islam learning theirs from Judaism, etc., in a Mid-East that was heavily wooded before being clear-cut by successive Mesopotamian empires).

6. Perkinson (2004, 9–20; 2005, xv–xxii).

7. Detroit is the only city I know where you might look overhead one day (as I did a couple of years ago) to see a hired airplane trailing a streamer advertising a phone number to call if you have scrap metal to sell!

8. Interestingly, Afrika Bambaataa and other early artists adopted a fashion they labeled "wild style."

9. For a startling theorization of this construct, see Ivan Illich's discussion, already in the 1970s, of an "energy crisis" that had not yet gained that name (Illich 1980, 133).

10. I am indebted to Larry Rasmussen for this way of speaking (Rasmussen 1997, 33).

11. This way of designating Otto's formula combines it with Wink's notion of the "Powers" as reimagined in their more "natural" settings in various eco-systems (as discussed in chapter 4).

12. I have written about this in some depth in the Abdul Karim Bangura edited *Pan-Africanism Caribbean Connections* and the Anthony B. Pinn and Monica R. Miller edited volume of *Culture and Religion*'s special issue on Hip-Hop and Religion (Perkinson 2007, 67–69, 75–76; 2009, 66–69).

13. Cf. Chang for sharp commentary on the way hip-hop's black cultural code, promulgated by a multicultural mélange of devotees, has leveraged a rainbow reality globally (Chang 2005, 418).

Bibliography

Abram, David. 1996. *The Spell of the Sensuous: Perception and Language in the More-Than-Human World*. New York: Vintage Books.

———. 2010. *Becoming Animal: An Earthly Cosmology*. New York: Pantheon Books.

Avens, Robert. 1984. *The New Gnosis: Heidegger, Hillman, and Angels*. Dallas: Spring Publications.

Baldwin, James. 1963. *The Fire Next Time*. New York: Dell Publishing Co.

Beardsley, John. 2007. *Connecting the Dots: Tyree Guyton's Heidelberg Project*. Detroit: Wayne State University Press, 38–47.

Benjamin, Walter. 1969. "Theses on the Philosophy of History," *Illuminations*. Trans. H. Zohn, Ed. H. Arendt. New York: Schoken, 253–264.

Boal, Augusto. 1979. *Theatre of the Oppressed*. Trans. C. A. & M. L. McBride. New York: Theatre Communications Group.

Boddy, Janice. 1989. *Wombs and Alien Spirits: Women, Men, and the Zar Cult in Northern Sudan*. Madison, WN: The University of Wisconsin Press.

Boggs, Grace Lee and Kurashige, Scott. 2011. *The Next American Revolution: Sustainable Activism for the Twenty-First Century*. Berkeley: University of California Press.

Borg, Marcus. 1994. *Meeting Jesus Again for the First Time: The Historical Jesus & the Heart of the Contemporary Faith*. San Francisco: Harper San Francisco.

Brennan, Teresa. 2003. *Globalization and Its Terrors: Daily Life in the West*. London: Routledge.

Brown, Frank, and Lucas, Phil. 1990. *Voyage of Rediscovery*. Vancouver: Moving Images Distribution (video).

———. 2004. *The Transmission of Affect*. Ithaca and London: Cornell University Press.

Buber, Martin. 1958. *Moses*. New York: Harper & Row.

Burhoe, Ralph Wendell, 1972. "Natural Selection and God," *Zygon* 7 (1972): 60.

Byron, Gay L. 2002. *Symbolic Blackness and Ethnic Difference in Early Christian Literature*. London: Routledge.

Chang, Jeff. 2005. *Can't Stop Won't Stop: A History of the Hip-Hop Generation*. New York: St. Martin's Press.

Chernetsov, Sevir.2004. "Ethiopian 'Magic Scrolls,'" *Manuscripta Orientalia* 10 (4): 40–159.

————. 2005. "Ethiopian Magic Scrolls," *Forum for Anthropology and Culture* No. 2 (2005). Peter the Great Museum of Anthropology and Ethnography, 188–200.

Clastres, Hélène. 1995 (1975). *The Land-Without-Evil: Tupi-Guarani Prophetism.* Trans. J. G. Brovender. Urbana and Chicago: University of Illinois Press.

Clottes, Jean and David Lewis-Williams. 1996. *The Shamans of Prehistory: Trance and Magic in the Painted Caves.* Text by Jean Clottes; Trans. Sophie Hawkes. New York: Harry N. Abrams, Inc., Publishers.

Cobb, Clifford W. and Daiz, Philippe. 2009. *Why Global Poverty? Think Again* (A Companion Guide to the Film, "The End of Poverty?"). New York: Robert Schalkenbach Foundation and Canoga Park, CA: Cinema Libre Studio.

Corbett, Jim. 1991. *Goatwalking.* New York: Viking Press.

————. 2005. *A Sanctuary for All Life: The Cowbalah of Jim Corbett.* Englewood, CO: Howling Dog Press.

Crossan, John Dominc. 1991. *The Historical Jesus: The Life of a Mediterranean Jewish Peasant.* San Francisco: Harper San Francisco.

Daneel, M. L. 1994. "African Independent Churches Face the Challenge of Environmental Ethics," *Eco-theology: Voices from South and North.* Ed. David G. Hallman. Maryknoll: Orbis, 248–263.

Davidson, Benjamin. 1970 (1848). *The Analytical Hebrew and Chaldee Lexicon.* Grand Rapids: Zondervan.

Davies, Stephan L. 1995. *Jesus the Healer: Possession, Trance, and the Origins of Christianity.* New York: Continuum Press.

Davis, Mike. 2006. *Planet of Slums.* New York: Verso.

Deloria, Vine. 1999. *For This Land: Writings on Religion in America.* New York: Routledge.

Deleuze, Gilles and Felix Guattari. 1980. *Mille plateaux. Capitalisme et schizophrene.* Paris. Tranls. in English as *A Thousand Plateaus: Capitalism and Schizophrenia,* 1987, Minneapolis: The University of Minnesoate Press.

de Plancy, Collin cf. End of section on Samaritan regarding Beelzebul; cf. Wikipedia Beelzebul.

Derrida, Jacques. 1989. "Psyche: Inventions of the Other," *Reading De Man Reading.* Eds. Waters and Godzich. Minneapolis: University of Minnesota Press, 25–64.

Diamond, Jared. 1999 (1997). *Guns, Germs, and Steel: The Fates of Human Societies.* New York: W. W. Norton & Co.

Du Bois, W. E. B. 1961. *The Souls of Black Folk.* New York: Fawcett Publications, Inc.

Dunbar, R. I. M. 1993. "Coevolution of Neocortical Size, Group Size and Language in Humans," *Behavioral and Brain Sciences* 16 (4): 681–735.

Dussel, Enrique. 1995. *The Invention of the Americas: Eclipse of "the Other" and the Myth of Modernity.* New York: Continuum.

Dyson, Michael Eric. 2001. *Holler If You Hear Me: Searching for Tupac Shakur.* New York: Basic Civitas Books.

Eisenberg, Evan. 1999. *The Ecology of Eden: An Inquiry into the Dream of Paradise and a New Vision of Our Role in Nature.* New York: Vintage Books.

Esaki, Brett. 2007. "Desperately Seeking Silence: Youth Culture's Unspoken Need," *CrossCurrents* 57 (3): 379–390.

Fanon, Frantz. 1963. *The Wretched of the Earth.* Trans. C. Farrington. New York: Grove Press.

Fox, Matthew. 1984. "Creation-Centered Spirituality from Hildegard of Bingen to Julian of Norwich," *Cry of the Environment.* Eds. P. N. Joranson and K. Butigan. Santa Fe: Bear & Co.

Freyne, Sean. 2011. "Jesus in Context: Galilee and Gospel," *Jesus of Galilee: Contextual Christology for the 21st Century.* Ed. R. Lassalle-Klein. Maryknoll: Orbis Books, 17–38.

Gentry, Howard. 1982. *Agaves of Continental North America.* Tuscon: University of Arizona Press.

Giesler, Patric V. 2004. *Shamanism: An Encyclopedia of World Beliefs, Practices, and Culture.* Eds M. Namba Walter and E. J. Neumann Fridman. Vol. 1. ABC-CLIO, Inc., 169–174.

Gordon, Avery F. 1997. *Ghostly Matters: Haunting and the Socioloical Imagination.* Berkeley: University of California Press.

Gowdy, John. 1998. *Limited Wants, Unlimited Means: A Reader on Hunter-Gatherer Economics and the Environment.* Ed. J. Gowdy. Washington, DC: Island Press, xv–xxxi.

Hall, James. 2009. *Sangoma: My Odyssey into the Spirit World of Africa.* New York: Sterling Ethos.

Hardt, Michael and Negri, Antonio. 2009. *Commonwealth.* Cambridge, MA: Belknap Press (Harvard University Press).

Harrison, Jane Ellen. 1963. *Mythology.* New York: Cooper Square.

Hemenway, Toby. 2009 (2000). *Gaia's Garden: A Guide to Home-Scale Permaculture.* Second Ed. White River Junction, VT: Chelsea Green Publishing Co.

Herron, Jerry. 2007. "Introduction: Getting to the Heidelberg Project on the 201st Anniversary of the Great Fire of 1805, or Manifesto for a New Detroit," *Connecting the Dots: Tyree Guyton's Heidelberg Project.* Detroit: Wayne State University Press, 1–9.

Herzog, William R. III. 1994. *Parables as Subversive Speech: Jesus as Pedagogue of the Oppressed.* Louisville, KY: Westminster John Knox Press.

———. 2000. *Jesus, Justice, and the Reign of God: A Ministry of Liberation.* Louisville, KY: Westminster John Knox Press.

Hiebert, Theodore. 1996. *The Yahwist's Landscape: Nature and Religion in Early Israel.* New York: Oxford University Press.

Hillel, Daniel. 2006. *The Natural History of the Bible: An Environmental Exploration of the Hebrew Scriptures.* New York: Columbia University Press.

Hillman, James. 1973. "Anima," *Spring*:122–123.

Hobbes, Thomas. 2010. *Leviathan.* Revised Edition, eds. A. P. Martinich and Brian Battiste. Peterborough, ON: Broadview Press.

hooks, bell. 1992. "Representations of Whiteness in the Black Imagination," *Black Looks: Race and Representation*. Boston: South End Press, 165–178.

Horsley, Richard A. 2011. *Jesus and the Powers: Conflict, Covenant, and the Hope of the Poor*. Minneapolis: Fortress Press.

Horsley, Richard A. and Hanson, John S. 1985. *Bandits, Prophets, and Messiahs: Popular Movements at the Time of Jesus*. San Francisco: Harper & Row.

Howard-Brook, Wes. 1994. *Becoming Children of God: John's Gospel and Radical Discipleship*. Maryknoll, NY: Orbis Books.

———. 2010. *Come Out My People: God's Call out of Empire in the Bible and Beyond*. Maryknoll: Orbis Books.

Howell, Sharon, 2013. "Beyond Detroit Future," *The Boggs Blog* (1/15/13).

Illich, Ivan. 1980. (1977). *Towards a History of Needs*. New York: Bantam Books.

Jackson, Marion E. 2007. "Trickster in the City," *Connecting the Dots: Tyree Guyton's Heidelberg Project*. Detroit: Wayne State University Press, 22–37.

Jackson, Wes. 2005. "Toward an Ignorance-Based Worldview," *The Land Report*, 14–16.

Jameson, Fredric. 1991. *Postmodernism: Or, the Cultural Logic of Late Capitalism*. Durham: Duke University Press.

Jensen, Derrick. 2001. "Saving the Indigenous Soul: An Interview with Martin Prechtel," http://www.thesunmagazine.org/issues/304/saving_the_indigenous_soul.

Jensen, Robert. 2008. "The Old Future's Gone: Progressive Strategy Amid Cascading Crises," http://uts.cc.utexas.edu/~rjensen/index.html.

Kobishchanov, Iurii M. 1978. "Axum," *The Early State*. Eds H. J. M. Claessen and P. Skalnik. Hague, the Netherlands: Mouton Publishers, printed in Great Britain, 151–168.

Kotting, Nancy. 2013 "The Power of Ruin: Detroit and the Artistic Mind," the Huffington Post (3/6/13), http://www.huffingtonpost.com/nancy-kotting/the-power-of-ruin-b_2820749.html.

Kovel, Joel. 2007. *The Enemy of Nature: The End of Capitalism or the End of the World?* London: Zed Books.

Kramer, Fritz. 1993 (1987). *The Red Fez: Art and Spirit Possession in Africa*. Trans. M. Green. London, New York: Verso.

LaDuke, Winona. 2005. *Recovering the Sacred: The Power of Naming and Claiming*. Cambridge, MA: South End Press.

Leacock, Eleanor. 1998. "Women's Status in Egalitarian Society: Implications for Social Evolution," *Limited Wants, Unlimited Means: A Reader on Hunter-Gatherer Economics and the Environment*. Washington, DC: Island Press, 139–164.

Loewen, James W. 1995 (2007). *Lies My Teacher Told Me: Everything Your American History Textbook Got Wrong*. New York: Touchstone.

Long, Charles. 1986. *Significations: Signs, Symbols, and Images in the Interpretation of Religion*. Philadelphia: Fortress Press.

Lynd, Stoughton. 1966. *Nonviolence in America: A Documentary History*. Indianapolis: Bobb-Merrill.

Markus, Robert A. 1990. "From Rome to the Barbarian Kingdoms," *The Oxford Illustrated History of Christianity*. Ed. J. MacManners. New York: Oxford University Press, 62–92.

Maté, Gabor. 1999. *Scattered: How Attention Deficit Disorder Originates and What You Can Do about It*. New York: Penguin Group.

———. 2010 (2008, 2009). *In the Realm of Hungry Ghosts: Close Encounters with Addiction*. Berkeley: North Atlantic Books.

———. 2012. Interview by Tracy Frisch, "What Ails Us: Gabor Maté Challenges the Way We Think about Chronic Illness, Drug Addiction, and Attention-Deficit Disorder," *The Sun Magazine* 440.

Mercier, Jacques. 1979. *Ethiopian Magic Scrolls*. Trans. R. Pevear. New York: George Braziller.

———. 1997. *Art that Heals: The Image as Medicine in Ethiopia*. Prestel (The Museum for African Art).

Mintz, Morton and Cohen, Jerry S. 1977. *Power, Inc*. Toronto: Bantam Books.

Myers, Ched. 1988. *Binding the Strong Man: A Political Reading of Mark's Story of Jesus*. Maryknoll, NY: Orbis Press.

———. 2001. *The Biblical Vision of Sabbath Economics*. Washington, DC: Church of the Savior.

———. 2005. "'The Cedar Has Fallen!': The Prophetic Word vs. Imperial Clear-Cutting," *Earth and Word: Classic Sermons on Saving the Planet*. Ed. D. Rhoads. New York: Continuum Press.

Newcomb, Steven T. 2008. *Pagans in the Promised Land: Decoding the Doctrine of Christian Discovery*. Golden, CO: Fulcrum.

Orenstein, Gloria. 1993. "Toward an Ecofeminist Ethic of Shamanism and the Sacred," *Ecofeminism and the Sacred*. Ed. Carol J. Adams. New York: Continuum, 172–190.

Pelikan, Jaroslav. 1997. *Jesus through the Centuries: His Place in the History of Culture*. New York (etc.): Harper & Row.

Peña, Devon G. 2006. "Toward a Critical Political Ecology of Latina/o Urbanism," http://www.acequiainstitute.org/images/Toward_a_political_ecology_of_Chicana-o_sustainable_urbanism_Draft_of_June_2006_.pdf.

Perkinson, James (Jim). 1996. "A Canaanitic Word in the Logos of Christ: or the Difference the Syro-Phoenician Woman Makes to Jesus," *Semeia* 75 (1996): 61–86.

———. 2004. *White Theology: Outing Supremacy in Modernity*, New York: Palgrave Macmillan Press.

———. 2005. *Shamanism, Racism, and Hip-Hop Culture: Essays on White Supremacy and Black Subversion*. New York: Palgrave Macmillan Press, 2005.

———. 2007a. "Kongo *Nkisi*/Canaanite Repartee/Black Savvy: Possession and Healing at the Crossroads," *CrossCurrents* 57 (3), 365–378.

———. 2007b. "Postcolonial Pan-Africanisms and Caribbean Connections: Behind Du Bois' Veil is Fanon's Muscle on a Herculoidian Trip," *Pan-Africanism Caribbean Connections*. Ed. Abdul Karim Bangura. New York: iUniverse, Inc., 64–75.

———. 2009. "Tupac Shakur as Ogou Achade: Hip-Hop Anger and Postcolonial Rancor Read From the Other Side," *Culture & Religion: An Interdisciplinary Journal* 10 (1) (Special Issue on Hip-Hop and Religion, ed. A. Pinn and M. Miller), 63–79.

———. 2010. "Hip-Hop Percussion and Cubist Vision: 'Africa' Climbing the Spine Like an Unwanted Mime at the Post-Colonial Crossroads," *CrossCurrents* 60 (2): 238–256.

———. 2011. "The 2010 US Social Forum as Sign of Martin King's Beloved Community: Ecumenism in the Hour of Planetary Crisis," *The Ecumenist* 48 (2) Spring, 8–15.

———. 2012. "Upstart Messiahs, Renegade Samaritans, and Temple Exorcisms: What Can Jesus' Peasant Resistance Movement in 1st Century Palestine Teach Us about Confronting 'Color-Blind' Whiteness Today?" *Christology and Whiteness: What Would Jesus Do?* Ed. G. Yancy. Milton Park, UK: Routledge Press, 136–155.

———. 2013. "Somewhere Underneath the MC's Wit and the Evangelical Word: Toward a Christian Ethical Evaluation of Hip Hop Polemic," *Urban God Talk: Constructing a Hip Hop Spirituality*. Ed. Andre. E. Johnson. Lanham: Lexington Books.

Pieris, Aloysius. 1987. "Speaking of the Son of God in Non-Church Cultures, e.g., in Asia," *An Asian Theology of Liberation*. Maryknoll: Orbis Books.

Prechtel, Martin. 2012. *The Unlikely Peace at Cuchumaquic: The Parallel Lives of People as Plants: Keeping the Seeds Alive*. Berkeley, CA: North Atlantic Books.

Prinzhorn, Hans. 1922. *Bildnerei der Geisteskranken. Ein Beitrag zur Psychologie und Psychopathologie der Gestaltung*. Berlin. Published in English 1995 (1972) as *Artistry of the Mentally Ill: A Contribution to the Psychology and Psychopathology of Configuration*. New York Heidelberg, and Berlin: Springer.

Quinn, Daniel. 1992. *Ishmael*. New York: Bantam Books.

———. 1996. *The Story of B: An Adventure of the Mind and Spirit*. New York: Bantam Deli.

Rasmussen, Larry. 1997. *Earth Community, Earth Ethics*. Maryknoll, NY: Orbis Press.

Rayan, Samuel. "Jesus and the Poor in the Fourth Gospel," *Readings in Indian Christian Theology I*. Eds R. S. Sugirtharajah and C. Hargreaves. SPCK International Study Guide 29 (Advanced). Indian Society for Promoting Christian Knowledge, 214–228.

Reichel-Dolmatoff, Gerardo. 1976. "Cosmology as Ecological Analysis: A View from the Rain Forest," *Man* 11 (3), 307–318.

Rose, Tricia. 1994. *Black Noise: Rap Music and Black Culture in Contemporary America*. Hanover, NH: Wesleyan University Press, Published by University Press of New England.

Schmookler, Andrew Bard. 1984. *The Parable of the Tribes*. Berkeley and Los Angeles: University of California Press.

Scott, Bernard Brandon. 1989. *Hear Then the Parable: A Commentary on the Parables of Jesus*. Minneapolis: Fortress Press.

Scott, James. 1976. *The Moral Economy of the Peasant: Rebellion and Subsistence in Southeast Asia.* New Haven and London: Yale University Press.

————. 1990. *Domination and the Arts of Resistance: Hidden Transcripts.* New Haven: Yale University Press.

Segundo, Juan Luis. 1986. *The Humanist Christology of Paul.* Trans. and Ed. J. Drury. Maryknoll, NY: Orbis Books, London: Sheed & Ward.

Shepard, Paul. 1982. *Nature and Madness.* Athens, GA: University of Georgia Press.

Shiva, Vandana. 2010 (1988). *Staying Alive: Women, Ecology and Development.* Boston: South End Press.

Sobrino, Jon. 1978. *Christology at the Crossroads: A Latin American Approach.* Trans. and Ed. J. Drury. Maryknoll: Orbis.

Spencer, Jon Michael. 1991. "Introduction," *The Emergency of Black and the Emergence of Rap* (A special issue of *Black Sacred Music: A Journal of Theomusicology*). Ed. J. M. Spencer. Durham, NC: Duke University Press, 1–11.

Spivak, Gayatri Chakravorty. 1999. *A Critique of Postcolonial Reason: Toward a History of the Vanishing Present.* Cambridge: Harvard University Press.

Sugrue, Thomas. 1996. *The Origins of the Urban Crisis: Race and Inequality in Postwar Detroit.* Princeton: Princeton University Press.

Stannard, David. 1992. *American Holocaust: The Conquest of the New World.* New York: Oxford University Press.

Taussign, Michael. 2009. *What Color is the Sacred?* Chicago: University of Chicago Press.

Taylor, Bradley. 2011. "Heidelberg and Community: A Space for Us All," *Heidelberg 25: A 25 Year Retrospective 1986–2011.* Detroit: Charles H. Wright Museum of African American History.

Taylor, Mark Lewis. 2011. *The Theological and the Political: On the Weight of the World.* Minneapolis: Fortress Press.

Thompson, Robert Farris. 1996. "Hip Hop 101," *Droppin' Science: Critical Essays on Rap Music and Hip-Hop Culture.* Ed. William E. Perkins. Philadelphia: Temple University Press, 211–219.

Tinker, George E. "Tink." 2008. *American Indian Liberation: A Theology of Sovereignty.* Maryknoll, NY: Orbis Books.

Turner III, Frederick. 1978 (1973). "Poetry and Oratory". *The Portable North American Indian Reader.* Penguin Book.

Weatherford, Jack. 1988. *Indian Givers: How the Indians of America Transformed the World.* New York: Fawcett Columbine.

Wells, Spencer. 2010. *Pandora's Seed: The Unforeseen Cost of Civilization.* New York: Random House.

Weyer, Johan cf. End of section on Samaritan regarding Beelzebul; cf. Wikipedia Beelzebul.

Wheaton, Henry. 1846. *Elements of International Law.* Third Ed. Philadelphia: Lea and Blanchard.

Willson, S. Brian. 2011. *Blood on the Tracks: The Life and Times of S. Brian Willson.* Oakland, CA: PM Press.

Wink, Walter. 1984. *Naming the Powers: The Language of Power in the New Testament*. Philadelphia: Fortress Press.

———. 1986. *Unmasking the Powers: The Invisible Forces that Determine Human Existence*. Philadelphia: Fortress Press.

———. 1992. *Engaging the Powers: Discernment and Resistance in a World of Domination*. Minneapolis: Fortress Press.

Woodcock, James. 1998. "Egalitarian Societies," *Limited Wants, Unlimited Means: A Reader on Hunter-Gatherer Economics and the Environment*. Ed. J. Gowdy. Washington, DC: Island Press, 87–110.

Young, John. 1997. *Peasant Revolution in Ethiopia: The Tigray People's Liberation Front, 1975–1991*. New York: Cambridge University Press.

Index

Abel, 1, 17, 27–32, 37, 50–2, 137, 183,
    205n24, 206n7, 210n10
Abraham (Abram), 2, 27, 32,
    34–5, 37–42, 59, 71, 87, 114–17,
    137, 142
    and hospitality, 40–1, 59, 72, 194
Abram, David, 176–8, 218n20
African Independent Churches,
    184, 230
agriculture, 6–16
    domestication, 8–9, 11, 100,
        109, 158
    mono-crop, 3–4, 7, 11–12, 15, 18,
        109–10
    settled, 3, 11–13, 15, 18, 27, 32, 34,
        39, 44, 60, 65, 100, 106–109, 126,
        132, 161, 168, 185
    subsistence (hoe), 4, 8, 10–14,
        16–18, 31–6, 39, 66, 77–9,
        82, 93, 109, 112, 116, 121,
        127–32, 172
    tenant farming, 11, 40, 72, 78
    See also Detroit
Allen, Will, 172
alliance(s) between humans and plants/
    animals, 7–8, 12, 15–17, 74, 93,
    106, 116, 161, 202n8, 203n9.
    See also christology; plant-people;
    symbiosis
anarcho-primitivism, 3
angel(s), 40, 43, 53, 80, 82
    and birds, 218n20, 226–7n5
    and logos, 117–26
    and magic scrolls, 139–59

and principalities, 102–17
and vision quest, 165–78
    See also possession; principalities
    (and powers)
animism, animistic, 13, 110, 151
anointing, xviii, xix, 23, 37, 39, 44, 47,
    60, 111, 120, 132, 160, 213n30
    and boundary stones, 37, 199n3
    and oils of animal/plant ancestors,
        xvii, 184, 202n8
    and rock, xix, 38, 97, 101, 111, 116,
        131, 177–8, 199, 215n8, 216n12,
        224n23
    and standing stones, 200n3, 222n13
Arab Spring, Tahrir Square, xxiv, 179,
    186, 200n4
artful, artfulness, xix, xx, xxii, xxxi, 21,
    23, 26–7, 30, 57–8, 66, 84, 161

Baal, 74, 82, 84, 209n8, 211n17,
    213n28, 212n25
Babylon, 23, 29, 32, 54, 85, 94, 211n18
band societies, 5, 116, 128
bedouin, 9, 11, 21, 32, 120,
    173, 207n13
Beelzebul, 56, 67, 81–4, 159, 209n8,
    212n25, 213n28, 213n29, 214n33,
    224n25
Benjamin, Walter, 66
Boal, Augusto, 204n20
Boddy, Janice, 133
Boggs, Grace Lee, 14, 188, 191–195
Brennan, Teresa, 98
Brown, Peter, 138

The manufacturer's authorised representative in the EU is Springer
Nature Customer Service Centre GmbH, Europaplatz 3, 69115 Heidelberg,
Germany. If you have any concerns regarding our products, please
contact ProductSafety@springernature.com

Printed and bound by CPI Group (UK) Ltd, Croydon, CR0 4YY

23/04/2026

02095595-0012